1997

SPINOZA

Purdue University Press Series in the History of Philosophy

General Editors

Arion Kelkel

Joseph J. Kockelmans

Adriaan Peperzak

Calvin O. Schrag

Thomas Seebohm

SPINOZA | The Way to Wisdom

Herman De Dijn

Purdue University Press
West Lafayette, Indiana

00   99   98   97   96   5   4   3   2   1

∞ The paper used in this book meets the minimum requirements of
American National Standard for Information Sciences—Permanence
of Paper Printed Library Materials, ANSI Z39.48-1992.

Printed in the United States of America

Interior design by Anita Noble

English translation of Spinoza's *Tractatus de intellectus emendatione*
from Curley, Edwin, trans., *The Collected Works of Spinoza*. Copyright
© 1985 by Princeton University Press. Reprinted by permission of
Princeton University Press.

Library of Congress Cataloging-in-Publication Data

De Dijn, H.
        Spinoza : the way to wisdom / Herman De Dijn.
            p.   cm. — (Purdue University Press series in the history of
        philosophy)
            Includes bibliographical references (p.   ) and index.
            ISBN 1-55753-081-5 (cloth : alk. paper). — ISBN 1-55753-082-3
        (pbk. : alk. paper)
            1. Spinoza, Benedictus de, 1632–1677. Tractatus de intellectus
        emendatione. 2. Science—Methodology. 3. Knowledge, Theory of.
        4. Spinoza, Benedictus de, 1632–1677. Ethica. 5. Ethics.
        I. Spinoza, Benedictus de, 1632–1677. Tractatus de intellectus
        emendatione. English. II. Title. III. Series.
        B3984.D55 1996
        199'.492—dc 20   95-46211
                                                                CIP

CONTENTS

PREFACE

The editors of the Purdue University Press Series in the History
of Philosophy suggested that I take as the basic text for the
Spinoza volume in the series the *Treatise on the Emendation of
the Intellect*. Spinoza wrote this text at the beginning of his philosophical career as a kind of introduction to his philosophy. However, the text remained unfinished, and was almost not included
in the *Opera Posthuma,* which was edited by Spinoza's friends
immediately after his death in 1677. There also is some debate as
to whether the Spinoza of the *Ethics* would have accepted this
text as a valuable introduction to his mature philosophy, especially as it seems to end in a kind of deadlock. Nevertheless, I
think the editors were right in their suggestion; it can be shown
that until the end of his life Spinoza valued this introductory
project and intended to complete it.

Furthermore, this text—as well as the title and content of
the *Ethics*—demonstrates the fundamental ethical intention of
Spinoza's philosophizing, however deeply it was influenced by
the new science, which was constituting itself at the beginning of
the modern age. I will try to show in this book that the *Treatise*
and the *Ethics* form one big project in which the ethical problematic of the beginning of the *Treatise* is returned to at the end of
the *Ethics*.

The text of the *Treatise* is notoriously difficult to understand
with respect both to its philosophical ideas and problems and to
its very structure and development. Fortunately, in the last few
years some new editions, commentaries, and studies have appeared that have made possible great progress in understanding
this difficult text. Information about these publications can be
found in the appendix and the bibliography. Although I have

struggled with the text of the *Treatise* at different intervals over many years, I still was able to learn a great deal from the recently published studies and commentaries of Theo Zweerman, Bernard Rousset, and Wolfgang Bartuschat.

The choice of the *Treatise on the Emendation of the Intellect* presented me with a problem: because the work is only the introduction to Spinoza's philosophy—anticipating, but not really developing, this philosophy itself—a commentary on the *Treatise* alone would not function as a presentation of Spinoza's fundamental ideas in their fully developed form. So it was necessary to add some chapters on the philosophical system (the *Ethics*) itself. Nevertheless, these chapters, forming the second part of the book, can be considered as part of my commentary on the *Treatise* because they show how the major problems and issues of the *Treatise* are treated or solved in the philosophical system itself. They are written so that the whole content of the *Ethics* is dealt with, however briefly, in a serious manner. Because it is impossible to include the entire text of the *Ethics* in this book, and because it would be pointless to insert only short excerpts of the various parts, the reader is referred to one of the many available translations.

I do not pretend that my notes on the Spinoza literature in the appendix are complete, but I hope it will serve as an adequate and reasonably up-to-date guide for further reading, especially taking into account valuable publications in French and German. Because much good scholarship has been published in these languages (as well as in Dutch and Italian) and is referred to in English publications, many titles in French and German (and even Dutch and Italian) are listed in the appendix and in the bibliography.

I have many debts of gratitude: to the National (Belgian) Foundation for Scientific Research, which financially supported the six-month sabbatical for the writing of this book; to Professor Joseph J. Kockelmans, for his trust that I would finish this book more or less on time; to Theo van der Werf, the secretary of the International Association "Het Spinozahuis," for various kinds of support, not only with respect to this book; to my colleagues at the Institute of Philosophy (Catholic University of Leuven), especially to the chairperson, Professor Carlos Steel, for their heartfelt encouragement; and to Princeton University Press, for permission to reprint Edwin Curley's translation of Spinoza's *Tractatus de intellectus emendatione*. Ms. Lut Kevers typed ever changing versions of the manuscript with great care and dedication. Dr. Paul Crowe was untiring in correcting my English and in preventing me from despair about its acceptability. Without the love and support of my wife and children, this book would never have been written.

I dedicate this book to the memory of the late Professors H. G. Hubbeling, Emilia Giancotti, and Alan Donagan. Each in his or her own way has done much for the study of Spinoza; each played an important role in the communication and friendship of the international group of Spinoza scholars who regularly meet at Spinoza conferences in different countries. They will not be forgotten.

The text of Spinoza reprinted in this book is the *Tractatus de intellectus emendatione* taken from Carl Gebhardt's four-volume edition of *Spinoza Opera*. When I refer directly to Gebhardt's edition, the references take the form "G, 1:107 (28-32)," the numbers indicating in this case volume 1, page 107, lines 28–32. In a few cases, Dutch words appear in the Latin text in brackets. These were inserted by Gebhardt to draw attention to additional words found in the original Dutch translation, entitled *De nagelate schriften,* of Spinoza's *Opera Posthuma*. Both the *Opera Posthuma* and *De nagelate schriften* appeared in Amsterdam in 1677, immediately after Spinoza's death. Gebhardt's edition, although intended as a critical edition, is unfortunately less than perfect. (A new critical edition is being prepared by the Groupe de Recherches Spinozistes in Paris, under the direction of Pierre-François Moreau, in cooperation with Dutch and Italian Spinoza scholars.) For example, the use of capitals for ordinary words (taken over in Edwin Curley's translation) does not have any real significance and is inconsistent (information obtained from Piet Steenbakkers, who is working on the new edition of the *Ethica*).

The translation of the *Tractatus de intellectus emendatione* reprinted here is Curley's translation as edited in his *The Collected Works of Spinoza,* volume 1, and based on Gebhardt's edition of the Latin text. References to Curley's edition take the form "Spinoza 1985, 37."

The paragraph numbers in brackets are those introduced by Curley (following an older, generally accepted usage) and are included for ease in making and following references. These paragraph numbers also have been introduced in the Latin text for the sake of parallelism and easy reference. Lettered footnotes are

Spinoza's and follow the lettering of Gebhardt's edition, although they are not entirely consecutive.

Quotations in English from the *Ethics,* the *Short Treatise,* and some *Letters* are also from Curley 1985. On very few occasions, I use material not found in Curley 1985. Reference then is made directly to the text of Gebhardt or to the critical edition of the *Korte Verhandeling* (*Short Treatise*) (Spinoza 1982). In referring to parts of the *Ethics,* I use a system of abbreviations (see list below) that refers to Spinoza's own reference system, allowing the reader to consult any text or translation of the *Ethica.*

TEI = *Treatise on the Emendation of the Intellect*

E = *Ethics or Ethica*

KV = *Korte Verhandeling*

ST = *Short Treatise*

PPC = *Renati Des Cartes Principia Philosophiae*

TTP = *Tractatus Theologico-Politicus*

TP = *Tractatus Politicus*

G = Gebhardt's edition of the *Opera,* vols. 1–4

E I P. 14, Sch. = *Ethics,* Part I, Proposition 14, Scholium

    Cor. = corollary

    Dem. = demonstration

    Pref. = preface

    Ax. = axiom

    Def. = definition

    Def. Aff. = definition of the affect

    Gen. Def. Aff. = general definition of the affects

    App. 31 = appendix, caput 31

    Post. = postulate

    Expl. = explanation

    Alt. Dem. = alternative demonstration

PART
ONE

Introduction

CHAPTER ONE | Spinoza's Life and Work

In his introduction to Spinoza's *Briefwisseling* (*Letters*), H. G. Hubbeling gives a survey of the real or fictional elements of Spinoza's life as found in his early biographies, in the *Letters*, and in various documents.[1] This survey shows that the older biographies contain many contradictions and should be used with great caution, even concerning the most basic elements of Spinoza's life. However, thanks to the discovery of many new documents, especially in recent years, we now know a great deal about Spinoza, even about his youth in the Jewish-Portuguese (or Sephardic) community in Amsterdam.

Spinoza was born on 24 November 1632 in Amsterdam into a merchant family. Together with many other Portuguese Jews, or "Marranos," who had outwardly professed Catholicism, his father, Michaël, had fled the Inquisition to the Netherlands at the end of the sixteenth century. Spinoza's mother, Hanna Debora, died when he was only six years old. His father was an important figure in the Sephardic community in Amsterdam; he belonged to the Parnassim, the group of synagogue elders. Spinoza was educated in the Talmud Tora school of the community but attended only the lower grades. The school had eminent teachers, such as the rabbis Saül Morteira and Menasseh ben Israël. After his father died in 1654, Spinoza and his stepbrother, Gabriël, headed the family business—the firm Bento y Gabriël de Spinoza, which traded in Oriental goods. Probably through his business contacts with freethinking Christians, Spinoza learned about the new philosophical and scientific ideas that were the object of lively discussions in the Netherlands, even among business people frequenting the stock market.

| 3

In 1656 Spinoza was permanently banned from the synagogue. There is much speculation about the reason for such a strong ban.[2] He was accused of holding abominable opinions and of engaging in detestable practices. The ban must be related to his unorthodox views (and behavior?) but probably in particular resulted from his unyielding reaction to the accusations raised against him.[3] How Spinoza arrived at these unorthodox views is not clear. But there were other dissidents in the Amsterdam community, before and after Spinoza, who also were banned, such as Uriel da Costa and Juan de Prado. De Prado was banned two years after Spinoza, and it is certain that de Prado and Spinoza kept in touch after Spinoza's exile.[4]

Around or after 1656, Spinoza was in close contact with Franciscus Van den Enden, an ex-Jesuit from Antwerp who ran a well-known Latin school in Amsterdam. Spinoza took lodgings with Van den Enden and studied Latin with him. Van den Enden was a notorious freethinker, and it is likely that Spinoza not only learned Latin here but also became more familiar with Cartesian ideas and the philosophies of Francis Bacon, Thomas Hobbes, and perhaps even Giordano Bruno.[5]

In consequence of the ban, Spinoza had to give up his business. He latinized his name from Baruch to Benedictus and, lacking any support, learned to grind lenses for various optical devices. He earned an international reputation for his skill, which led Gottfried Leibniz to send him a note on optics (letter 45). It is certain that he became quickly and deeply engaged in philosophy, since by 1661–62 identifiably Spinozistic ideas can be recognized.

In the spring of 1661, Spinoza came to live in Rijnsburg, near the university town of Leiden, where, as in other universities in the Netherlands, René Descartes's views were strongly debated and sometimes mixed with Scholastic ideas (the *philosophia novantiqua*).[6] Rijnsburg also was the gathering place of an unorthodox Christian sect, the Collegiants, some of whom became involved in Spinoza's circle of friends, discussing his philosophical ideas, as expressed especially in the *Korte Verhandeling van God, de mensch en deszelfs welstand* (*Short Treatise on God, Man, and His Well-Being*, which I shall abbreviate as *Short Treatise*). This Dutch translation of a Latin text (which was lost) was discovered in manuscript only in the late nineteenth century and may be seen as a proto-*Ethics*. The first appendix to the *Short Treatise* is written *more geometrico*—that is, in a geometrical, or axiomatic-deductive, way—showing that Spinoza already was trying to express his philosophical ideas in a "scientific" manner. Many of Spinoza's philosophical friends were familiar with Cartesianism and had liberal religious tendencies. The most important, Lodewijk Meyer, published works of his own on philosophy and religion and was appointed director of the Amsterdam Theater in 1665.[7]

There still is debate on whether the *Short Treatise* was written before or after the *Tractatus de intellectus emendatione* (*Treatise on the Emendation of the Intellect,* which I shall abbreviate as *Treatise*).[8] I maintain that the *Short Treatise* came before the *Treatise,* and that both texts were written by 1662. The *Treatise* was intended as an introduction to philosophy, but it also was a reaction to the predominant ideas of Descartes and Bacon (and perhaps even of Hobbes).

Spinoza lived a quiet existence in Rijnsburg, a way of life that allowed him to develop his philosophical ideas. This does not mean that he was completely secluded. During the whole of his life, he had personal or epistolary contact with many people in the learned world—for example, with Henry Oldenburg, who became the first secretary of England's famous Royal Society (and who functioned as a mediator between Spinoza and one of the founders of chemistry, Robert Boyle); and with philosophers, such as Leibniz and Walter von Tschirnhaus; scientists, such as Christian Huygens; and politicians, such as Johannes Hudde. From Spinoza's correspondence, it is evident that he followed their publications, including those on probability calculus, mathematics, and physics. Indeed, his interest in these subjects was so great that two short pieces, *Stelkonstige Reeckening van den Regenboog* (*On the Rainbow*) and *Reeckening van Kanssen* (*On the Calculation of Chances*), were until recently ascribed to Spinoza.[9]

Spinoza's growing reputation was further established with the publication in 1663 of the *Renati Des Cartes Principia Philosophiae (Principia),* an exposition of Descartes's *Principles,* parts 1 and 2, published with a preface by Meyer. The origin of this text was Spinoza's tutoring of a young man studying Descartes's philosophy at Leiden University. Attached to the *Principia* was an appendix containing *Cogitata Metaphysica,* a mixture of Scholastic and Cartesian philosophy typical of the period. Spinoza did not hesitate to take a personal standpoint vis-à-vis the ideas exposed, announcing his own philosophical ideas.

In the spring of 1663, Spinoza moved to Voorburg, near The Hague. It is clear from his correspondence of this period that parts of his major work—the *Ethics*—were already circulating among his friends. From letter 28, we know that a substantial portion of the *Ethics* was finished by 1665, although this work eventually contained more parts. From 1665 to 1670, Spinoza worked on his *Tractatus Theologico-Politicus,* although he probably kept refining the *Ethics* in the meantime. The *Tractatus* was intended as a plea for freedom of thinking and, indirectly, as support for the policy of Johan de Witt, the councillor pensionary of the United Provinces.

Probably written in connection with the *Tractatus Theologico-Politicus* is Spinoza's work on Hebrew grammar, *Compendium Grammatices Linguae Hebraeae* (around 112 pages in the *Opera Posthuma*). The only work that Spinoza published under his own name was the *Principia.* Of the other works, only the *Tractatus Theologico-Politicus* was published during Spinoza's lifetime. Although there was some tolerance of freedom of thought at the time, the publication of the *Tractatus Theologico-Politicus* produced real outrage, and people soon knew who the author was. Spinoza tried to prevent the appearance of a Dutch translation because he feared it would mean the prohibition of the book. It was nonetheless banned officially in 1674, but that did not prevent it from becoming known all over Europe.[10] It played a significant role in the enlightened critique of religion. Probably because of protection from such highly placed people as Johan and Cornelius de Witt, Spinoza did not get into trouble, even though one of his disciples, Adriaan Koerbagh, had died in prison in 1669, convicted for his "blasphemous and abominable" doctrines and publications (in Dutch). It is not surprising that Spinoza published his *Tractatus* anonymously and in Latin; the first Dutch translation, by Jan Hendriksz Glazemaker, appeared in 1693.

Probably in 1670, Spinoza moved for the last time, to The Hague, where he lived until his death in 1677. In 1672, the United Provinces faced wars with England, Münster, Cologne, and France. After the outbreak of the war against France, the De Witt brothers were viciously murdered by an Orangist-Calvinist mob, which desecrated their corpses. The political situation had changed, with growing popular support for the Prince of Orange, William III.[11]

After 1670, Spinoza continued work on the *Ethics,* and in 1675, he made a trip to Amsterdam to see about having his work published. But hostile rumors about the publication of his new book made him decide to postpone publication (letter 68, of 1675 to Oldenburg). In 1673, he received an invitation from the professor of theology J. Ludwig Fabritius, counselor to the Elector Palatine Karl Ludwig, offering him a chair of philosophy at the

University of Heidelberg. Fearing that teaching would interfere with his philosophizing and doubting there would be enough freedom of thought, Spinoza politely refused.[12]

In the same year, Spinoza made a mysterious trip to Utrecht (then under French occupation), at the invitation of the prince of Condé. When he arrived, the prince was away from Utrecht and consequently the (probably diplomatic) mission was of no avail. The fundamental change in the political situation forced Spinoza to rethink the political ideas expressed in the *Tractatus Theologico-Politicus*. So in his last years, he began writing his *Tractatus Politicus*, his major work of political theory, which remained incomplete at his death in 1677. This work influenced political ideas in revolutionary eighteenth-century France. Emmanuel-Joseph Sieyès, one of the leading theoreticians of the French Revolution, wrote a constitution that strongly resembles the ideas expressed in the *Tractatus Politicus*.[13] Although Spinoza's political philosophy is interesting and original, it often is neglected in surveys of major political thinkers.

In February 1677, Spinoza, having been ill for some time, died of tuberculosis, which probably was exacerbated by the inhalation of glass dust from his lens grinding and polishing. Although considered a notorious atheist—and certainly not a Christian—he was buried in a rented grave in the New Church in The Hague. Two houses in which he lived are preserved as museums. According to Spinoza's wish, after his death his manuscripts were sent to the printer Rieuwerts at Amsterdam, where they appeared the same year under the title *B. D. S. Opera Posthuma*. At the same time, a complete Dutch translation, partly made by the well-known translator J. H. Glazemaker, appeared under the title *De nagelate schriften van B. D. S.*[14] By 1678, the *Opera Posthuma* were banned in Holland.

I NOTES

1. Spinoza 1977, 29-67. Hubbeling includes in his discussion Jacob Freudenthal's *Lebensgeschichte Spinoza's in Quellenschriften, Urkunden und Nichtamtlichen Nachrichten* (1899) and A. M. Vaz Dias and W. G. van der Tak's *Spinoza, mercator et autodidactus* (1932).

2. The document pronouncing the ban is in the town archives of Amsterdam. For ample information and further references about the ban, see Kasher & Biderman 1990; Wesselius 1990a, 1990b.

3. Wesselius 1990b, 201–2.

4. See Revah 1959, 1964.

5. Recently, anonymous texts have been discovered that must be attributed to Van den Enden. The editor, Wim Klever, claims that they

"demonstrate" Spinoza's enormous debt to Van den Enden, whom he calls a proto-Spinoza; see Klever 1991; Van den Enden 1992. However, Klever's views cannot be considered conclusive; see De Dijn 1994 also for references to other critics.

6. Descartes died in 1650 in Sweden but lived for many years in the Netherlands. On the *philosophia novantiqua,* see De Dijn 1983.

7. For more information about Spinoza's philosophical friends, see Meinsma 1980, 1983; about Meyer, see Spinoza 1977, 43–44.

8. See Mignini 1979; and Mignini's introduction to Spinoza 1986; but also Bartuschat's introduction to Spinoza 1993.

9. See De Vet 1983, 1986.

10. For a brief account of the immediate reception of the *Tractatus Theologico-Politicus* and of similar publications before the *Tractatus,* see the introduction by Brad Gregory to Spinoza 1989, 27–36; see also Siebrand 1988.

11. For a short presentation of Spinoza's historic context in the Netherlands, see Gregory's introduction to Spinoza 1989, 18–26; for a full account, see De Vries.

12. See letters 47 and 48 (Spinoza 1977).

13. See Pariset 1906 (and Vernière 1982). I owe this information to Frank Vanden Berghe.

14. About the editorial history of the *Opera Posthuma,* see Steenbakkers 1994, chap. 1.

Spinoza's *Treatise on the Emendation of the Intellect* is his introduction to philosophy. For a seventeenth-century thinker like Spinoza, philosophy was fundamentally the same as science. As a *unified* science, it has at least three tasks. The first is to provide the ontological foundation of the *scienza nuova,* or new science, recently discovered by Nicolaus Copernicus, Galileo Galilei, William Harvey, and others. As Descartes and Hobbes—the founders of the new philosophy—realized, philosophy has, as a second task, the justification of *itself*—both negatively, against the illusory philosophizing of premodern thinking; and positively, by showing itself to be a valid metaphysics. Finally, philosophy has to provide a new scientific ethics and politics that leads people into the new (modern) age; in other words, it must replace the traditional way of living, which excessively exposed people to the accidents of fate, with a scientifically based way of life that leads to self-mastery.

Although Spinoza stands squarely in this modern context and engages in all three tasks, his philosophy is peculiar in that the ethical aim is central. This is clear from some of the titles of his works: *Short Treatise on God, Man, and His Well-Being* and *Ethics.* As we will see, his *Treatise on the Emendation of the Intellect* is also "ethical" through and through. It is important to clarify what I mean by "ethical." Ethics refers here not primarily to norms or principles governing our relation to others but to ideals and prescriptions concerning the best way of life for the individual—that is, a way of life leading to real happiness.

What may appear strange from a contemporary perspective is that Spinoza links ethics with knowledge—more precisely with a metaphysical theory and a theory of man strongly associated with the new science. (Edwin Curley therefore rightly translates the title *Ethica* as *The Metaphysical Moralist*.) In their metaphysics, modern philosophers reacted to the advent of the new science and what this implied for human life and human culture. Often this metaphysics served (as for Descartes) not only to give a foundation for the new sciences but especially to defuse the threat that this new science seemed to pose to traditional religious culture. Spinoza's metaphysics constitutes a totally different approach. Not only is there no need for a separate justification of the new, scientific way of thinking—certainly not one arrived at through the proof of a personal, benevolent God—but, for Spinoza, it also is possible to use this new, neutral, and purely objective way of thinking to reflect about being and man[1] (as Hobbes did) and even about God (as nobody had dared to do). However, what is most peculiar about Spinoza is that for him the solution to the ethical problem of real happiness is squarely situated in a confrontation with this "naturalistic" conception of God and man.[2] Paradoxically, it is somehow through this naturalistic conception that people can find real security and inner peace.

The problem for modern philosophers was to introduce people into the new way of thinking and living, to seduce them into modernity. This pedagogy may take different forms. Descartes thought the best introduction was a kind of stylized autobiography (as in his *Discourse* and even his *Meditations*), showing in an exemplary way how to change from old to new. Hobbes, in his *De Corpore*, hoped that the best way of teaching was to demonstrate the truth immediately, starting from the right, fundamental principles. Spinoza employed both pedagogical devices. In his *Treatise*, he took the Cartesian approach; in the *Short Treatise* and *Ethics*, the Hobbesian line. The difference is probably due to the public he wrote for. The *Short Treatise* and even the *Ethics* were written not for the general public but for "the friends,"[3] who were sufficiently freethinking not to be shocked and scared away by new meanings given to such fundamental terms as substance, God, or freedom, and sufficiently intelligent to agree and operate with these new concepts. Even here, there is an element of seduction and introduction. The way Spinoza presented his basic definitions and axioms was such that a kind of "semantic revolution" was brought about.[4] Familiar terms, and even familiar interpretations of such terms, were transformed into unexpected new interpretations, having astounding consequences (for example, the equation God or nature—*Deus sive Natura*). The "friends," of course, were not restricted to the small group around Spinoza asking his guidance in their reading and discussion of his texts. Like Ludwig Wittgenstein, Spinoza undoubtedly thought that he was "writing for friends who are scattered throughout the corners of the globe" and throughout time.[5]

Since the philosopher has himself changed from a nonknower to a knower, and since, from his own experience, he knows which factors were decisive in this change, he may develop a pedagogy for a wider audience: those already familiar with the modern way of thinking (and capable of reading Latin) and having at the same time a deep ethical interest. It was for these "honnêtes gens"[6] that Spinoza wrote his *Principia Philosophiae Cartesianae* together with the *Cogitata Metaphysica*. It was for these people—who were already interested in the new philosophy as discussed even at the old universities (blended there with Scholastic thought into a *philosophia novantiqua*)—that he wrote his *Treatise,* as an introduction to his philosophy,[7] which, he claimed, is perhaps not the best, but undoubtedly the true philosophy.[8]

It is not absolutely clear whether the *Treatise* was conceived as an introduction to the *Short Treatise* or to the *Ethics;* perhaps the *Philosophia* that Spinoza had in mind while writing the *Treatise* cannot be identified with either work but rather with an idea that was never realized in the form in which it was conceived.[9] Nevertheless, we know that until the end of his life, Spinoza intended to complete the *Treatise* as an introduction to his mature philosophy.[10] As we will see, the *Treatise* can be read as a perfect introduction to the *Ethics.*

Like Descartes, Spinoza wants to introduce the reader to philosophy by telling the story (or fable, as Descartes puts it) of his own experience, which may serve as an example of how one can come to master the new way of thinking for oneself. Unlike Descartes, however, Spinoza does not write out of dissatisfaction with old (premodern, Scholastic) ways of thinking or of how to really think for oneself in a methodical way to yield real scientific thought. The story that Spinoza tells is one of an ethical experience, with parallels in Stoic thinking—a story that was very popular in the sixteenth and seventeenth centuries. Alexandre Koyré and other commentators have stressed that this story should not be taken as strictly biographical. It clearly is meant as a paradigm, in which one can in principle recognize oneself.[11] Spinoza relates a life experience in which the pursuit of "ordinary goods"— such as honor, wealth, and sensual pleasure—leads to deep dissatisfaction.[12] Such a life can be experienced as a deadly illness from which one seeks to escape, for which one desperately wants a therapy.

Descartes wanted to introduce people into autonomous scientific thinking by demonstrating the inadequacy of traditional forms of thinking, and through the use of a device he had discovered: methodical doubt. What seems to bother Spinoza, primarily, is not the uncertainty of traditional knowledge or the question of how to obtain a real foundation for the new science but rather the Stoic question of the good life: how to find it and how to escape the deadly obsession with the pursuit of ordinary goods.[13] (For the Stoics, clever argumentation, erudition, and science are numbered among the "goods" that do not yield the good life, which is rather the result of a kind of nondoing [*ataraxia*].[14]) Spinoza wants us to employ a kind of methodical doubt in the moral domain. Strangely enough, as for Descartes, it will be in the doubting process itself that the beginnings of the solution will somehow be found. Furthermore, the ultimate ethical solution will consist in arriving at a certain stage of knowledge, not the scientific knowledge rejected by the Stoics but a kind of contemplative knowledge. It is not easy for us today to understand how knowledge provides real happiness.[15]

For Descartes, ethical security is secondary to the problem of epistemic certainty, which, in his philosophy, seems to depend on an anthropomorphic idea of God. For Blaise Pascal, this security can only be found in faith in an inscrutable God, which reveals the limited nature of scientific certainty. For Spinoza, real certainty seems connected with a kind of knowledge that not just provides unshakable scientific evidence but also transforms one's life. The very possessing of it constitutes security and peace of mind, even though it seems to contain a "picture" of God that is fundamentally anti-anthropomorphic, and even though it seems to contain a "picture" of ourselves that denies our most cherished ideas, such as anthropocentric ideas of freedom and special election by God. This explains why the method of "moral doubt" will lead to the search for a method of *thinking* properly, a method for "the emendation of the intellect" that tells us *the truth* about ourselves and the world in which we live. It is this search that gives this introduction to philosophy its proper title.

I have already mentioned that Spinoza links the question of the good life to the theme of illness and good health. Just as there is medicine for the body (*medicina corporis*), there is a therapy for the mind, which is nothing but logic: "to show how the intellect must be perfected, or in what way the Body must be cared for, so that it can perform its function properly. The former is the concern of Logic, and the latter of Medicine" (*Ethics* V, Pref.). This theme of a *medicina animi* (or *mentis*) is a traditional one—certainly going back to Cicero—and is taken up by modern philosophers; sometimes it is understood as a logic,[16] sometimes as an ethics.[17] Spinoza distinguishes logic from ethics (see *Ethics* V, Pref.) but links the two closely. What we are looking for is a therapy for curing the mind's false desires. Paradoxically, this therapy turns out to consist in an *emendatio intellectus,* a logic that leads as soon as possible into metaphysics, which in turn will provide the ultimately ethical solution.[18]

The *Treatise* clearly is Spinoza's logic. This term should not be confused with what we today call "formal logic." In seventeenth-century philosophy, it is used for a combination of epistemological and methodological considerations of the different sorts of ideas or forms of thinking people have, and of the right way to methodically develop scientific thinking. (In this way the term is used not only in Spinoza's *Treatise* but also in the first chapter of Hobbes's *De Corpore* and in Descartes's *Meditations* and in *La logique de Port-Royal.*[19]) Logical considerations function as an introduction to metaphysics, or the unified science, and as a guide to the way in which philosophy or science is to be developed.

As Edwin Curley mentions in a footnote, the translation of the title of the *Treatise* is disputed. According to some, the Latin term "emendatio" should not be rendered "emendation" because the intellect as such cannot be "improved"; it should be rendered, as H. H. Joachim claims, "purification," as the *Treatise* is the project of restoring the intellect to its "natural perfection, by eliminating from it . . . ideas which are not its own but have come to it from an external source."[20] According to others, "purification" is not much better because if the intellect as such cannot be improved, it cannot be purified, either; it is pure by definition.[21] Spinoza himself speaks both of the emendation and of the purification of the intellect, although he considers the intellect as pure in itself. The image that Spinoza seems to have had of the work of the logician is that of a surgeon, removing hindrances to the healthy growth of an organism or one of its parts but largely relying on the intrinsic power of the organism to come into full blossom. The evolution that the reader should make in order to understand philosophy is described by Theo Zweerman as a removal and a kind of homecoming:[22] it is like establishing oneself in one's own element (the intellect), no longer being alienated in dispersion. This coming into one's own will give real peace of mind (*acquiescentia in se ipso*).[23] This removal and homecoming is guided by the philosopher, who has already succeeded in performing this move and in reaching real peace and security.

This understanding of Spinoza's philosophy as a whole shows it to consist of a huge circular movement, determined by the alpha and omega of his philosophizing—the obtaining of real peace of mind. The beginning of the philosophical endeavor is the existential quest for real salvation. Paradoxically, this quest leads to the development of a logic or purification of the intellect, which itself becomes philosophy proper as soon as possible. This philosophy contains a metaphysics and a theory of man as necessary steps toward an ethics that shows us how to obtain salvation, real peace of mind. If we really consist, deep inside, in intellect, this whole movement is not as paradoxical as it seems. The ethical quest is ultimately a quest to "know thyself."

The unity between *logica* and *philosophia* determines the structure of this book. In the next part, we will analyze Spinoza's logic, which is the introduction to philosophy proper. This logic deals in reversed order, as it were, with the fundamental topics of his philosophy: ethics, the human mind as imagination and intellect, and God.

The next six chapters closely follow the structure of the *Treatise*, as indicated in the text itself (§ 49):

General aim, means, and way (§§ 1–48): from ethical considerations to logic

chapter 3 (§§ 1–17): discovery of the end, which is to obtain the highest good (that is, to obtain another human nature, together with others) (§ 14)

chapter 4 (§§ 18–29): discovery of the means to obtain this end (that is, an emendation of the intellect, "rendering it capable of understanding things in the way the attainment of our end requires") (§ 18)

chapter 5 (§§ 30–49): indication of the way to move toward the end (this way is tied up with the method studied in the second section, §§ 50–end).

The Method needed on the way (§§ 50–end): from logic to metaphysics

chapter 6 (§§ 50–90): first part of the method: "show how to distinguish a true idea from all other perceptions, and to restrain the mind from those other perceptions"

chapter 7 (§§ 91–98): second part of the method: "teach rules so that we may perceive things unknown according to such a standard"

chapter 8 (§§ 99–end): third part of the method: "establish an order, so that we do not become weary with trifles"

The third part of this book will summarize the insights of philosophy, properly speaking (as developed in the *Ethics,* to which the *Treatise* is the introduction). This philosophy is a move from metaphysics to ethics.

chapter 9 (*Ethics* I): metaphysics
chapter 10 (*Ethics* II): theory of human knowledge
chapter 11 (*Ethics* III–V): ethics

I N O T E S

1. Where Spinoza uses *homo* or *homines,* I use the word "man" or "men" for want of a better one. I do not mean to imply gender specificity.
2. De Dijn 1991.
3. *ST* II, conclusion.
4. I borrow this expression from M. Walther.
5. Wittgenstein 1980, 6e.
6. I borrow this expression from Bernard Rousset.
7. There are frequent references to "my philosophy" in the text of the *TEI* (e.g., notes k and l).
8. Letter 76 to Albert Burgh, from the end of 1675 to the beginning of 1676.
9. These matters are discussed in De Dijn 1974b; Spinoza 1992; Mignini 1979, 1988.
10. See, for example, letter 37, of 1666, to J. Bouwmeester, and letter 60, of 1675, to Tschirnhaus, which was written after the completion of the *Ethics.*
11. See Koyré's comment in Spinoza 1990, 97.
12. The three goods are a classical triad; see Bartuschat's comment in Spinoza 1993, 102; Busche 1991, 171.
13. About Spinoza and Stoic philosophy, see Kristeller 1985; Graeser 1991; Proietti 1985, 1989.
14. Aurelius 1964, 8.1.
15. About this problem, see Oakeshott 1984.
16. See Tschirnhaus's *Medicina mentis.*
17. This is Leibniz's understanding of *medicina mentis;* see Busche 1991, 171.
18. Kristeller 1985, 2–3.

19. De Dijn 1974b, 2 n. 2.

20. About this dispute, see Curley's note to the *TEI* title (Spinoza 1985, 7). Francis Bacon already understood his work *Novum Organon* (1620) as a *"Doctrina de expurgatione Intellectus."* See Bartuschat's introduction in Spinoza 1993, xxxii–xxxiii (with a reference to Gebhardt 1905).

21. Eisenberg 1971, 171–75.

22. Zweerman 1993, 260–61.

23. *E* V, P. 27.

P A R T
T W O

The Way

| **The Introduction (§§ 1–17):
The General Aim of the *Treatise***

Text
Admonitio ad lectorem

Tractatus, quem de Intellectus Emendatione, &c. imperfectum
hic tibi damus, Benevole Lector, jam multos ante annos ab
Auctore fuit conscriptus. In animo semper habuit eum perficere:
At, aliis negotiis praepeditus, & tandem morte abreptus, ad
optatum finem perducere non potuit. Cum vero multa prae-
clara, atque utilia contineat, quae Veritatis sincero indagatori
non parum e re futura esse, haudquaquam dubitamus, te iis
privare noluimus; &, ut etiam multa obscura, rudia adhuc, &
impolita, quae in eo hinc inde occurrunt, condonare non gra-
veris, horum ne inscius esses, admonitum te quoque esse
voluimus. Vale.

Tractatus de intellectus emendatione, et de via, qua optime in veram rerum cognitionem dirigitur

[1]   Postquam me Experientia docuit, omnia, quae in communi
vita frequenter occurrunt, vana, & futilia esse: cum viderem
omnia, a quibus, & quae timebam, nihil neque boni, neque mali
in se habere, nisi quatenus ab iis animus movebatur, constitui
tandem inquirere, an aliquid daretur, quod verum bonum, & sui
communicabile esset, & a quo solo, rejectis caeteris omnibus,
animus afficeretur; imo an aliquid daretur, quo invento, &
acquisito, continua, ac summa in aeternum fruerer laetitia.

| Notice to the Reader

This *Treatise on the Emendation of the Intellect* etc., which we give you here, kind reader, in its unfinished [that is, defective] state, was written by the author many years ago now. He always intended to finish it. But hindered by other occupations, and finally snatched away by death, he was unable to bring it to the desired conclusion. But since it contains many excellent and useful things, which — we have no doubt — will be of great benefit to anyone sincerely seeking the truth, we did not wish to deprive you of them. And so that you would be aware of, and find less difficult to excuse, the many things that are still obscure, rough, and unpolished, we wished to warn you of them. Farewell.

| Treatise on the Emendation of the Intellect and on the way by which it is best directed toward the true knowledge of things

[1] After experience had taught me that all the things which regularly occur in ordinary life are empty and futile, and I saw that all the things which were the cause or object of my fear had nothing of good or bad in themselves, except insofar as [my] mind was moved by them, I resolved at last to try to find out whether there was anything which would be the true good, capable of communicating itself, and which alone would affect the mind, all others being rejected — whether there was something which, once found and acquired, would continuously give me the greatest joy, to eternity.

The notice to the reader was written by the editors of the *Opera Posthuma*.

[2] Dico, *me tandem constituisse:* primo enim intuitu inconsultum videbatur, propter rem tunc incertam certam amittere velle: videbam nimirum commoda, quae ex honore, ac divitiis acquiruntur, & quod ab iis quaerendis cogebar abstinere, si seriam rei alii novae operam dare vellem: & si forte summa felicitas in iis esset sita, perspiciebam, me ea debere carere; si vero in iis non esset sita, eisque tantum darem operam, tum etiam summa carerem felicitate.

[3] Volvebam igitur animo, an forte esset possibile ad novum institutum, aut saltem ad ipsius certitudinem pervenire, licet ordo, & commune vitae meae institutum non mutaretur; quod saepe frustra tentavi. Nam quae plerumque in vita occurrunt, & apud homines, ut ex eorum operibus colligere licet, tanquam summum bonum aestimantur, ad haec tria rediguntur; divitias scilicet, honorem, atque libidinem. His tribus adeo distrahitur mens, ut minime possit de alio aliquo bono cogitare.

[4] Nam quod ad libidinem attinet, ea adeo suspenditur animus, ac si in aliquo bono quiesceret; quo maxime impeditur, ne de alio cogitet; sed post illius fruitionem summa sequitur tristitia, quae, si non suspendit mentem, tamen perturbat, & hebetat.

Honores, ac divitias persequendo non parum etiam distrahitur mens, praesertim, ubi[a] hae non nisi propter se quaeruntur, quia tum supponuntur summum esse bonum;

[5] honore vero multo adhuc magis mens distrahitur: supponitur enim semper bonum esse per se, & tanquam finis ultimus, ad quem omnia diriguntur. Deinde in his non datur, sicut in libidine, poenitentia; sed quo plus utriusque possidetur, eo magis augetur laetitia, & consequenter magis ac magis incitamur ad utrumque augendum: si autem spe in aliquo casu frustremur, tum summa oritur tristitia.

Est denique honor magno impedimento, eo quod, ut ipsum assequamur, vita necessario ad captum hominum est dirigenda, fugiendo scilicet, quod vulgo fugiunt, & quaerendo, quod vulgo quaerunt homines.

---

a. Potuissent hac latius, & distinctius explicari, distinguendo scilicet divitias, quae quaeruntur vel propter se, vel propter honorem, vel propter libidinem, vel propter valetudinem, & augmentum scientiarum & artium; sed hoc ad suum locum reservatur, quia hujus loci non est, haec adeo accurate inquirere.

[2]   I say that *I resolved at last*—for at first glance it seemed ill-advised to be willing to lose something certain for something then uncertain. I saw, of course, the advantages that honor and wealth bring, and that I would be forced to abstain from seeking them, if I wished to devote myself seriously to something new and different; and if by chance the greatest happiness lay in them, I saw that I should have to do without it. But if it did not lie in them, and I devoted my energies only to acquiring them, then I would equally go without it.

[3]   So I wondered whether perhaps it would be possible to reach my new goal—or at least the certainty of attaining it—without changing the conduct and plan of life which I shared with other men. Often I tried this, but in vain. For most things which present themselves in life, and which, to judge from their actions, men think to be the highest good, may be reduced to these three: wealth, honor, and sensual pleasure. The mind is so distracted by these three that it cannot give the slightest thought to any other good.

[4]   For as far as sensual pleasure is concerned, the mind is so caught up in it, as if at peace in a [true] good, that it is quite prevented from thinking of anything else. But after the enjoyment of sensual pleasure is past, the greatest sadness follows. If this does not completely engross, still it thoroughly confuses and dulls the mind.

The mind is also distracted not a little by the pursuit of honors and wealth, particularly when the latter[a] is sought only for its own sake, because it is assumed to be the highest good. [5] But the mind is far more distracted by honor. For this is always assumed to be good through itself and the ultimate end toward which everything is directed.

Nor do honor and wealth have, as sensual pleasure does, repentance as a natural consequence. The more each of these is possessed, the more joy is increased, and hence the more we are spurred on to increase them. But if our hopes should chance to be frustrated, we experience the greatest sadness. And finally, honor has this great disadvantage: to pursue it, we must direct our lives according to other men's powers of understanding—fleeing what they commonly flee and seeking what they commonly seek.

---

a. I could explain this more fully and distinctly, by distinguishing wealth that is sought for its own sake, or for the sake of honor, or for the sake of sensual pleasure or for the sake of health and the advancement of the arts and sciences. But I reserve this for its own place; such an exact investigation is not appropriate here.

[6]   Cum itaque viderem, haec omnia adeo obstare, quominus operam novo alicui instituto darem, imo adeo esse opposita, ut ab uno, aut altero necessario esset abstinendum, cogebar inquirere, quid mihi esset utilius; nempe, ut dixi, videbar bonum certum pro incerto amittere velle. Sed postquam aliquantulum huic rei incubueram, inveni primo, si, hisce omissis, ad novum institutum accingerer, me bonum sua natura incertum, ut clare ex dictis possumus colligere, omissurum pro incerto, non quidem sua natura (fixum enim bonum quaerebam), sed tantum quoad ipsius consecutionem:

[7]   Assidua autem meditatione eo perveni, ut viderem, quod tum, modo possem penitus deliberare, mala certa pro bono certo omitterem. Videbam enim me in summo versari periculo, & me cogi, remedium, quamvis incertum, summis viribus quaerere; veluti aeger lethali morbo laborans, qui ubi mortem certam praevidet, ni adhibeatur remedium, illud ipsum, quamvis incertum, summis viribus cogitur quaerere, nempe in eo tota ejus spes est sita; illa autem omnia, quae vulgus sequitur, non tantum nullum conferunt remedium ad nostrum esse conservandum, sed etiam id impediunt, & frequenter sunt causa interitus eorum, qui ea possident [(indien men dus mag spreken)],[b] & sempter causa interitus eorum, qui ab iis possidentur.

[8]   Permulta enim exstant exempla eorum, qui persecutionem ad necem usque passi sunt propter ipsorum divitias, & etiam eorum, qui, ut opes compararent, tot periculis sese exposuerunt, ut tandem vita poenam luerent suae stultitiae. Neque eorum pauciora sunt exempla, qui, ut honorem assequerentur, aut defenderent, miserrime passi sunt. Innumeranda denique exstant exempla eorum, qui prae nimia libidine mortem sibi acceleraverunt.

[9]   Videbantur porro ex eo haec orta esse mala, quod tota felicitas, aut infelicitas in hoc solo sita est; videlicet, in qualitate objecti, cui adhaeremus amore. Nam propter illud, quod non amatur, nunquam orientur lites, nulla erit tristitia, si pereat, nulla invidia, si ab alio possideatur, nullus timor, nullum odium, &, ut verbo dicam, nullae commotiones animi; quae quidem omnia contingunt in amore eorum, quae perire possunt, uti haec omnia, de quibus modo locuti sumus.

---

b. Haec accuratius sunt demonstranda.

[6]   Since I saw that all of these things stood in the way of my working toward this new goal, indeed were so opposed to it that one or the other must be given up, I was forced to ask what would be more useful to me. For as I say, I seemed to be willing to lose the certain good for the uncertain one. But after I had considered the matter a little, I first found that, if I devoted myself to this new plan of life, and gave up the old, I would be giving up a good by its nature uncertain (as we can clearly infer from what has been said) for one uncertain not by its nature (for I was seeking a permanent good) but only in respect to its attainment.

[7]   By persistent meditation, however, I came to the conclusion that, if only I could resolve, wholeheartedly, [to change my plan of life], I would be giving up certain evils for a certain good. For I saw that I was in the greatest danger, and that I was forced to seek a remedy with all my strength, however uncertain it might be—like a man suffering from a fatal illness, who, foreseeing certain death unless he employs a remedy, is forced to seek it, however uncertain, with all his strength. For all his hope lies there. But all those things men ordinarily strive for, not only provide no remedy to preserve our being, but in fact hinder that preservation, often cause the destruction of those who possess them,[b] and always cause the destruction of those who are possessed by them.

[8]   There are a great many examples of people who have suffered persecution to the death on account of their wealth, or have exposed themselves to so many dangers to acquire wealth that they have at last paid the penalty for their folly with their life. Nor are there fewer examples of people who, to attain or defend honor, have suffered most miserably. And there are innumerable examples of people who have hastened their death through too much sensual pleasure.

[9]   Furthermore, these evils seemed to have arisen from the fact that all happiness or unhappiness was placed in the quality of the object to which we cling with love. For strife will never arise on account of what is not loved, nor will there be sadness if it perishes, nor envy if it is possessed by another, nor fear, nor hatred—in a word, no disturbances of the mind. Indeed, all these happen only in the love of those things that can perish, as all the things we have just spoken of can do.

---

b. These things are to be demonstrated more accurately.

[10]   Sed amor erga rem aeternam, & infinitam sola laetitia pascit animum, ipsaque omnis tristitiae est expers; quod valde est desiderandum, totisque viribus quaerendum. Verum non absque ratione usus sum his verbis: *modo possem serio deliberare*. Nam quamvis haec mente adeo clare perciperem, non poteram tamen ideo omnem avaritiam, libidinem, atque gloriam deponere.

[11]   Hoc unum videbam, quod, quamdiu mens circa has cogitationes versabatur, tamdiu illa aversabatur, & serio de novo cogitabat instituto; quod magno mihi fuit solatio. Nam videbam illa mala non esse talis conditionis, ut remediis nollent cedere. Et quamvis in initio haec intervalla essent rara, & per admodum exiguum temporis spatium durarent, postquam tamen verum bonum magis ac magis mihi innotuit, intervalla ista frequentiora, & longiora fuerunt; praesertim postquam vidi nummorum acquisitionem, aut libidinem, & gloriam tamdiu obesse, quamdiu propter se, & non, tanquam media ad alia, quaeruntur; si vero tanquam media quaeruntur, modum tunc habebunt, & minime oberunt, sed contra ad finem, propter quem quaeruntur, multum conducent, ut suo loco ostendemus.

[12]   Hic tantum breviter dicam, quid per verum bonum intelligam, & simul quid sit summum bonum. Quod ut recte intelligatur, notandum est, quod bonum, & malum non, nisi respective, dicantur; adeo ut una, eademque res possit dici bona, & mala secundum diversos respectus, eodem modo ac perfectum, & imperfectum. Nihil enim, in sua natura spectatum, perfectum dicetur, vel imperfectum; praesertim postquam noverimus, omnia, quae fiunt, secundum aeternum ordinem, & secundum certas Naturae leges fieri.

[13]   Cum autem humana imbecillitas illum ordinem cogitatione sua non assequatur, & interim homo concipiat naturam aliquam humanam sua multo firmiorem, & simul nihil obstare videat, quominus talem naturam acquirat, incitatur ad media quaerendum, quae ipsum ad talem ducant perfectionem: & omne illud, quod potest esse medium, ut eo perveniat, vocatur verum bonum; summum autem bonum est eo pervenire, ut ille cum aliis individuis, si fieri potest, tali natura fruatur. Quaenam autem illa sit natura, ostendemus suo loco, nimirum esse[c] cognitionem unionis, quam mens cum tota Natura habet.

---

c. Haec fusius suo loco explicantur.

[10]   But love toward the eternal and infinite thing feeds the mind with a joy entirely exempt from sadness. This is greatly to be desired, and to be sought with all our strength.

But not without reason did I use these words *if only I could resolve in earnest*. For though I perceived these things [that is, this evil] so clearly in my mind, I still could not, on that account, put aside all greed, desire for sensual pleasure and love of esteem.

[11]   I saw this, however: that so long as the mind was turned toward these thoughts, it was turned away from those things, and was thinking seriously about the new goal. That was a great comfort to me. For I saw that those evils would not refuse to yield to remedies. And although in the beginning these intervals were rare, and lasted a very short time, nevertheless, after the true good became more and more known to me, the intervals became more frequent and longer—especially after I saw that the acquisition of money, sensual pleasure, and esteem are only obstacles so long as they are sought for their own sakes, and not as means to other things. But if they are sought as means, then they will have a limit, and will not be obstacles at all. On the contrary, they will be of great use in attaining the end on account of which they are sought, as we shall show in its place.

[12]   Here I shall only say briefly what I understand by the true good, and at the same time, what the highest good is. To understand this properly, it must be noted that good and bad are said of things only in a certain respect, so that one and the same thing can be called both good and bad according to different respects. The same applies to perfect and imperfect. For nothing, considered in its own nature, will be called perfect or imperfect, especially after we have recognized that everything that happens happens according to the eternal order, and according to certain laws of Nature.

[13]   But since human weakness does not grasp that order by its own thought, and meanwhile man conceives a human nature much stronger and more enduring than his own, and at the same time sees that nothing prevents his acquiring such a nature, he is spurred to seek means that will lead him to such a perfection. Whatever can be a means to his attaining it is called a true good; but the highest good is to arrive—together with other individuals if possible—at the enjoyment of such a nature. What that nature is we shall show in its proper place: that it is the knowledge[c] of the union that the mind has with the whole of Nature.

---

c.   These things will be explained more fully in their place.

[14]   Hic est itaque finis, ad quem tendo, talem scilicet naturam acquirere, &, ut multi mecum eam acquirant, conari, hoc est, de mea felicitate etiam est operam dare, ut alii multi idem, atque ego intelligant, ut eorum intellectus, & cupiditas prorsus cum meo intellectu, & cupiditate conveniant; utque hoc fiat,[d] necesse est [Vooreerst] tantum de Natura intelligere, quantum sufficit, ad talem naturam acquirendam; deinde formare talem societatem, qualis est desideranda, ut quamplurimi quam facillime, & secure eo perveniant.

[15]   Porro [, ten darden,] danda est opera Morali Philosophiae, ut & Doctrinae de puerorum Educatione; &, quia Valetudo non parvum est medium ad hunc finem assequendum, concinnanda est [, ten vierden,] integra Medicina; & quia arte multa, quae difficilia sunt, facilia redduntur, multumque temporis, & commoditatis in vita ea lucrari possumus, ideo [ten vijfden,] Mechanica nullo modo est contemnenda.

[16]   Sed ante omnia excogitandus est modus medendi intellectus, ipsumque, quantum initio licet, expurgandi, ut feliciter res absque errore, & quam optime intelligat. Unde quisque jam poterit videre, me omnes scientias ad unum finem,[e] & scopum velle dirigere, scilicet, ut ad summam humanam, quam diximus, perfectionem perveniatur; & sic omne illud, quod in scientiis nihil ad finem [et scopum] nostrum nos promovet, tanquam inutile erit rejiciendum, hoc est, ut uno verbo dicam, omnes nostrae operationes, simul & cogitationes ad hunc sunt dirigendae finem.

[17]   Sed quia, dum curamus eum consequi, & operam damus, ut intellectum in rectam viam redigamus, necesse est vivere, propterea ante omnia cogimur quasdam vivendi regulas, tanquam bonas, supponere, has scilicet.

I.   Ad captum vulgi loqui, & illa omnia operari, quae nihil impedimenti adferunt, quominus nostrum scopum attingamus. Nam non parum emolumenti ab eo possumus acquirere, modo ipsius captui, quantum fieri potest, concedamus; adde, quod tali modo amicas praebebunt aures ad veritatem audiendam.

---

    d. Nota, quod hic tantum curo enumerare scientias ad nostrum scopum necessarias, licet ad earum seriem non attendam.
    e. Finis in scientiis est unicus, ad quem omnes sunt dirigendae.

[14]   This, then, is the end I aim at: to acquire such a nature, and to strive that many acquire it with me. That is, it is part of my happiness to take pains that many others may understand as I understand, so that their intellect and desire agree entirely with my intellect and desire. To do this it is necessary,[d] *first,* to understand as much of Nature as suffices for acquiring such a nature; *next,* to form a society of the kind that is desirable, so that as many as possible may attain it as easily and surely as possible.

[15]   *Third,* attention must be paid to Moral Philosophy and to Instruction concerning the Education of children. Because Health is no small means to achieving this end, *fourthly,* the whole of Medicine must be worked out. And because many difficult things are rendered easy by ingenuity, and we can gain much time and convenience in this life, *fifthly,* Mechanics is in no way to be despised.

[16]   But before anything else we must devise a way of healing the intellect, and purifying it, as much as we can in the beginning, so that it understands things successfully, without error and as well as possible. Everyone will now be able to see that I wish to direct all the sciences toward one end[e] and goal, viz. that we should achieve, as we have said, the highest human perfection. So anything in the sciences which does nothing to advance us toward our goal must be rejected as useless—in a word, all our activities and thoughts are to be directed to this end.

[17]   But while we pursue this end, and devote ourselves to bringing the intellect back to the right path, it is necessary to live. So we are forced, before we do anything else, to assume certain rules of living as good:

1. To speak according to the power of understanding of ordinary people, and do whatever does not interfere with our attaining our purpose. For we can gain a considerable advantage, if we yield as much to their understanding as we can. In this way, they will give a favorable hearing to the truth.

---

d. Note that here I take the trouble only to enumerate the sciences necessary for our purpose, without attending to their order.

e. In the sciences there is only one end, toward which they must all be directed.

II. Deliciis in tantum frui, in quantum ad tuendam valetudinem sufficit.

III. Denique tantum nummorum, aut cujuscunque alterius rei quaerere, quantum sufficit ad vitam, & valetudinem sustentandam, & ad mores civitatis, qui nostrum scopum non oppugnant, imitandos.

2. To enjoy pleasures just so far as suffices for safeguarding our health.

3. Finally, to seek money, or anything else, just so far as suffices for sustaining life and health, and conforming to those customs of the community that do not conflict with our aim.

I Commentary

In a penetrating and beautiful study, Zweerman demonstrates that the first section of the *Treatise* is carefully built following the ancient rules of rhetoric so as to give maximum force to the attempt to seduce readers into a new way of life and of thinking.[1] This is done in a highly stylized, quasi-autobiographical account. It presents the reader with the dramatic story of a kind of exemplary conversion from ordinary life to a life of wisdom.[2] In §§ 1–11, the reader is first confronted, as in a mirror, with an autobiographical "I." This "I" is the "I" of Everyman, with whom the reader can easily identify. In the next passage, §§ 12–13, the perspective changes drastically; the reader now is confronted with the "I" of the master, who has already reached the goal and presents us with the way to reach it ourselves. This "I," speaking in an objective, almost impersonal fashion, describes a truly philosophical perspective (the perspective of the lover of wisdom). He does this only briefly (§ 12), because the ordinary reader cannot immediately comprehend this perspective in full. The fact that the master seems to know so well what is going on in ordinary human life has the result that, however briefly he tells us about the right perspective, we will attempt to reorganize our lives accordingly. So in §§ 14–17, the "I" of the first section reappears and, with the master, draws the conclusions concerning the implementation of the philosophical perspective.

As Zweerman and Bernard Rousset have noticed, the changes in perspective are accompanied by changes in vocabulary. In the first perspective, the vocabulary has a strong Cartesian flavor (words like "meditation," "persistent meditation," "distraction," "attention," and "clear perception"). In the perspective of the master, we are introduced to words that are distinctively Spinozistic ("to understand" [*intelligere*], "Nature," "true good," and "highest good").

I The Perspective of Everyman (§§ 1–11)

In this section, Spinoza recalls an ethical experience that has paradigmatic value: experiencing the futility of pursuing ordinary goods. Some have seen this section as an account of Spinoza's personal experience as *Mercator Sapiens Amstelodamensis,*[3] the wise Jewish merchant of Amsterdam. The text is replete with talk about goods and calculations concerning them, and with considerations of the personal "economy" of happiness.

Harry Frankfurt, on the other hand, has claimed that in this section Spinoza reveals himself as anxiety-ridden with respect to powerful sexual desires and competitive urges and as displaying an Oedipal syndrome.[4] Frankfurt links this to the thesis that a certain motivation underpins rationalist systems such as Descartes's and Spinoza's. Both attempt to come to terms with a chaotic, irrational world, either outside (Descartes) or inside oneself (Spinoza). Descartes solves his problem by withdrawing to an orderly inner world; Spinoza does so by substituting the order of the universe for the chaos within himself. These are speculative, overgeneralizing theses, and it is difficult to take them seriously. This section is not strictly autobiographical but rather a highly stylized, traditional, and paradigmatic account of human life. And as we have seen in chapter 1, Spinoza is not at all the withdrawn, ascetic philosopher one sometimes imagines him to be. He strongly rejects asceticism[5] and is quite capable of enjoying ordinary life and company; in a word, he appears to be more of a "realist." A careful reading of the whole of this section reveals that ordinary goods are not rejected in and of themselves (§ 11); they are rejected when they excessively occupy our mind. Spinoza's thought seems to be in full accord here with other religious traditions, which tell us not to reject "worldly" goods but not to be possessed by them, either.[6]

Whether the perspective of Everyman opens itself to the intervention of the master depends upon a particular self-experience and its development. The course of ordinary life normally brings about a certain disillusionment and a certain wisdom: an experience of the futility of ordinary pursuits and the realization that the things we fear or hope for are not good or bad in themselves (§ 1). This leads to the idea that there may be a *real* good, which continuously gives the greatest joy. But this idea does not immediately lead to the decision to search for this real good, for we realize that in this search we might have to lose a certain good for the sake of obtaining something uncertain (§ 2). The attempt to have it both ways fails, however, because the pursuit of ordinary goods occupies the mind too strongly and makes our happiness depend excessively on extrinsic factors (§§ 3–5).

The resolution at last to find out whether there is a true or certain good and to go after it (§ 1) depends on two new considerations. The first concerns the distinction between "a good by its nature uncertain" and a good "uncertain not by its nature . . . but only in respect of its attainment" (§ 6). The second, more important consideration, obtained after persistent meditation, is that there is no real choice but to pursue the *real,* certain good, whatever it may be (§ 7). This second consideration depends on the insight that the pursuit of ordinary goods is actually a kind of possession, a kind of folly: the pursuit not of a good uncertain by its nature but of a certain evil. Avarice, ambition, and lust "are nothing but species of madness, although they are not enumerated among diseases" (*Ethics* IV, P. 44, Sch). The move from uncertain good to certain evil is demonstrated in §§ 7–8.

So the only real option is to look for the second kind of good, however uncertain we may be as to its attainment: it is all or nothing. In this search, we are like people suffering from a fatal illness, whose only hope is to find a real remedy (§ 7). Anticipating a fundamental truth from the theory of emotions in the *Ethics* (IV, P. 47, Sch.), at this stage Spinoza attributes to Everyman the insight that the way out of this fluctuation between fear and hope is love —not the love of ordinary things but the love directed toward something eternal and infinite (§§ 8–10). Unfortunately, knowing this does not seem to be enough to master it (§ 10).

The way out of a life of dreams into real life and health is not found so easily: considerations such as the foregoing do not immediately help people put aside old habits. The removal from one way of life (*institutum:* § 3),[7] with its own peculiar emotional economy (pursuit of ordinary goods), into the new (*novum institutum,* § 11), with its new economy (of certain, true goods) and its new *ethos* (of love), will depend on yet another crucial experience and discovery. The very intervals of meditation on human life and its real good prove unexpectedly to be a real comfort (*solatio*[8]) for the mind. In this way, the discovery is made that there are remedies against the evils of the old habits.

This kind of thinking is a way of looking at (one's own) human life "from outside," as it were, from beyond the dream: it requires a certain estrangement from our ordinary selves.[9] But at the same time, the activity in which this estrangement happens is lived as a discovery of our true selves, is experienced as a kind of happiness, a kind of comfort. We discover here a force in us that we did not know but that was always already there; the remedy is not something external to us.[10] These intervals can even become more frequent and longer, especially, says Spinoza, after the insight into the true good dawns upon us, and after we realize that ordinary goods can be pursued harmlessly, as steps toward the true good (§ 11). This true good will turn out to be that which makes us *independent* of extrinsic determinations. The true good will turn out to be *autonomy,* which consists in pure understanding and the joy accompanying it. The new way of life is not one in which the ordinary goods are left behind, which is quite impossible (see section 3). It is a sort of life in which the pursuit of ordinary goods is accompanied by a distancing attitude toward them. In this way the attitude present in the thinking that proves to be a remedy can also somehow extend itself into ordinary life.

All this shows how different Spinoza's starting point is from Descartes's. The latter's philosophical conversion consists in a dissatisfaction with all traditional learning and the attempt to reach certainty in one's own thinking through methodical doubt. Spinoza's conversion more resembles Pascal's wager: it is concerned with the "reckoning of chances" for real happiness. Yet the solution is completely different: for Pascal, it is a leap of faith, a faith containing the promise of a reward to be fulfilled only in the afterlife; for Spinoza, it is a certain kind of understanding, an activity that is its own reward, the breakthrough of eternity in time, in this life. The alternative is not this life or the afterlife; it is the choice between ordinary life—which is a form of madness, leading inexorably to the death one feared—or the new life of pure understanding, in which death is feared no longer (*Ethics* IV, P. 67; V, P. 41).

The Philosophical Perspective (§§ 12–13)

With § 12 the perspective changes drastically; the tone of voice is different, more solemn, more impersonal. Now it is the master speaking. He lifts the veil of deeper insights, but not yet completely: the philosophical (ethical) perspective is indicated here only briefly.

What does the master have to say? First, "it must be noted" that good or bad, perfect or imperfect, can be said of things not as they are in themselves, considered according to what they really are, but only from the perspective of man as inevitably striving to preserve himself. Second, "everything that happens happens according to the eternal order, and according to certain laws of Nature"; everything is determined.

Surely, these two truths are not commonly accepted, even among philosophers. So Spinoza seems to ask quite a lot of his readers. The supposition seems to be that the reader is by now so impressed with the way the master has been telling the story of his own life that he or she is prepared to make a real jump: to listen to the master also when he speaks from a perspective that is quite uncommon, and to draw certain conclusions with him that will allow Everyman to adopt this philosophical perspective. Perhaps

Spinoza's expectations with respect to his readers were not that extravagant after all. In those days thought was not totally unfavorable toward determinism: Calvinists preached the idea of predestination (a concept playing an important role in Spinoza's *Short Treatise*), and since the Renaissance, Stoic ideas about fate had been revived and played a role in the common culture.[11]

Paragraph 13 indicates how, notwithstanding the truth of determinism, an ethical perspective is possible and inescapable. This has to do with the *interim* position of man (an idea introduced by the word "meanwhile"). People are on their way toward their destination, but without knowing exactly what this will be concretely, because they cannot know the precise order of causes or where time will bring them. "In the meantime," they cannot stop striving for whatever it is that they see as the ideal.

Even the philosopher (the master) forms this ethical perspective because first, he does not grasp the eternal order of Nature, the weakness of his thought not allowing him to understand why things actually follow from each other the way they do (to understand this would require an infinite regress); second, he inevitably forms the idea of "a human nature much stronger and more enduring than his own" as an ideal toward which he strives;[12] and, finally, he "sees that nothing prevents his acquiring such a nature, [so] he is spurred to seek means that will lead him to such a perfection."

In the preface of *Ethics* IV, Spinoza will repeat that rational people know that things are neither good nor bad in and of themselves, neither perfect nor imperfect, and that these notions do not express anything real. Yet even rational people continue to form the notion of an ideal person, and with it the related ideas of good and bad that express our true knowledge of what promotes or hinders the coming about of this ideal. Why is this? Knowledge about the truth of determinism does not eliminate one's striving to persist in one's own being, one's *conatus*.[13] This *conatus* gives rise to conscious desires for what was experienced before as good or bad (pleasurable or painful). Even the *conatus* of the rational man remains a conscious striving, but one determined by rational insight into man's real nature and capacities and into what is, or is not, compatible with the acquisition of such a nature and capacities. Rational insight into human nature (as provided in *Ethics* II and III) teaches us that each human individual is a mind, a thinking thing that can arrive at a stage of knowing, providing a level of satisfaction that goes far beyond the pleasures produced by ordinary goods. The *desirability* of such a nature (that is, of such a development of human nature) makes it into an ideal and changes the means to obtain this perfection into a good (and the opposite into something bad).

The desirability of the ideal depends, of course, on somehow having the *experience* of the satisfaction accompanying thinking and on the insight that "nothing prevents [our] acquiring such a nature." Both requirements are fulfilled, not only in the master but also somehow in the pupil, at least if he or she has had the experience of meditating described in § 11: this experience demonstrated not only the satisfaction of thinking but also the fact that this joy is not impossible for us to obtain. Of course, if we knew exactly the real order of nature—the actual causal order of things—we could not desire what is perhaps impossible. But the weakness of our thought, even in rational people, does not allow this knowledge. On the basis of our *conatus,* we inevitably desire an ideal, which is a kind of possibility, not proven to be unreachable (because in fact we reached it already somehow in the past).

This ideal, which as such has no ontological significance (it is not the idea of something real), is the ideal that all human beings have in common *insofar as* they are capable of understanding and of desiring understanding (see also *Ethics* IV, P. 29–37).

At this point Spinoza can explain what is a true good and what is the highest good. (In *Ethics* IV, P. 27–28, he again distinguishes between "a certain good" and "the highest good.") A *true good* is "whatever can be a means to his [man's] attaining it [the model of a perfect human nature]." *The highest good* is "to arrive—together with other individuals if possible—at the enjoyment of such a [perfect] nature." Spinoza adds that, "in its proper place," he will give further details as to what this ideal human nature is (in the last propositions of *Ethics* IV, he calls this the ideal of "the free man"). The highest good is the realization of the ideal by means of true goods. Since it is an ideal common to all rational people, it is not surprising that it is realized in community with others and under the guidance of a master.

At this stage, Spinoza briefly indicates the content of the ideal: "it is the knowledge of the union that the mind has with the whole of Nature." Again, in a footnote, he adds that this will be explained more fully in its right place, in the philosophy properly speaking. The link between the highest good and the enjoyment of a nature, which is identified with a kind of knowledge, will indeed be found in *Ethics* IV, P. 26–28, and a second time in book V of the *Ethics.*[14] It is clear already from the *Treatise* that the highest good is seen as the enjoyment of a "perfect" human nature— that is, the realization of a human capacity to know, which knowledge goes together with real happiness. This knowledge is a kind of self-conscious relating of oneself to Nature. It is a kind of *activity* in which one enjoys oneself, in which one finds inner peace and security. This knowledge will turn out to be of the kind in which one *distances* oneself from one's ordinary life and consciousness (this is already implied in §§ 11 and 12). We will have to raise the question of how such knowledge can ever constitute highest happiness (this will require an analysis of *Ethics* V, in particular).

The philosophical perspective that Spinoza presents here is paradoxical: it is an ethical perspective introduced within a naturalistic philosophy. It has been said that it constitutes a new kind of humanism, a "naturalized humanism" that escapes the anthropocentric ideas of Christian humanism,[15] but perhaps also those of ordinary, enlightened humanism, even of the present day.[16] This philosophical perspective is a blend of a naturalistic philosophy and a kind of humanism. Man is ultimately an element of nature, which itself has no ends in view, certainly not the happiness of mankind. Nevertheless, being a *conatus* that is somehow the expression of nature, which is itself immanent in man, one can reach a certain way of life (*institutum*) in which one enjoys real happiness. This happiness consists in knowing, in recognizing, what one really is. "To become what one really is (in knowing what one really is)"—this is the message of the philosopher. Although nature is not there for man, yet *in* man nature is powerful as knowledge, and in this knowledge man can somehow find real happiness, realizing he exists as a part of nature for no further reason: As the seventeenth-century German mystic Silesius wrote, "Die Ros ist ohne warum" (Roses are there for no reason whatsoever).

The Program for Real Happiness (§§ 14–17)

If the true and the highest good are really what we have just been told they are, then we can and must set up a plan to acquire it. The plan is geared toward the acquisition of a certain state of knowledge; so it is not surprising that the strategy to reach the end should consist largely in the acquisition of knowledge. Actually, the plan contains all the sciences, all sorts of learning as well as the related techniques ("activities and thoughts"): it forms a real "cybernetics,"[17] or steering device, directing us to our life's goal (§ 16).

At the beginning of this section (§ 14), and taking up an idea expressed at the end of the previous section, Spinoza indicates, without much explanation, that my happiness is linked to others' also acquiring real understanding, or at least to my striving to bring about such good company. Agreement (*convenientia*) with others in "intellect and desire" is said to be extremely important for obtaining one's own end. As Spinoza will explain later in the *Ethics* (IV, P. 35–37), this is not simply because, from a utilitarian perspective, people who live under the guidance of reason are most useful to each other. More important is that they "share the same nature" (*Ethics* IV, P. 35, Cor. 1) and that the enjoyment of this nature is enhanced by noticing that others love what one loves oneself (*Ethics* IV, P. 37, second proof). This idea of a *convenientia,* an agreement in nature between all people (*Ethics* IV, P. 31, 32), reminds one of Stoic ideas.[18] The *convenientia* of intellects is no longer based on the ordinary desire for honor; it is characterized by virtues and desires, such as being honorable (*honestas*) (*Ethics* IV, P. 37, Sch. 1), which is practically the same as nobility (*generositas*), which is in turn a subspecies of strength of character (*fortitudo*) (*Ethics* IV, P. 73, Sch., referring to III, P. 59, Sch.: all of these desires are, for Spinoza, forms of "the desire by which each one strives, solely from the dictate of reason, to aid other men and join them to him in friendship").

To change oneself into a knower and to form such a community of friends, a complex machinery has to be put to work, a kind of *universitas scientiarum (et artium),* a whole system of the sciences, including arts and technology.[19] We are reminded here of the old image of the tree of knowledge, also used by Bacon, Descartes, Hobbes, and others. Spinoza does not put the arts and sciences in a logical order but simply enumerates them. It is important to stress the specific character of this program: only those things that contribute to the end are included, and only to the degree they really do this (§ 16). Once more, it is evident that Spinoza's ultimate preoccupation is *ethical* in the broad sense indicated. Spinoza distinguishes formally between end (*finis*) and goal (*scopus*): *finis* indicates the overall end, which is happiness; *scopus* indicates the end as specified in a more precise way, that is, as goal. The distinction again derives from Stoic philosophy.[20]

The program contains the following:

1. a metaphysics, "to understand as much of Nature as suffices for acquiring such a[n ideal] nature." Notice there is no mention of a physics; in *Ethics* II Spinoza will introduce rudimentary elements of a physics (*Ethics* II, P. 13, Sch.), but he adds that his intention is not "to deal expressly

with body," because this is "not necessary for the things I wish to demonstrate."[21]

2. the plan to form a society "of the kind that is desirable, so that as many as possible may attain it [the ideal human nature] as easily and surely as possible." This looks like a purely practical aim, but it is likely that Spinoza had in mind the development of a theoretical understanding of politics as well as the practice of politics. His own political theory—both in the *Tractatus Theologico-Politicus* and in the *Tractatus Politicus*—is a practical science.

3. "Moral Philosophy" and the "Instruction concerning the Education of Children." What Spinoza meant here is the sort of practical ethics we find in *Ethics* IV and V. As to education, it is likely that he was thinking of the sort of humanistic education he himself got in the Latin School of Van den Enden.

4. "the whole of Medicine," again a combination of science and practical arts.

5. "Mechanics," to "gain much time and convenience in this life"; through this, "many difficult things are rendered easy by ingenuity." Inevitably one thinks of Bacon's idea of mastering nature by cleverly obeying it.

6. "before anything else, we must devise a way of healing the intellect, and purifying it, as much as we can in the beginning, so that it understands things successfully, without error and as well as possible." This part of the program can be called a *logica* in its two elements: to separate truth from error and to understand as perfectly as possible.

It is illuminating to compare this "cybernetic" program to other programmatic passages in Spinoza. In the third chapter of the *Tractatus Theologico-Politicus*, Spinoza indicates the three fundamental aims of human beings: to understand things through their first cause, to master the passions or to acquire the habit of virtue, and to live in security and good health.[22] The first and second have to do with metaphysics and ethics and are said to lie in man's power. The third—good health and security—has to do with medicine and politics and are known to be gifts of fortune (notwithstanding the fact that in medicine and politics we try to master fortune as much as possible). If only the first and second aim are really in our power, it is of particular importance to develop metaphysics and ethics as soon as possible. The means to get there in a way that is not itself dependent on fortune is

logic. The opposition between the cunning of learning and fortune (*ars* as against *fortuna*) plays a central role in the logic itself. The whole point of the logic is to escape the influence of
fortune in one's thinking by acquiring the means to operate the
cybernetic machine leading us to our end. The art allowing us to
do this turns out to be our *innate* power to think. This power is
"activated" in the artful "purification" of our intellect, which is
performed in a persistent meditation on true ideas already in our
mind. Although certain external conditions have to be fulfilled
before *ars* can take its course (a level of economic, social, cultural,
and individual development), the mastery of the art itself is the
work of the innate capacities of the individual.

What does it mean "before anything else," to "devise a way of
healing the intellect, and purifying it"? We will learn this in the
rest of the *Treatise.* The steps are precisely described—in reverse
order—in a letter (37) to Johannes Bouwmeester, who asked
Spinoza whether there is a real method to skillfully (*arte*) im-
prove the understanding, or whether we are dependent on fortune (*fortuna*). The steps are as follows: (1) to gain reflexive
knowledge of pure intellect and of its nature and laws; (2) to pu-
rify the intellect by distinguishing intellect and imagination, or
true ideas and fictitious, false, and dubious ideas; (3) to engage in
a short description of the mind and its ideas (*historiola mentis*) in
the way Bacon has taught us; and (4) to decide on a way of life
according to a fixed plan. The following sections of the *Treatise*
are an exact implementation of points 3 to 1 in the letter to Bouwmeester.[23] The fourth point is worked out in the last paragraph (§
17) of this section: it develops a provisional morality in three
rules.

In paragraph 16 we learned that, before anything else, we
must engage in logic or "devise a way of healing the intellect, and
purifying it." But "while we . . . devote ourselves to bringing the
intellect back to the right path, it is necessary to live," says paragraph 17. Therefore, there is yet another task to perform "before
anything else": "to assume certain rules of living as good," to
adopt a *provisional morality.* When we read the rules carefully,
we see that they refer to the three goods that were discussed at
the beginning of this section (thus rhetorically constituting a nice
circle). The rules require moderation with respect to honor, sensual pleasure, and wealth. As we have seen in § 11, the pursuit of
these goods as a means to something else does no harm. On the
contrary, because these goods are basic ones (concerning contact,
health, and nourishment), it is essential to continue to obtain
them, albeit with the right attitude. Even the philosopher has to

live. This provisional morality will therefore turn out to remain a full part of the interim morality (discussed in §§ 12–13 and to be developed in *Ethics* IV[24]).

I NOTES

1. Zweerman 1993.
2. The word "sapientia" is used, for example, in *TEI* § 31.
3. Van Suchtelen 1985.
4. Frankfurt 1986.
5. *E* IV, P. 45, Sch.
6. It is remarkable how many insights about human life and emotionality expressed in *Ethics* IV are present in this section.
7. Curley translates *institutum* as "plan" or "goal"; along with Zweerman, I prefer "institution."
8. This is possibly an echo of Boethius's *De consolatione philosophiae.*
9. This problematic is dealt with extensively in Nagel 1986. The title of his book, *The View from Nowhere,* (deliberately?) echoes Spinoza's view of things *sub specie aeternitatis.*
10. The notion of remedy that I use here will return in *E* V, P. 20, Sch.
11. A "stoical" poem of the seventeenth-century Dutch poet P. C. Hooft with the title "Noodlot" (Fate) was quoted by Spinoza's friend Jarig Jelles in the preface of the *Nagelate Schriften.* (For the important role played by Justius Lipsius in the spread of Stoic ideas in the Renaissance and early modernity, see Zanta 1914; Abel 1978; and Saunders 1955.)
12. There are similar ideas in Arnold Geulincx's *Ethica* (which Spinoza must have read); see De Vleeschauwer 1964 (reference found in Zweerman 1993, 163n.14).
13. The notion of *conatus* is clearly present in the *Treatise;* see, for example, §§ 7, 14.
14. Questions inevitably arise as to why Spinoza had to express this twice, and what the difference is between the two accounts. As we will discuss later, the second account (*Ethics* V) implies that the striving toward an (external) ideal is somehow overcome, and that a life beyond longing is possible.
15. Zweerman 1974.
16. De Dijn 1993.
17. Zweerman 1993, 187.
18. Zweerman 1993, 190n.11 (reference to the Stoic theme of "consentment").
19. Koyré (Spinoza 1990, 98, 99) refers here to Bacon (and his expression *propter augmentum scientiarum et artium*), to Descartes, and to Rosicrucian thinking. See also Spinoza 1992, 168, where Rousset refers further to Aristotle, Hobbes, and Geulincx; Zweerman (1993, 185–88) notices that Spinoza does not include in his list of arts and sciences theology or fine arts.
20. Rousset notes this in Spinoza 1992, 182.
21. Spinoza 1985, 462, 458.

22. G 3:46 (28–31). These aims are a version of the traditional distinction between *logos — ethos — pathos;* see Zweerman 1993, 231.

23. The *Treatise* implements all three points. This proves that the *Treatise,* although unfinished, cannot have been far from completion.

24. On this provisional morality or interim morality, see also Zweerman 1993, 197–209.

A Short Survey of the Mind (§§ 18–29): The Means to Obtain the End

| Text

[18] Hisce sic positis, ad primum, quod ante omnia faciendum est, me accingam, ad emendandum scilicet intellectum, eumque aptum reddendum ad res tali modo intelligendas, quo opus est, ut nostrum finem assequamur. Quod ut fiat, exigit ordo, quem naturaliter habemus, ut hic resumam omnes modos percipiendi, quos hucusque habui ad aliquid indubie affirmandum, vel negandum, quo omnium optimum eligam, & simul meas vires, & naturam, quam perficere cupio, noscere incipiam.

[19] Si accurate attendo, possunt omnes ad quatuor potissimum reduci.

I. Est Perceptio, quam ex auditu, aut ex aliquo signo, quod vocant ad placitum, habemus.

II. Est Perceptio, quam habemus ab experientia vaga, hoc est, ab experientia, quae non determinatur ab intellectu; sed tantum ita dicitur, quia casu sic occurrit, & nullum aliud habemus experimentum, quod hoc oppugnat, & ideo tanquam inconcussum apud nos manet.

III. Est Perceptio, ubi essentia rei ex alia re concluditur, sed non adaequate; quod fit,^f cum vel ab aliquo effectu

---

f. Hoc cum fit, nihil de causa intelligimus praeter id, quod in effectu consideramus: quod satis apparet ex eo, quod tum causa non nisi generalissimis terminis explicetur, nempe his, *Ergo datur aliquid, Ergo datur aliqua potentia, &c.* Vel etiam ex eo, quod ipsam negative exprimant, *Ergo non est hoc, vel illud, &c.* In secundo casu aliquid causae tribuitur propter effectum, quod clare concipitur, ut in exemplo ostendemus; verum nihil praeter propria, non vero rei essentia particularis.

[18]   Having laid down these rules, I come now to what must be done first, before all else: emending the intellect and rendering it capable of understanding things in the way the attainment of our end requires. To do this, the order we naturally have requires me to survey here all the modes of perceiving which I have had up to now for affirming or denying something without doubt, so that I may choose the best of all, and at the same time begin to know my powers and the nature that I desire to perfect.

[19]   If I consider them accurately, I can reduce them all to four main kinds:

1.   There is the Perception we have from report or from some conventional sign.

2.   There is the Perception we have from random experience, that is, from experience that is not determined by the intellect. But it has this name only because it comes to us by chance, and we have no other experiment that opposes it. So it remains with us unshaken.

3.   There is the Perception that we have when the essence of a thing is inferred from another thing, but not adequately. This happens, either[f] when we infer the cause

---

f.   When this happens, we understand nothing about the cause except what we consider in the effect. This is sufficiently evident from the fact that then the cause is explained only in very general terms, *e.g., Therefore there is something, Therefore there is some power, etc.* Or also from the fact that the terms express the cause negatively, *Therefore it is not this, or that, etc.* In the second case something clearly conceived is attributed to the cause on account of the effect, as we shall show in an example; but nothing is attributed to it except *propria,* not the essence of a particular thing.

causam colligimus, vel cum concluditur ab aliquo universali, quod semper aliqua proprietas concomitatur.

IV. Denique Perceptio est, ubi res percipitur per solam suam essentiam, vel per cognitionem suae proximae causae.

[20] Quae omnia exemplis illustrabo. Ex auditu tantum scio meum natalem diem, & quod tales parentes habui, & similia; de quibus nunquam dubitavi. Per experientiam vagam scio me moriturum: hoc enim ideo affirmo, quia vidi alios mei similes obiisse mortem, quamvis neque omnes per idem temporis spatium vixerint, neque ex eodem morbo obierint. Deinde per experientiam vagam etiam scio, quod oleum sit aptum alimentum ad nutriendam flammam, quodque aqua ad eam extinguendam apta sit; scio etiam, quod canis sit animal latrans, & homo animal rationale, & sic fere omnia novi, quae ad usum vitae faciunt.

[21] Ex alia vero re hoc modo concludimus: postquam clare percipimus, nos tale corpus sentire, & nullum aliud, inde, inquam, clare concludimus animam unitam[g] esse corpori, quae unio est causa talis sensationis; sed[h] quaenam sit illa sensatio, & unio, non absolute inde possumus intelligere.

Vel postquam novi naturam visus, & simul, eum habere talem proprietatem, ut unam, eandemque rem ad magnam distantiam minorem videamus, quam si eam cominus intueamur, inde concludimus Solem majorem esse, quam apparet, & alia his similia.

[22] Per solam denique rei essentiam res percipitur; quando ex eo, quod aliquid novi, scio, quid hoc sit aliquid nosse, vel ex eo, quod novi essentiam animae, scio eam corpori esse

---

g. Ex hoc exemplo clare videre id est, quod modo notavi. Nam per illam unionem nihil intelligimus praeter sensationem ipsam, effectus scilicet, ex quo causam, de qua nihil intelligimus, concludebamus.

h. Talis conclusio, quamvis certa sit, non tamen satis tuta est, nisi maxime caventibus. Nam nisi optime caveant sibi, in errores statim incident: ubi enim res ita abstracte concipiunt, non autem per veram essentiam, statim ab imaginatione confunduntur. Nam id, quod in se unum est, multiplex esse imaginantur homines. Nam iis, quae abstracte, seorsim, & confuse concipiunt, nomina imponunt, quae ab ipsis ad alia magis familiaria significandum usurpantur; quo fit, ut haec imaginentur eodem modo, ac eas res imaginari solent, quibus primum haec nomina imposuerunt.

from some effect, or when something is inferred from some universal, which some property always accompanies.

4. Finally, there is the Perception we have when a thing is perceived through its essence alone, or through knowledge of its proximate cause.

[20]   I shall illustrate all of these with examples. I know only from report my date of birth, and who my parents were, and similar things, which I have never doubted. By random experience I know that I shall die, for I affirm this because I have seen others like me die, even though they had not all lived the same length of time and did not all die of the same illness. Again, I also know by random experience that oil is capable of feeding fire, and that water is capable of putting it out. I know also that the dog is a barking animal, and man a rational one. And in this way I know almost all the things that are useful in life.

[21]   But we infer [one thing] from another in this way: after we clearly perceive that we feel such a body, and no other, then, I say, we infer clearly that the soul is united[g] to the body, which union is the cause of such a sensation; but we cannot understand absolutely from this what[h] that sensation and union are. Or after we have come to know the nature of vision, and that it has the property that we see one and the same thing as smaller when we look at it from a great distance than when we look at it from close up, we infer that the sun is larger than it appears to be, and other things of the same kind.

[22]   Finally, a thing is perceived through its essence alone when, from the fact that I know something, I know what it is to know something, or from the fact that I know the essence of the soul, I know that it is united to the body. By the same kind of

----

g. We see clearly from this example what I have just noted. For we understand nothing through that union except the sensation itself, that is, the effect, from which we inferred the cause, concerning which we understand nothing.

h. Although such a conclusion is certain, it is still not sufficiently safe, unless we take the greatest care. For those who do not take such care will immediately fall into errors. When things are conceived so abstractly, and not through their true essence, they are immediately confused by the imagination. What in itself is one, men imagine to be many. For to the things they conceive abstractly, separately, and confusedly, they give names which they use to signify other more familiar things. Hence they imagine these things in the same way as they are accustomed to imagine the things to which the names were first given.

unitam. Eadem cognitione novimus duo & tria esse quinque, &, si dentur duae lineae uni tertiae parallelae, eas etiam inter sese parallelas, &c. Ea tamen, quae hucusque tali cognitione potui intelligere, perpauca fuerunt.

[23]　Ut autem haec omnia melius intelligantur, unico tantum utar exemplo, hoc scilicet. Dantur tres numeri: quaerit quis, quartum, qui sit ad tertium, ut secundus ad primum. Dicunt hic passim mercatores, se scire, quid sit agendum, ut quartus inveniatur, quia nempe eam operationem nondum oblivioni tradiderunt, quam nudam sine demonstratione a suis magistris audiverunt; alii vero ab experientia simplicium faciunt axioma universale, scilicet ubi quartus numerus per se patet, ut in his 2, 4, 3, 6, ubi experiuntur, quod ducto secundo in tertium, & producto deinde per primum diviso fiat quotiens 6; & cum vident eundem numerum produci, quem sine hac operatione noverant esse proportionalem, inde concludunt operationem esse bonam ad quartum numerum proportionalem semper inveniendum.

[24]　Sed Mathematici vi demonstrationis Prop. 19. lib. 7. Euclidis sciunt, quales numeri inter se sint proportionales, scilicet ex natura proportionis, ejusque proprietate, quod nempe numerus, qui fit ex primo, & quarto aequalis sit numero, qui fit ex secundo, & tertio; attamen adaequatam proportionalitatem datorum numerorum non vident, & si videant, non vident eam vi illius Propositionis, sed intuitive, [of] nullam operationem facientes.

[25]　Ut autem ex his optimus eligatur modus percipiendi, requiritur, ut breviter enumeremus, quae sint necessaria media, ut nostrum finem assequamur, haec scilicet.

I. Nostram naturam, quam cupimus perficere, exacte nosse, & simul tantum de rerum natura, quantum sit necesse.

II. Ut inde rerum differentias, convenientias, & oppugnantias recte colligamus.

III. Ut recte concipiatur, quid possint pati, quid non.

IV. Ut hoc conferatur cum natura, & potentia hominis. Et ex istis facile apparebit summa, ad quam homo potest pervenire, perfectio.

knowledge, we know that two and three are five, and that if two lines are parallel to a third line, they are also parallel to each other, etc. But the things I have so far been able to know by this kind of knowledge have been very few.

[23]   That you may understand all these things better, I shall use only one example. Suppose there are three numbers. Someone is seeking a fourth, which is to the third as the second is to the first. Here merchants will usually say that they know what to do to find the fourth number, because they have not yet forgotten that procedure which they simply heard from their teachers, without any demonstration.

Others will construct a universal axiom from an experience with simple numbers, where the fourth number is evident through itself—as in the numbers 2, 4, 3, and 6. Here they find by trial that if the second is multiplied by the third, and the product then divided by the first, the result is 6. Since they see that this produces the same number which they knew to be the proportional number without this procedure, they infer that the procedure is always a good way to find the fourth number in the proportion.

[24]   But Mathematicians know, by the force of the demonstration of Proposition 19 in Book VII of Euclid, which numbers are proportional to one another, from the nature of proportion, and its property, *viz.* that the product of the first and fourth numbers is equal to the product of the second and third. Nevertheless, they do not see the adequate proportionality of the given numbers. And if they do, they see it not by the force of that Proposition, but intuitively, [or] without going through any procedure.

[25]   To choose the best mode of perceiving from these, we are required to enumerate briefly the means necessary to attain our end:

1. To know exactly our nature, which we desire to perfect, and at the same time,
2. [To know] as much of the nature of things as is necessary,
    (a) to infer rightly from it the differences, agreements and oppositions of things,
    (b) to conceive rightly what they can undergo and what they cannot,
    (c) to compare [the nature of things] with the nature and power of man.

This done, the highest perfection man can reach will easily manifest itself.

[26]   His sic consideratis videamus, quis modus percipiendi nobis sit eligendus.

Quod ad primum attinet. Per se patet, quod ex auditu, praeterquam quod sit res admodum incerta, nullam percipiamus essentiam rei, sicuti ex nostro exemplo apparet; & cum singularis existentia alicujus rei non noscatur, nisi cognita essentia, uti postea videbitur: hinc clare concludimus omnem certitudinem, quam ex auditu habemus, a scientiis esse secludendam. Nam a simplici auditu, ubi non praecessit proprius intellectus, nunquam quis poterit affici.

[27][i]   Quoad secundum. Nullus etiam dicendus est, quod habeat ideam illius proportionis, quam quaerit. Praeterquam quod sit res admodum incerta, & sine fine, nihil tamen unquam tali modo quis in rebus naturalibus percipiet praeter accidentia, quae nunquam clare intelliguntur, nisi praecognitis essentiis. Unde etiam & ille secludendus est.

[28]   De tertio autem aliquo modo dicendum, quod habeamus ideam rei, deinde quod etiam absque periculo erroris concludamus; sed tamen per se non erit medium, ut nostram perfectionem acquiramus.

[29]   Solus quartus modus comprehendit essentiam rei adaequatam, & absque erroris periculo; ideoque maxime erit usurpandus. Quomodo ergo sit adhibendus, ut res incognitae tali cognitione a nobis intelligantur, simulque, ut hoc quam compendiose fiat, curabimus explicare:

------

i.   Hic aliquanto prolixius agam de experientia; & Empiricorum, & recentium Philosophorum procedendi Methodum examinabo.

[26]   Having considered these requirements, let us see which mode of perceiving we ought to choose.

As for the first, it is evident in itself that from report—apart from the fact that it is a very uncertain thing—we do not perceive any essence of a thing, as is clear from our example. And since the existence of any singular thing is not known unless its essence is known (as we shall see afterwards), we can clearly infer from this that all the certainty we have from report is to be excluded from the sciences. For no one will ever be able to be affected by simple report, unless his own intellect has gone before.

[27]   As for the second,[i] again, no one should be said to have the idea of that proportion which he is seeking. Apart from the fact that it is a very uncertain thing, and without end, in this way no one will ever perceive anything in natural things except accidents. But these are never understood clearly unless their essences are known first. So that also is to be excluded.

[28]   Concerning the third, on the other hand, we can, in a sense, say that we have an idea of the thing, and that we can also make inferences without danger of error. But still, it will not through itself be the means of our reaching our perfection.

[29]   Only the fourth mode comprehends the adequate essence of the thing and is without danger of error. For that reason, it is what we must chiefly use. So we shall take care to explain how it is to be used, that we may understand unknown things by this kind of knowledge and do so as directly as possible;

---

i.   Here I shall discuss experience somewhat more fully, and examine the Method of proceeding of the Empiricists and of the new Philosophers.

I Commentary

As we have seen, the first task in respect of the ultimate end, happiness, is "before all else: emending the intellect and rendering it capable of understanding things in the way the attainment of our end requires. To do this, the order we naturally have requires me to survey here all the modes of perceiving which I have had up to now for affirming or denying something without doubt, so that I may choose the best of all, and at the same time begin to know my powers and the nature that I desire to perfect" (§ 18). In letter 37 Spinoza calls this task a short description of the mind and its ideas (*historiola mentis*) "in the way of Bacon."[1] This description must provide us with the means to find our way toward the end toward which we are striving.

This "short history" of the mind consists of an enumeration of four modes of perceiving, of "affirming or denying something without doubt."[2] No justification is given for the enumeration; the reader is supposed to find it straightforward and corresponding to fact.

As for Descartes, the term "perception" has a broad meaning for Spinoza, equivalent to the term "idea" or "cognition" (in the *Ethics,* Spinoza distinguishes three kinds of cognition, or knowledge in the broad sense). A perception or idea is the *apprehension* of an object or of a relation of objects. A perception or idea is the *acquaintance* with an object (or relation of objects) in thought, in which the object or objects are automatically affirmed to be (or not to be) thus and such (or related in such and such a way), unless the presence of another idea or perception prevents this affirmation.[3] Spinoza calls affirmation or negation a form of *willing* intrinsic to an idea (or perception): idea and willing (of this sort) are one.[4]

Like ideas or acts of willing, emotions or affects also are called modes of thought; but they necessarily presuppose ideas or perceptions in the sense defined, whereas ideas can exist without consequent emotions (but not without affirmation or negation, or the suspension of them in doubt and fiction).[5]

Like "idea" or "perception," the equivalent term "knowledge" (*cognitio*) also is used by Spinoza in a broad sense: it again refers to different sorts of acts of knowing involving an affirmation or negation. For Spinoza, conceiving or understanding something normally goes together with affirming or denying what one understands or conceives; these acts are part of a process of thinking that results in the affirmation or negation of something. For

Spinoza, real understanding (*intellectio*) is the same as real knowledge (*cognitio; scientia*).

Spinoza surveys only those kinds of perception that are characterized as affirmation or denial *without doubt*. Only judgments with no doubt involved are possible means toward our end—the end being knowledge of our power and nature (*scopus*) in which we somehow find happiness (*finis*). We will see that the kinds of perception Spinoza enumerates, although all exempt from doubt, differ as to the character of their certainty, their "clearness and distinctness."[6] For Spinoza, certainty and clearness and distinctness of ideas should be understood not so much in terms of their capacity to withstand Cartesian doubt but in terms of the intrinsic characteristics of the ideas, those which make them into real ideas. So although much Cartesian vocabulary is used (perception, certainty, and clearness and distinctness), this does not automatically mean that we are being presented with a Cartesian problematic, even on the epistemological or methodological levels.

Spinoza distinguished four main kinds (or modes) of perception. In the *Short Treatise*[7] and in the *Ethics*,[8] Spinoza only makes a threefold distinction as to ways of knowing: the first and second kinds in the *Treatise* are grouped together as the first. Concerning the second (third) and third (fourth) kinds, there are subtle changes from one book to another. As Rousset rightly points out, the reason for this difference is undoubtedly that a *historiola mentis* is different from a real *theory* of the different kinds of human knowing. In a theory, one would have to demonstrate their difference on the basis of an explanatory insight into man's nature and capacities.[9] Another reason may be that the second kind of knowing—that "from random experience" (§ 19.2)—is here singled out, so that it becomes a separate object of criticism, in fact a critique of Baconian empiricism.[10]

I Perception of the First Kind

This is "the Perception we have from report or from some conventional sign" (§ 19.1). Spinoza includes as examples: "I know only from report my date of birth, and who my parents were, and similar things, which I have never doubted" (§ 20).

This kind of knowing, through verbal or written signs, is the least important (§ 26); Spinoza's remarks here constitute an implicit critique of Hobbes and of Scholastic thinking.[11] Later (§§ 88–89), Spinoza will point out that language of itself is a dangerous tool because the signification of words is arbitrary and at the same time adapted to the unsophisticated level of thinking of the common people. Sometimes accidental combinations of words stuck in the memory suggest fanciful conceptions; this is the source of much (sometimes even serious) error. In science we should use language with great care.[12] However, as we will see, Spinoza is not condemning language in general.

In his examples of this kind of perception, Spinoza uses the word *scire* ("to know") because the perceptions are indubitable for us. This type of knowledge, related to learning from report and tradition, is quite sufficient for everyday living, and it is ridiculous to apply Cartesian doubt to it. Together with the second type, it belongs (as we will see in § 84) to the *imaginatio* as opposed to the *intellectus* (§ 86). The *imaginatio* is the capacity to form *imaginationes* — apprehensions of, and judgments concerning, objects derived from sense experience, memory, and fantasy. In the first part of the method (§§ 52–90), Spinoza ranks under the *imaginatio* all knowing based on false, dubious, and fictitious ideas and on memory and language not guided by the intellect. As we have seen, a major task of the *Treatise* is a purification of the intellect, its separation from the imagination. The *intellectus* is the capacity to form apprehensions/judgments based on clear and distinct ideas or perfectly intelligible ideas, which are called true (§ 84) and adequate (a term especially used in the *Ethics*). In the *Ethics,* the *imaginatio* will be strongly criticized as the source of all sorts of illusions (for example, it is the source of belief in miracles). Nevertheless, this criticism should be understood in the context of a search for real knowledge. In daily life, this kind of knowledge based on report and tradition is absolutely necessary; when Spinoza discusses daily life and its common sense (as in the *Tractatus Theologico-Politicus*), he speaks much more favorably about this kind of knowledge.[13]

| Perception of the Second Kind

This is "the Perception we have from random experience [*experientia vaga*], that is, from experience that is not determined by the intellect. But it has this name only because it comes to us by chance, and we have no other experience that opposes it. So it remains with us unshaken" (§ 19.2). For example, Spinoza says, "By random experience I know that I shall die, . . . that oil is capable of feeding fire, and that water is capable of putting it out. I know also that the dog is a barking animal, and man a rational one. And in this way I know almost all the things that are useful in life" (§ 20). Curley rightly translates *experientia vaga* not as "vague" but as "random experience." The second characteristic is negative: it is experience *not* determined by the intellect, and only indubitable because nothing has ever opposed it (and put it in doubt). This suggests that there is knowledge from experience that can be determined by the intellect and is indubitable not by accident but through intellectual thinking (see § 102).

This kind of knowledge probably is singled out to afford an opportunity to criticize empiricists, such as Bacon, who take this kind of knowing as a solid basis for science (see Spinoza's critique of Bacon in letters 4 and 6). As Spinoza later indicates (§ 27), this kind of perception is "very uncertain" and "without end," teaching us only accidental characteristics of things that cannot be properly understood except within a proper scientific context (in Spinoza's sense[14]). The understanding reached here is "without end": it can be increased endlessly without ever leading to a real understanding of things, because it proceeds without order and without providing real insight into the links between things. It is "very uncertain" because it can be jeopardized by new experience.

The examples that Spinoza gives repeat traditional definitions of "the dog" and of "man." This is an implicit critique of the use made in scientific thinking of abstractions, general notions, and universals and of related axioms (explicitly criticized in *Ethics* II, P. 40, Sch. 1, where all these are distinguished from *notiones communes,* which are the basis of science). In § 23 we are given an example of the unsatisfactory nature of abstractions based on experience and of the use of such axioms in arithmetic.

I Perception of the Third Kind

This is "the Perception that we have when the essence of a thing is inferred from another thing, but not adequately. This happens, either when we infer the cause from some effect, or when something is inferred from some universal, which some property always accompanies" (§ 19.3).

This third kind of indubitable perception is not accidental or random; it proceeds in an orderly fashion. It has to do with understanding in terms of causes and effects or consists in proofs, both of which are intellectual ways of knowing. Yet this kind of knowing is not really *adequate* (a Spinozistic term indicating complete knowledge of a thing) because it does not lead to a real insight into the essence of things. Spinoza is using here Aristotelian-Scholastic terminology to express his own ideas. Understanding things has to do with understanding their essence and properties. This understanding is arrived at in proofs, or in reasonings concerning cause and effect. In § 85 he approvingly quotes an old Aristotelian-Scholastic saying: "veram scientiam procedere a causa ad effectus" (true scientific knowledge proceeds from causes to effects). Cause and effect are actually epistemic terms here: "cause" refers to that which makes a thing into what it is (a thing with such and such an essence); "effect" refers to what follows from the thing's essence, that is, certain properties. This is why there is such a close connection between thinking in terms of cause and effect and proof (Spinoza even sometimes uses the expression "cause or reason" ("causa sive ratio," *Ethics* I, P. 11, Dem. 2). There really is no difference, epistemically speaking, between cause, essential trait, and principle, on the one hand, and effect, property, and consequence, on the other. To understand and explain things by way of proofs, by the derivation of consequences from principles, is the same as properly explaining characteristics of things on the basis of an apprehension of their essence, which is the same as knowing *why* things are what they are and why they have the properties they have. "Proof" should be taken here in the Scholastic sense as consisting in syllogisms, in which the link between something and some property is demonstrated on the basis of a middle term giving the "cause or reason" for the combination of the subject term and the predicate in the conclusion.

How is it possible for a perception that consists of proof, or of knowing in terms of causes and effects, not to be adequate? This becomes clear when we consider the two cases that Spinoza distinguishes in this kind of knowing.[15] The first is "when we infer the cause from some effect." In footnote f, Spinoza clarifies this as follows: "When this happens, we understand nothing about the cause except what we consider in the effect. This is sufficiently evident from the fact that then the cause is explained only in very general terms, e.g., *Therefore there is something, Therefore there is some power, etc.* Or also from the fact that the terms express the cause negatively, *Therefore it is not this, or that, etc.*" In § 21 Spinoza gives the example of sensation: the moment we have a sensation, we can infer as its cause the union of mind and body. But this inference gives no insight into the precise nature of the sensation or into the union.

Footnote g shows how this example demonstrates the inadequacy of this kind of knowing:[16] the "cause" inferred is not really understood because this "inference" provides no more insight into the "effect" than we already had. Footnote h adds that although the conclusion of the inference "is certain, it is still not sufficiently safe, unless we take the greatest care." Whence this danger? If we think things without first having an insight into their true nature or into the nature of their causes, we conceive them abstractly. To think things *abstractly* is to think them without knowing that they are effects that cannot properly be understood *in separation* from their causes, or that what we think about them is a consequence that requires the understanding of principles. Spinoza does not elaborate on this here (he will do so later; see chapter 6 below). He simply points out the dangers of such abstract thinking through an example. The principal danger is confusion of intellectual thinking with the data of the imagination, particularly with what is thought under abstract terms.

The example that Spinoza uses here is clearly a Cartesian one. With this example Spinoza wants to demonstrate two things: that in itself the inference is correct (certain), but that it does not give real insight (into the "cause"); and that it contains certain dangers. The conclusion does not add more insight than we have already in the premises. (*Major:* Sensation requires a union; *minor:* There is sensation; *conclusion:* There is a union.) In this way, we have no real explanation of the *effect,* the sensation ("that we feel such a body, and no other"), which is known only *abstractly,* as separated from its causes. So we have no real insight into the *cause,* the union of mind and body. Indeed, there is a great danger here: since we do not come to a more adequate understanding of the sensation, we will not have an accurate insight into the union. This insight will be easily confused with other images of union through the influence of abstract terms (such as "union"). This is actually what happened to Descartes, who came to think of the union of mind and body as a kind of blending of two different substances.[17] Implicitly Spinoza demonstrates the necessity of separating pure intellect from imagination.

The second case (of inferential knowledge that is not really adequate) is "when [the cause] is inferred (*colligere*[18]) from some universal, which some property always accompanies." In footnote f this is clarified as follows: "In the second case something clearly conceived is attributed to the cause on account of the effect, as we shall show in an example; but nothing is attributed to it except *propria,* not the essence of a particular thing."

In Spinoza's second example, that of the nature of vision and our consequent inference about the sun (§ 21), we start from a universal and a property concerning an effect and infer a property concerning its cause. The effect is a certain vision of the sun, of which we know that—as all cases of vision—it has the property indicated. From all this we infer that the sun is much larger than it appears.[19] The same goes for the example in § 24: the general proportionality of numbers, combined with a certain property, allows us, if applied to concrete numbers, to infer the missing number and to know the rationale (or "cause") of the "effect" (or problem of the missing number).

The fact that Spinoza can give examples from such vastly different domains as psychology and arithmetic indicates that his "cause-effect" terminology is epistemological, or methodological. A cause is always that which really explains, a *rationale: causa sive ratio.* In quasi-Aristotelian language one could say that "cause" means "formal cause," and that, even when "efficient causation" is involved (as in the case of sensation or vision), to *understand* it is to be able to reduce it to "formal causation," to rational insight and inference.[20]

The third kind of knowledge gives us "an idea of the thing, and [allows us to] also make inferences without danger of error [if we are careful enough]." Yet it is not "through itself . . . the means of reaching our perfection" (§ 28). In the *Ethics,* the account of the corresponding (second) kind of knowledge seems at first to be very different from the one given here. In the *Ethics,* the second kind of knowledge (*ratio*) is between *imaginatio* and *scientia intuitiva;* it is knowledge based on common notions (*notiones communes*), which are distinguished carefully from universal notions and the like (*Ethics* II, P. 40, Sch. 1, 2). This *ratio*[21] seems to play an important role in the properly ethical part of the *Ethics* (*Ethics* IV and V), as regards the attainment of our perfection, our ultimate end. It looks as if Spinoza completely revised his conception of the meaning and the importance of this indubitable kind of knowledge. (Some, such as Gilles Deleuze, even claim that the discovery of *notiones communes* is the reason that Spinoza left the *Treatise* unfinished.[22]) Perhaps, following Alexandre Matheron, one should not overemphasize the absence of the concept of "common notion."[23] After all, Spinoza gives here only a survey of the kinds of perception that everyone is supposed to be familiar with in terminology adapted to the matter at hand, a *historiola mentis.* Nothing indicates that the Cartesian-Baconian presentation of this third kind of knowledge could not be amended in a Spinozistic way. Furthermore, even in the *Ethics,* the second kind of knowledge (*ratio*) is not really the proper means to the ethical end of salvation.[24]

| The Fourth Kind of Perception

"Finally, there is the Perception we have when a thing is perceived through its essence alone, or through knowledge of its proximate cause" (§ 19.4). For example, "a thing is perceived through its essence alone when, from the fact that I know something, I know what it is to know something, or from the fact that I know the essence of the soul, I know that it is united to the body. By the same kind of knowledge, we know that two and three are five, and that if two lines are parallel to a third line, they are also parallel to each other, etc." (§ 22; see also the mathematical example in § 24).

The mathematical examples are not adequate to the definition of this kind of perception.[25] They are supposed to draw attention to the *intuitive* character of this kind of knowledge ("without going through any procedure," § 24). Intuitive knowledge, of course, does not exclude knowledge of a complex relation between objects; on the contrary, all the examples Spinoza gives here are of such complex relations. For a full account of this type of knowledge—which does not belong in this short survey—we have to wait until later (§§ 72, 95).

When Spinoza ends his examples, he adds: "the things I have so far been able to know by this kind of knowledge have been very few." This indicates that the mathematical examples serve only as analogies: in principle, one can give many such examples, whereas Spinoza confesses that he knows very few things in the fourth way. Yet Spinoza considered mathematics as a bridge between prephilosophical and philosophical thinking.[26] Mathematics teaches us in an exemplary way what real thinking means, even though it is not yet real thinking of reality itself.

The other examples that Spinoza adduces are to "know what it is to know something" (which is in a sense the topic of the *Treatise* itself), and the union of mind and body (an example from *Philosophia*). The second example seems the same as the one given in connection with the third kind of perception. Yet there is a fundamental difference, because the basis of this intuitive knowledge is not Cartesian sensation but, supposedly, knowledge of the *essence* of the mind. Knowing the human mind is knowing the union adequately, because the mind is nothing but the idea of an object that is the human body; from which it follows "that the human Mind is united to the Body, but also what should be understood by the union of Mind and Body" (*Ethics* II, P. 13, Cor. and Sch.).

The first example is of a perception where a thing is known "through its essence alone"; the second of a perception where a thing is known "through knowledge (*cognitio*) of its proximate cause" (that is, as we will see later, through those intrinsic determinations which explain the thing's essence). Notice that, in the whole enumeration, this is the first time that Spinoza uses the term *cognitio*. In this type of "perception" things are known *really*, not superficially—that is, *through* their *intrinsic* determinations, making them into *what* they are. Therefore, this type of perception yields truth (see § 71). As Rousset points out, only at this point does Spinoza use the word through (*per*) instead of from (*ex, ab*).[27] That there is something (the essence) through which a thing *is* really *what* it *is* is put forward without more ado, as something self-evident and indisputable.[28]

Again Spinoza uses here common, Scholastic distinctions. A thing that can be perceived perfectly "through its essence alone" clearly does not have to be perceived "through its proximate cause," and a thing to be perceived "through its proximate cause" cannot be perceived "through its essence alone" (see §§ 92ff.). This means that, strictly speaking, the first example is not really to the point, because to know that one knows *does* have a proximate cause. We are confronted anew with the fact that this exposition is only an enumeration with a limited purpose, using examples that guide the reader to a certain level of comprehension.

Again we see that Spinoza expresses his ideas about knowledge in terms of causation. Again this must be understood as a search, in the comprehension of things, not for their *concrete, efficient* causes but for those elements that give a rationale for why the thing is what it is (thereby explaining also *that* it is?). In the second part of the *Methodology* (§§ 91ff.), Spinoza discusses how this is to be understood.

I Conclusion (§§ 25–29)

This survey of the different modes of perfection is part of a strategy toward an end (happiness) that is itself dependent on *knowledge,* both of our own nature and of our power (in comparison to other things). So the sort of perception or knowledge we have to choose in order to reach the ultimate end (*finis*) must put at our disposal the means: (1) to know exactly our nature, which we desire to perfect, and at the same time as much of the nature of things as is necessary (see *Ethics* I and II); (2) to infer rightly from it the differences, agreements, and oppositions of things (see *Eth-*

ics II and III); (3) to conceive rightly what they can undergo and what not (see *Ethics* III and IV); and (4) to compare the nature of things with the nature and power of man (see *Ethics* IV and V).[29]

According to Rousset, this enumeration given in § 25 corresponds to that given in the *Ethics*.[30] To infer from the nature of things "the differences, agreements and oppositions" (point 2)[31] is what Spinoza seems to be doing in *Ethics* II and III, where, on the basis of experiential data (expressed in some of the axioms and postulates) he discusses similarities and differences between human beings and other things. In *Ethics* II, P. 29, Sch., Spinoza opposes the confused, inadequate knowledge of ourselves, of our own body, and of external bodies—which is the product of *imaginatio*—to another kind of knowledge, one in which the mind "is determined internally, from the fact that it regards a number of things at once, to understand their agreements, differences, and oppositions . . . then it [the mind] regards things clearly and distinctly." In the *Ethics* this capacity of the mind is closely connected with the formation of *notiones communes*. It is difficult to attribute this knowledge of differences, agreements, and oppositions to the fourth kind of perception; on the other hand, it plays a crucial role in the movement toward our end. This seems to allow for the idea that the third kind could and should play a certain role within the fourth kind (as will be the case in the *Ethics*).

The evaluation of the four kinds of perception as possible means (steps) toward our end leads to the conclusion that we have to rely *chiefly* on the fourth kind of knowledge (§ 29). "So we shall take care to explain how it is to be used, that we may understand unknown things by this kind of knowledge and do so as directly as possible" (this question is taken up again in the second part of the Method: see § 49). Spinoza says that the third sort of perception is not "through itself" a good means, and that the fourth is the chief means to our end. This suggests that already at the time of the *Treatise,* Spinoza may have accepted some sort of cooperation between the two sorts of knowledge. Later, this becomes the cooperation between knowledge based on *notiones communes* and intuitive knowledge.[32]

There is much left to be explained about various elements in this quick survey of the different sorts of perceptions; much will become clearer in the following phases of the logic. Spinoza intended this survey mainly as a device to make sure that on our way toward our end, we put ourselves on the right track, using the right vehicle: perception of the fourth kind.

I NOTES

1. De Dijn 1974b, 12n. 1.
2. Parallels can be found in Descartes, Geulincx, the Port Royal school, and older sources; see Rousset's comment in Spinoza 1992, 181.
3. *E* II, P. 49, Sch.
4. *TEI* § 34n. u; *E* II, P. 49, Cor.
5. *E* II, Def. 3.
6. The Cartesian expression "clear and distinct" is identical to the typical Spinozistic expression "adequate."
7. *ST* II, chaps. 1 and 2 (Spinoza 1985, 97–99).
8. *E* II, P. 40, Sch. 2.
9. Spinoza 1992, 180.
10. Bartuschat makes this point in Spinoza 1993, 105 (referring to Bacon, *Novum Organon* 1.100).
11. Rousset notes this in Spinoza 1992, 182.
12. Concerning Spinoza and language, see Mark 1978, § 8 (with references given to the discussion between G. H. R. Parkinson and D. Savan); also Donagan 1988, 49–53.
13. For a well-argued defense of the importance of the first kind of knowledge according to Spinoza, see De Deugd 1966.
14. See the discussion of *TEI* §§ 102–3 in chapter 8.
15. Matheron (1988, 105) claims these two cases come down to the same thing.
16. This is not the same as "inadequacy" as understood in the *Ethics*.
17. Spinoza's conception of "union" is explained in *E* II, P. 13, Sch. (see also Bartuschat's explanation in Spinoza 1993, 106).
18. *Colligere,* as in the tables of Bacon; see Rousset's comment in Spinoza 1992, 184.
19. The example comes from Bacon, as Rousset points out (Spinoza 1992, 189).
20. In footnote i, Spinoza says: "Here I shall discuss experience somewhat more fully, and examine the Method of proceeding of the Empiricists and of the new Philosophers." He never worked this out. See, however, his correspondence with Boyle (through Oldenburg, the secretary of the Royal Society) on the nature of science (letters 6, 11, 13, and 15); see also Bartuschat's reference to studies of Franco Biasutti and Elhanan Yakira concerning Spinoza and experimental science in Spinoza 1993, 107; and Rousset's comments in Spinoza 1992, 202. Concerning Spinoza and science in general, see Grene and Nails 1986, and the other works mentioned in the appendix.
21. See chapter 10.
22. Deleuze 1968, 271–72.
23. Matheron 1988.
24. De Dijn 1992a; see also chapter 11.
25. Concerning Spinoza's conception of mathematics, see Medina 1985; Matheron 1986.
26. This is clear also from the *Ethics* I, App., and from other passages of the *Treatise*.
27. Spinoza 1992, 185.
28. Bartuschat notes this in Spinoza 1993, 105.

29. I followed here the order of the Latin text, not of Curley's translation (which adopts H. H. Joachim's emendation of the numbering and punctuation); see Spinoza 1985, 15n. 22.

30. Spinoza 1992, 199–201.

31. Rousset points out that this kind of inference can also be found in Stoic philosophy and in Bacon; see Spinoza 1992, 199.

32. See my interpretation of *TEI* § 100 in chapter 8.

The Way and the Method
(§§ 30–49): Spinoza's Methodology

| Text

[30]   [dat is] postquam novimus, quaenam Cognitio nobis sit necessaria, tradenda est Via, & Methodus, qua res, quae sunt cognoscendae, tali cognitione cognoscamus. Quod ut fiat, venit prius considerandum, quod hic non dabitur inquisitio in infinitum; scilicet, ut inveniatur optima Methodus verum investigandi, non opus est alia Methodo, ut Methodus veri investigandi investigetur; &, ut secunda Methodus investigetur, non opus est alia tertia, & sic in infinitum: tali enim modo nunquam ad veri cognitionem, imo ad nullam cognitionem perveniretur. Hoc vero eodem modo se habet, ac se habent instrumenta corporea, ubi eodem modo liceret argumentari. Nam, ut ferrum cudatur, malleo opus est, & ut malleus habeatur, eum fieri necessum est; ad quod alio malleo, aliisque instrumentis opus est, quae etiam ut habeantur, aliis opus erit instrumentis, & sic in infinitum; & hoc modo frustra aliquis probare conaretur, homines nullam habere potestatem ferrum cudendi.

[31]   Sed quemadmodum homines initio innatis instrumentis quaedam facillima, quamvis laboriose, & imperfecte, facere quiverunt, iisque confectis alia difficiliora minori labore, & perfectius confecerunt, & sic gradatim ab operibus simplicissimis ad instrumenta, & ab instrumentis ad alia opera, & instrumenta pergendo, eo pervenerunt, ut tot, & tam difficilia parvo labore perficiant; sic etiam intellectus[k] vi sua nativa facit sibi instrumenta intellectualia, quibus alias vires acquirit ad

---

k. Per vim nativam intelligo illud, quod in nobis a causis externis non causatur, quodque postea in mea Philosophia explicabimus.

[30]   [I.e.,] after we know what Knowledge is necessary for us, we must teach the Way and Method by which we may achieve this kind of knowledge of the things that are to be known.

To do this, the first thing we must consider is that there is no infinite regress here. That is, to find the best Method of seeking the truth, there is no need of another Method to seek the Method of seeking the truth, or of a third Method to seek the second, and so on, to infinity. For in that way we would never arrive at knowledge of the truth, or indeed at any knowledge.

Matters here stand as they do with corporeal tools, where someone might argue in the same way. For to forge iron a hammer is needed; and to have a hammer, it must be made; for this another hammer, and other tools are needed; and to have these tools too, other tools will be needed, and so on to infinity; in this way someone might try, in vain, to prove that men have no power of forging iron.

[31]   But just as men, in the beginning, were able to make the easiest things with the tools they were born with (however laboriously and imperfectly), and once these had been made, made other, more difficult things with less labor and more perfectly, and so, proceeding gradually from the simplest works to tools, and from tools to other works and tools, reached the point where they accomplished so many and so difficult things with little labor, in the same way the intellect, by its inborn power,[k] makes intellectual tools for itself, by which it acquires other pow-

---

k. By inborn power I understand what is not caused in us by external causes. I shall explain this afterwards in my Philosophy.

alia opera[1] intellectualia, & ex iis operibus alia instrumenta, seu potestatem ulterius investigandi, & sic gradatim pergit, donec sapientiae culmen attingat.

[32] Quod autem intellectus ita sese habeat, facile erit videre, modo intelligatur, quid sit Methodus verum investigandi, & quaenam sint illa innata instrumenta, quibus tantum eget ad alia ex iis instrumenta conficienda, ut ulterius procedat. Ad quod ostendendum sic procedo.

[33] Idea[m] vera (habemus enim ideam veram) est diversum quid a suo ideato: Nam aliud est circulus, aliud idea circuli. Idea enim circuli non est aliquid, habens peripheriam, & centrum, uti circulus, nec idea corporis est ipsum corpus: & cum sit quid diversum a suo ideato, erit etiam per se aliquid intelligibile; hoc est, idea, quoad suam essentiam formalem, potest esse objectum alterius essentiae objectivae, & rursus haec altera essentia objectiva erit etiam in se spectata quid reale, & intelligibile, & sic indefinite.

[34] Petrus ex. gr. est quid reale; vera autem idea Petri est essentia Petri objectiva, & in se quid reale, & omnino diversum ab ipso Petro. Cum itaque idea Petri sit quid reale, habens suam essentiam peculiarem, erit etiam quid intelligibile, id est, objectum alterius ideae, quae idea habebit in se objective omne id, quod idea Petri habet formaliter, & rursus idea, quae est ideae Petri, habet iterum suam essentiam, quae etiam potest esse objectum alterius ideae, & sic indefinite. Quod quisque potest experiri, dum videt se scire, quid sit Petrus, & etiam scire se scire, & rursus scit se scire, quod scit, &c. Unde constat, quod, ut intelligatur essentia Petri, non sit necesse ipsam ideam Petri intelligere, & multo minus ideam ideae Petri; quod idem est, ac si dicerem, non esse opus, ut sciam, quod sciam me scire, & multo minus esse opus scire, quod sciam me scire; non magis, quam ad intelligendam essentiam trian-

---

1. Hic vocantur opera: in mea Philosophia, quid sint, explicabitur.

m. Nota, quod hic non tantum curabimus ostendere id, quod modo dixi, sed etiam nos hucusque recte processisse, & simul alia scitu valde necessaria.

ers for other intellectual works,[1] and from these works still other tools, or the power of searching further, and so proceeds by stages, until it reaches the pinnacle of wisdom.

[32]   It will be easy to see that this is the situation of the intellect, provided we understand what the Method of seeking the truth is, and what those inborn tools are, which it requires only to make other tools from them, so as to advance further. To show this, I proceed as follows.

[33]   A true idea[m] (for we have a true idea) is something different from its object. For a circle is one thing and an idea of the circle another—the idea of the circle is not something which has a circumference and a center, as the circle does. Nor is an idea of the body the body itself. And since it is something different from its object, it will also be something intelligible through itself; that is, the idea, as far as its formal essence is concerned, can be the object of another objective essence, and this other objective essence in turn will also be, considered in itself, something real and intelligible, and so on, indefinitely.

[34]   Peter, for example, is something real; but a true idea of Peter is an objective essence of Peter, and something real in itself, and altogether different from Peter himself. So since an idea of Peter is something real, having its own particular essence, it will also be something intelligible, i.e., the object of a second idea, which will have in itself, objectively, whatever the idea of Peter has formally; and in turn, the idea which is [the idea] of the idea of Peter has again its essence, which can also be the object of another idea, and so on indefinitely. Everyone can experience this, when he sees that he knows what Peter is, and also knows that he knows, and again, knows that he knows that he knows, etc.

From this it is evident that to understand the essence of Peter, it is not necessary to understand an idea of Peter, much less an idea of an idea of Peter. This is the same as if I said that, in order for me to know, it is not necessary to know that I know, much less necessary to know that I know that I know—no more than it is necessary to understand the essence of a circle in order

---

1.   Here they are called works. In my Philosophy, I shall explain what they are.

m.   Note that here we shall take care to show not only what we have just said, but also that we have so far proceeded rightly, and at the same time other things that it is quite necessary to know.

guli opus sit essentiam circuli^n intelligere. Sed contrarium
datur in his ideis. Nam ut sciam me scire, necessario debeo
prius scire.

[35]   Hinc patet, quod certitudo nihil sit praeter ipsam
essentiam objectivam; id est, modus, quo sentimus essentiam
formalem, est ipsa certitudo. Unde iterum patet, quod ad
certitudinem veritatis nullo alio signo sit opus, quam veram
habere ideam: Nam, uti ostendimus, non opus est, ut sciam,
quod sciam me scire. Ex quibus rursum patet, neminem posse
scire, quid sit summa certitudo, nisi qui habet adaequatam
ideam, aut essentiam objectivam alicujus rei; nimirum, quia
idem est certitudo, & essentia objectiva.

[36]   Cum itaque veritas nullo egeat signo, sed sufficiat
habere essentias rerum objectivas, aut, quod idem est, ideas, ut
omne tollatur dubium, hinc sequitur, quod vera non est Methodus signum veritatis quaerere post acquisitionem idearum, sed
quod vera Methodus est via, ut ipsa veritas, aut essentiae
objectivae rerum, aut ideae (omnia illa idem significant) debito
ordine^o quaerantur.

[37]   Rursus Methodus necessario debet loqui de Ratioci-
natione, aut de intellectione; id est, Methodus non est ipsum
ratiocinari ad intelligendum causas rerum, & multo minus est
τò intelligere causas rerum; sed est intelligere, qui sit vera idea,
eam a caeteris perceptionibus distinguendo, ejusque naturam
investigando, ut inde nostram intelligendi potentiam noscamus,
& mentem ita cohibeamus, ut ad illam normam omnia intelligat, quae sunt intelligenda; tradendo, tanquam auxilia, certas
regulas, & etiam faciendo, ne mens inutilibus defatigetur.

---

n. Nota, quod hic non inquirimus, quomodo prima essentia objectiva nobis innata sit. Nam id pertinet ad investigationem naturae, ubi
haec fusius explicantur, & simul ostenditur, quod praeter ideam nulla
datur affirmatio, neque negatio, neque ulla voluntas.
o. Quid quaerere in anima sit, explicatur in mea Philosophia.

to understand the essence of a triangle.[n] Indeed, in these ideas the opposite is the case. For to know that I know, I must first know.

[35]   From this it is clear that certainty is nothing but the objective essence itself, i.e., the mode by which we are aware of the formal essence is certainty itself. And from this, again, it is clear that, for the certainty of the truth, no other sign is needed than having a true idea. For as we have shown, in order for me to know, it is not necessary to know that I know. From which, once more, it is clear that no one can know what the highest certainty is unless he has an adequate idea or objective essence of some thing. For certainty and an objective essence are the same thing.

[36]   Since truth, therefore, requires no sign, but it suffices, in order to remove all doubt, to have the objective essences of things, or, what is the same, ideas, it follows that the true Method is not to seek a sign of truth after the acquisition of ideas, but the true Method is the way that truth itself, or the objective essences of things, or the ideas (all those signify the same) should be sought[o] in the proper order.

[37]   Again, the Method must speak about Reasoning, or about the intellection; i.e., Method is not the reasoning itself by which we understand the causes of things; much less the understanding of the causes of things, it is understanding what a true idea is by distinguishing it from the rest of the perceptions; by investigating its nature, so that from that we may come to know our power of understanding and so restrain the mind that it understands, according to that standard, everything that is to be understood; and finally by teaching and constructing certain rules as aids, so that the mind does not weary itself in useless things.

---

n. Note that here we are not asking how the first objective essence is inborn in us. For that pertains to the investigation of nature, where we explain these things more fully, and at the same time show that apart from the idea there is neither affirmation, nor negation, nor any will.

o. In my Philosophy, I shall explain what seeking is in the soul.

[38]   Unde colligitur, Methodum nihil aliud esse, nisi cognitionem reflexivam, aut ideam ideae; & quia non datur idea ideae, nisi prius detur idea, ergo Methodus non dabitur, nisi prius detur idea. Unde illa bona erit Methodus, quae ostendit, quomodo mens dirigenda sit ad datae verae ideae normam. Porro cum ratio, quae est inter duas ideas, sit eadem cum ratione, quae est inter essentias formales idearum illarum, inde sequitur, quod cognitio reflexiva, quae est ideae Entis perfectissimi, praestantior erit cognitione reflexiva caeterarum idearum; hoc est, perfectissima ea erit Methodus, quae ad datae ideae Entis perfectissimi normam ostendit, quomodo mens sit dirigenda.

[39]   Ex his facile intelligitur, quomodo mens, plura intelligendo, alia simul acquirat instrumenta, quibus facilius pergat intelligere. Nam, ut ex dictis licet colligere, debet ante omnia in nobis existere vera idea, tanquam innatum instrumentum, qua intellecta intelligatur simul differentia, quae est inter talem perceptionem, & caeteras omnes. Qua in re consistit una Methodi pars. Et cum per se clarum sit, mentem eo melius se intelligere, quo plura de Natura intelligit, inde constat, hanc Methodi partem eo perfectiorem fore, quo mens plura intelligit, & tum fore perfectissimam, cum mens ad cognitionem Entis perfectissimi attendit, sive reflectit.

[40]   Deinde, quo plura mens novit, eo melius & suas vires, & ordinem Naturae intelligit: quo autem melius suas vires intelligit, eo facilius potest seipsam dirigere, & regulas sibi proponere; & quo melius ordinem Naturae intelligit, eo facilius potest se ab inutilibus cohibere; in quibus tota consistit Methodus, uti diximus.

[41]   Adde quod idea eodem modo se habet objective, ac ipsius ideatum se habet realiter. Si ergo daretur aliquid in Natura, nihil commercii habens cum aliis rebus, ejus etiam si daretur essentia objectiva, quae convenire omnino deberet cum formali, nihil etiam[p] commercii haberet cum aliis ideis, id est,

---

p. Commercium habere cum aliis rebus est produci ab aliis, aut alia producere.

[38]   From this it may be inferred that Method is nothing but a reflexive knowledge, or an idea of an idea; and because there is no idea of an idea, unless there is first an idea, there will be no Method unless there is first an idea. So that Method will be good which shows how the mind is to be directed according to the standard of a given true idea.

Next, since the relation between the two ideas is the same as the relation between the formal essences of those ideas, it follows that the reflexive knowledge of the idea of the most perfect Being will be more excellent than the reflexive knowledge of any other ideas. That is, the most perfect Method will be the one that shows how the mind is to be directed according to the standard of the given idea of the most perfect Being.

[39]   From this you will easily understand how the mind, as it understands more things, at the same time acquires other tools, with which it proceeds to understand more easily. For, as may be inferred from what has been said, before all else there must be a true idea in us, as an inborn tool; once this true idea is understood, we understand the difference between that kind of perception and all the rest. Understanding that difference constitutes one part of the Method.

And since it is clear through itself that the mind understands itself the better, the more it understands of Nature, it is evident, from that that this part of the Method will be more perfect as the mind understands more things, and will be most perfect when the mind attends to, *or* reflects on, knowledge of the most perfect Being.

[40]   Next, the more the mind knows, the better it understands its own powers and the order of Nature. The better the mind understands its own powers, the more easily it can direct itself and propose rules to itself; the better it understands the order of Nature, the more easily it can restrain itself from useless pursuits. In these things, as we have said, the whole of the Method consists.

[41]   Moreover, the idea is objectively in the same way as its object is really. So if there were something in Nature that did not interact with other things, and if there were an objective essence of that thing which would have to agree completely with its formal essence, then that objective essence would not interact[p]

---

p.   To interact with other things is to produce, or be produced by, other things.

nihil de ipsa poterimus [verstaan noch] concludere; & contra,
quae habent commercium cum aliis rebus, uti sunt omnia, quae
in Natura existunt, intelligentur, & ipsorum etiam essentiae
objectivae idem habebunt commercium, id est, aliae ideae ex eis
deducentur, quae iterum habebunt commercium cum aliis, & sic
instrumenta, ad procedendum ulterius, crescent. Quod conaba-
mur demonstrare.

[42] Porro ex hoc ultimo, quod diximus, scilicet quod idea
omnino cum sua essentia formali debeat convenire, patet iterum, quod, ut mens nostra omnino referat Naturae exemplar,
debeat omnes suas ideas producere ab ea, quae refert originem,
& fontem totius Naturae, ut ipsa etiam sit fons caeterarum
idearum.

[43] Hic forte aliquis mirabitur, quod nos, ubi diximus,
bonam Methodum eam esse, quae ostendit, quomodo mens sit
dirigenda ad datae verae ideae normam, hoc ratiocinando
probemus: id quod ostendere videtur, hoc per se non esse notum. Atque adeo quaeri potest, utrum nos bene ratiocinemur?
Si bene ratiocinamur, debemus incipere a data idea, & cum
incipere a data idea egeat demonstratione, deberemus iterum
nostrum ratiocinium probare, & tum iterum illud alterum, & sic
in infinitum.

[44] Sed ad hoc respondeo: quod si quis fato quodam sic
processisset, Naturam investigando, scilicet ad datae verae
ideae normam alias acquirendo ideas debito ordine, nunquam
de sua veritate^q dubitasset, eo quod veritas, uti ostendimus, se
ipsam patefacit, & etiam sponte omnia ipsi affluxissent. Sed
quia hoc nunquam, aut raro contingit, ideo coactus fui illa sic
ponere, ut illud, quod non possumus fato, praemeditato tamen
consilio acquiramus, & simul, ut appareret, ad probandam
veritatem, & bonum ratiocinium, nullis nos egere instrumentis,
nisi ipsa veritate, & bono ratiocinio: Nam bonum ratiocinium
bene ratiocinando comprobavi, & adhuc probare conor.

---

q. Sicut etiam hic non dubitamus de nostra veritate.

with other ideas, i.e., we could not infer anything about it. And conversely, those things that do interact with other things (as everything that exists in Nature does) will be understood, and their objective essences will also have the same interaction, i.e., other ideas will be deduced from them, and these again will interact with other ideas, and so the tools for proceeding further will increase, which is what we were trying to demonstrate.

[42] Next, from what we have just said, that an idea must agree completely with its formal essence, it is evident that for our mind to reproduce completely the likeness of Nature, it must bring all of its ideas forth from that idea which represents the source and origin of the whole of Nature, so that that idea is also the source of the other ideas.

[43] Here, perhaps, someone will be surprised that, having said that a good Method is one which shows how the mind is to be directed according to the standard of a given true idea, we should prove this by reasoning. For that seems to show that this is not known through itself. So it may be asked whether our reasoning is good? If our reasoning is good, we must begin from a given [true?] idea; and since to begin from a given [true?] idea requires a demonstration, we must again prove our reasoning, and then once more prove that other reasoning, and so on to infinity.

[44] To this I reply that if, by some fate, someone had proceeded in this way in investigating Nature, i.e., by acquiring other ideas in the proper order, according to the standard of the given true idea, he would never have doubted[q] the truth he possessed (for as we have shown, the truth makes itself manifest) and also everything would have flowed to him of its own accord.

But because this never or rarely happens, I have been forced to lay things down in this way, so that what we cannot acquire by fate, we may still acquire by a deliberate plan, and at the same time so that it would be evident that to prove the truth and good reasoning, we require no tools except the truth itself and good reasoning. For I have proved, and still strive to prove, good reasoning by good reasoning.

---

q. As we also do not here doubt the truth we possess.

[45]   Adde, quod etiam hoc modo homines assuefiant
meditationibus suis internis. Ratio autem, cur in Naturae
inquisitione raro contingat, ut debito ordine ea investigetur, est
propter praejudicia, quorum causas postea in nostra Philosophia explicabimus. Deinde quia opus est magna, & accurata
distinctione, sicut postea ostendemus; id quod valde est laborio-
sum. Denique propter statum rerum humanarum, qui, ut jam
ostensum est, prorsus est mutabilis. Sunt adhuc alia rationes,
quas non inquirimus.

[46]   Si quis forte quaerat, cur ipse statim ante omnia
veritates Naturae isto ordine ostenderim: nam veritas se ipsam
patefacit? Ei respondeo, simulque moneo, ne propter Paradoxa,
quae forte passim occurrent, ea velit tanquam falsa rejicere; sed
prius dignetur ordinem considerare, quo ea probemus, & tum
certus evadet, nos verum assequutos fuisse, & haec fuit causa,
cur haec praemiserim.

[47]   Si postea forte quis Scepticus & de ipse prima
veritate, & de omnibus, quas ad normam primae deducemus,
dubius adhuc maneret, ille profecto aut contra conscientiam
loquetur, aut nos fatebimur, dari homines penitus etiam animo
occaecatos a nativitate, aut a praejudiciorum causa, id est,
aliquo externo casu. Nam neque seipsos sentiunt; si aliquid
affirmant, vel dubitant, nesciunt se dubitare, aut affirmare:
dicunt se nihil scire; & hoc ipsum, quod nihil sciunt, dicunt se
ignorare; neque hoc absolute dicunt: nam metuunt fateri, se
existere, quamdiu nihil sciunt; adeo ut tandem debeant obmu-
tescere, ne forte aliquid supponant, quod veritatem redoleat.

[48]   Denique cum ipsis non est loquendum de scientiis:
nam quod ad vitae, & societatis usum attinet, necessitas eos
coegit, ut supponerent, se esse, & ut suum utile quaererent, &
jurejurando multa affirmarent, & negarent. Nam, si aliquid
ipsis probetur, nesciunt, an probet, aut deficiat argumentatio.
Si negant, concedunt, aut opponunt; nesciunt se negare, conce-
dere, aut opponere; adeoque habendi sunt tanquam automata,
quae mente omnino carent.

[45]   Moreover, in this way men become accustomed to their own internal meditations.

But the reason why Nature is rarely investigated in the proper order, is, first, that men have prejudices whose causes we shall explain afterwards in our Philosophy. And then, the task requires a considerable capacity for making accurate distinctions (as we shall show later) and much effort. Finally, there is the condition of human affairs, which are quite changeable, as we have already shown. There are still other reasons, which we shall not go into.

[46]   If, by chance, someone should ask why I did [not] immediately, before anything else, display the truths of Nature in that order—for does not the truth make itself manifest?—I reply to him and at the same time I warn him not to try to reject these things as false because of Paradoxes that occur here and there; he should first deign to consider the order in which we prove them, and then he will become certain that we have reached the truth; and this was the reason why I have put these things first.

[47]   But perhaps, afterwards, some Skeptic would still doubt both the first truth itself and everything we shall deduce according to the standard of the first truth. If so, then either he will speak contrary to his own consciousness, or we shall confess that there are men whose minds also are completely blinded, either from birth, or from prejudices, i.e., because of some external chance. For they are not even aware of themselves. If they affirm or doubt something, they do not know that they affirm or doubt. They say that they know nothing, and that they do not even know that they know nothing. And even this they do not say absolutely. For they are afraid to confess that they exist, so long as they know nothing. In the end, they must be speechless, lest by chance they assume something that might smell of truth.

[48]   Finally, there is no speaking of the sciences with them. (For as far as the needs of life and society are concerned, necessity forces them to suppose that they exist, and to seek their own advantage, and in taking oaths, to affirm and deny many things.) For, if someone proves something to them, they do not know whether the argument is a proof or not. If they deny, grant, or oppose, they do not know that they deny, grant, or oppose. So they must be regarded as automata, completely lacking a mind.

[49]   Resumamus jam nostrum propositum. Habuimus hucusque primo finem, ad quem omnes nostras cogitationes dirigere studemus. Cognovimus secundo, quaenam sit optima perceptio, cujus ope ad nostram perfectionem pervenire possimus. Cognovimus tertio, quaenam sit prima via, cui mens insistere debeat, ut bene incipiat; quae est, ut ad normam datae cujuscunque verae ideae pergat, certis legibus inquirere. Quod ut recte fiat, haec debet Methodus praestare: Primo veram ideam a caeteris omnibus perceptionibus distinguere, & mentem a caeteris perceptionibus cohibere. Secundo tradere regulas, ut res incognitae ad talem normam percipiantur. Tertio [en eindelijk] ordinem constituere, ne inutilibus defatigemur. Postquam hanc Methodum novimus, vidimus quarto hanc Methodum perfectissimam futuram, ubi habuerimus ideam Entis perfectissimi. Unde initio illud erit maxime observandum, ut quanto ocius ad cognitionem talis Entis perveniamus.

[49]   Let us now return to our subject. First [§§ 1–17], we have treated the end toward which we strive to direct all our thoughts; second [§§ 18–29], we learned which is the best perception, by whose aid we can reach our perfection; third [§§ 30–48], we learned which is the first path our mind must enter on to begin well—which is to proceed in its investigation according to certain laws, taking as a standard a given true idea.

If this is to be done properly, the Method must, first [§§ 50–90], show how to distinguish a true idea from all other perceptions, and to restrain the mind from those other perceptions; second [§§ 91–98], teach rules so that we may perceive things unknown according to such a standard; third [§§99–?], establish an order, so that we do not become weary with trifles. When we came to know this Method [§ 38], we saw, fourth, that it will be most perfect when we have the idea of the most perfect Being. So in the beginning we must take the greatest care that we arrive at knowledge of such a Being as quickly as possible.

| Commentary

Once we know which of the different sorts of indubitable perceptions is to be preferred, we must concentrate on the method to
engage in this kind of knowledge on our way toward our end (§
29). Spinoza makes a formal distinction between *way* and
method, although the method itself can be considered as a kind of
way (and is so considered by Spinoza[1]). In these paragraphs,
Spinoza is particularly concerned with a certain paradox, which
he tries to elucidate: we seem to need a method, and yet this
method cannot be anything external to our knowledge, justifying
it from outside, because if so, we would ask what is the method to
justify this method, and so on ad infinitum.

| The Possibility of a Method
| (§§ 30–37)

In order to find the method of seeking the truth (according to the
model of the fourth kind of perception), "there is no need of another Method to seek the Method of seeking the truth, or of a
third Method to seek the second, and so on, to infinity." If this
were the case, "we would never arrive at knowledge of the truth,
or indeed at any knowledge" (§ 30).

How, then, do we find the method? Spinoza's answer consists
of an analogy with "corporeal tools" needed to reach practical
ends (§§ 30–32). If, in order to make certain instruments, one always needs other instruments, how can one ever get going? The
answer is that people possess "inborn tools," which are the origin
of ever more complicated and sophisticated tools.[2] The situation
is the same in the domain of knowledge. Here, too, man *as intellect* has an "inborn power" (*vis nativa*[3]), not caused by external
causes (footnote k). Through this power, the intellect produces
"intellectual tools for itself, by which it acquires other powers [*vires*] for other intellectual works, and from these works still other
tools, or the power [*potestas*[4]] of searching further, and so proceeds by stages, until it reaches the pinnacle of wisdom." The innate power of the intellect is not a pure possibility but an active
capacity to form "intellectual tools," by which new powers are acquired for other "intellectual works," and so on. The intellectual
tools made by the inborn power of the intellect are "true ideas,"
which are *never* considered purely provisional (§ 39). In footnote
l, Spinoza says that in his *Philosophia* he will explain what "intellectual works" are: it is not too farfetched to think that he may
have had in mind the *notiones communes.*[5] Not only the power of

the intellect is described as "inborn"; so are the intellectual instruments: the power cannot fail to be activated. Instead of a vicious infinite regress, we discover the capacity of a real progress, culminating in wisdom (*sapientia*).

The reality of the human intellect possessing a real power to understand will be further explained in the *Philosophia* (footnote k), which will take the form of the *Ethics*. Here Spinoza explains the intellect both as *part* of God's intellect, through which God perfectly understands everything, and as an immanent *effect* of the divine substance under the attribute of thought (*Cogitatio*). The cogitative power of the divine substance (God as having the attribute *Cogitatio*) is an immanent cause of its effects; this immanent power constitutes the innermost force of the modifications of thinking. The inner power of each thing, of the human mind as intellect, for example, *cannot* be the product of *external* modal causes.[6]

Yet the nature of the intellect is already partly elucidated in the following paragraphs, which prepare a kind of phenomenology of the intellect (§§ 50–90, 108–9). According to Spinoza, the intellect should not be considered as an abstract faculty (cf. *Ethics* II, P. 48, Sch.: the intellect *is* its ideas). As the inborn power of the mind expressing itself inevitably in ideas, it can rightfully be identified with its true ideas or acts of apprehension.

There is no vicious regress in our search for the method because the method is not something external to our knowledge but rather is intrinsic to the knowing process itself: to know intellectually (to have perceptions of the fourth kind) is, in principle, to know what it is to know intellectually. *Method is the same as reflexive knowledge.* So to discover the method, it is sufficient to have intellectual (true and indubitable) ideas and reflexively to study their nature and properties. That we *have* such ideas is affirmed without more ado: "for we have a true idea" (§ 33). The proof of how and why we come to have them pertains to "the investigation of nature," where it will also be shown that idea and will belong together (§ 34n. u; see also *Ethics* II, P. 48–49). Spinoza can, of course, affirm that we have true ideas in view of his previous survey of perceptions, especially in view of what was said about the fourth kind of perception. To understand the method and its possibility, Spinoza now has to investigate what a true idea is, since it is the basis of reflection and therefore of method. The nature of a true idea will be clarified by analyzing the relation between such an idea and its "formal" (that is, real) object and between such an idea and the idea of itself.

I The Idea and Its Real Object

Let us take a true idea of something—for example, the idea of a real circle. There is a difference "in nature" between the idea and its *ideatum* (or real object). The circle is a body, a modification of extension; the idea of it is a modification of thought (§ 33). Yet it is precisely in and through its idea that the circle is thought as it really is in itself according to its "formal" essence and properties. The idea of the circle expresses the "formal" reality of the circle in thought: it is the *essentia objectiva* of the real circle, in which the circle is fully known as it really is (§ 34).

Spinoza uses the Scholastic-Cartesian opposition between "formal," "formally" (*formalis; formaliter*) and "objective," "objectively" (*objectivus; objective*). "Formal" has the meaning of "real" (having a *forma*); "objective" means "what is given in the mind" or "what is before the mind's eye"—literally "what lies before." A thing's "formal" essence is its real essence; the "objective essence" of a thing is the presentation of the thing's "formal" reality in the mind, its idea. Notice that the *essence* of a thing is a real aspect of the thing, that which makes the thing into *what* it is: it is something individual and particular, which can, however, be the same in many things of the same sort.[7]

As we will see, as the objective essence of the circle, the idea of the circle is a reality in its own right with *mental* characteristics different from the bodily characteristics of the circle presented in the idea of the circle. It is precisely through these mental characteristics that the idea is capable of *presenting* bodies in thought. The peculiar reality of the idea of the circle can in turn become the object of thought in the idea of the idea of the circle; as we will see, this "reduplication" is not an accidental characteristic of thought. Since the idea of the circle is an acquaintance with the real circle in which the circle is fully known, the questions, Does the idea of the circle correspond to the circle itself? or Is the idea true? are answered in advance. Being the presentation of the whole reality of the circle in thought, of course its idea is true (§ 36). All this shows Spinoza's conception of idea and the relationship between *idea* and *ideatum* (or reality) to be different from Descartes's.[8]

In Spinoza's conception, a real idea is the presentation of an object; it is not a representation, which would allow the possibility that what is presented—and in that presentation regarded as formally real—might not correspond (might not really be "hooked on") to reality. Spinoza's conception of thinking or of an idea is very peculiar, even from a contemporary perspective. He rejects the position that an idea is an image or pictorial reflection that may (more or less successfully) or may not at all succeed in referring to and in portraying external reality (*Ethics* II, P. 48, Sch.). On the contrary, an idea is the "formation" of a thing in thought, it is an activity that, if unhindered, automatically expresses and presents a reality in thought (constituting an "objective" reality). This is why a well thought-out project (for example, of a machine) can be called a true idea, even if we do not know whether or not the machine exists (§ 69). For Spinoza, it is not the truth of ideas that is a problem but rather their falsehood (about falsehood, see §§ 67ff.). True and false ideas are not primarily distinguished by an extrinsic factor, that is, by whether they correspond to external reality or not. They are distinguished by "denominations," or characteristics *intrinsic* to the ideas as such, without relation to other things (§§ 69, 77). The distinction between truth and falsehood depends fundamentally on the difference between true and false ideas as such, as *expressions* of things in thought; it depends on whether the nature and power of intellectual thinking is fully present or not. The "form of the true thought must be placed in the same thought itself without relation to other things" (§ 71). Even if an idea is true in the sense that it "corresponds to the facts" but does so only extrinsically or accidentally, it is not *really* true,[9] because it is not really the full presentation of what it is supposed to express (§ 69): "there is something real in ideas, through which the true are distinguished from the false" (§ 70). Accordingly, false ideas are not in the first place characterized by their failure to correspond perfectly. They are ideas in which the formation of an "objective essence" is somehow obstructed or incomplete.

Already in the *Treatise* this *intrinsic* feature characterizing true ideas is called *adequacy* (*adaequata idea,* §§ 35, 73). In the *Ethics* (II, Def. 4), this is defined as follows: "By adequate idea I understand an idea which, insofar as it is considered in itself, without relation to an object, has all the properties, or intrinsic denominations of a true idea." An adequate idea or objective essence (§ 35) is therefore an idea that is complete, so that truth (or correspondence with things) follows from it.

In letter 60, to Tschirnhaus, Spinoza explicitly states that, for him, adequacy and truth come down to the same thing, except that *truth* refers to the correspondence of an idea to reality, whereas adequacy primarily refers to the nature of the idea itself, which makes truth possible. It is the intrinsic force of an idea as being a real objective essence that is the basis of the extrinsic characteristic of truth.

It is clear that Spinoza's theory of truth is not the usual correspondence theory of truth. Truth is an *intrinsic* characteristic of an idea—the presence of a real "objective essence." Yet truth as correspondence is not denied (see *Ethics* I, Ax. 6; letter 60). Spinoza's ontology implies that an idea, being a real objective essence, necessarily corresponds to an *ideatum:* "the idea is objectively in the same way as its object is really" (§ 41); a "true idea must agree with its object" (*Ethics* I, Ax. 6). The ontological basis of this epistemology can be found in *Ethics* II. Here the relation between idea and its object is understood as the relationship between two modifications of two different attributes—*Cogitatio* and *Extensio*—of the same substance. This substance produces *in the same act* two *automatically* corresponding modes, according to its two attributes: a body (in extension) and its idea (in thought). The idea *is* the *essentia objectiva* of the body's *essentia formalis*. The *essentia formalis* is the "formal" (real) essence of the body, through which the body is what it is and has the properties or activities it does really have. The *essentia objectiva* is the essence as *thought* or as *known* in the activity of thinking that is "the idea of the body." The idea is nothing but the presentation of the body in thought, as "objected" to or in thought.

If truth is an intrinsic as well as an extrinsic feature of ideas,[10] then, for this reason alone, Spinoza's theory of truth cannot be called a coherence theory of truth, at least not if such a theory is defined as the view that coherence is *all* there is to truth.[11] A coherence theory is said to come down to this: "for *p* to be the case in the material world is for the idea that *p* to belong in the coherent system [of ideas]."[12] Although the "order and connection of ideas is the same as the order and connection of things" (*Ethics* II, P. 7), it does not mean simply that the material world is to be equated with coherent thought about it.[13] The material world, although *substantially* the same as the world of ideas, belongs to a *really different* attribute of substance.

The mind as intellect is the self-conscious activity of linking objective essences in such a way that the intelligible order of real (formal) things is expressed in thought (*Ethics* I, P. 30). However, the concrete activity of the human intellect is complicated because the human mind also engages in constructions that are false (such as we inevitably experience in our mental life), and even in constructions that are known to be "pure" constructions not existing as such in nature (for example, geometrical constructions). According to Spinoza, this should not lead to generalized doubt about whether our thought constructions ever *really* express "formal" reality. But it does lead to the desire to demonstrate that our constructions, at least in certain domains, do correspond to reality. In geometry, "intrinsic" truth or constructibility is enough; but in philosophy, we desire to form not only well-formed thoughts but thoughts that are certain to express "physical" things. This requires taking care "not to mix up the things that are only in the intellect with those that are real" (§ 93), even though these "things in the intellect" are well-formed thoughts. As we will see, the deductive activity of thought is of great help here, especially when it can link its ideas to the idea of a being that exists necessarily. The difference between sorts of well-formed thought is clearly present in letter 9, to Simon de Vries (1663): "For example, if someone asks me for a description of the Temple of Solomon, I ought to give him a true description of the temple . . . unless I want to talk nonsense to him. But if I have constructed in my mind some temple which I want to build, and if I infer from its description that I must buy land of such a kind and so many thousand stones and other materials, will anyone in his right mind tell me that I have drawn a bad conclusion because I have perhaps used a false definition? Or will anyone require me to prove my definition?"

Paradoxically, Spinoza's conception of an idea as the having of a real "objective essence" automatically expressing formal reality is compatible with his conception of truth as *correspondence*. This correspondence of ideas has to be demonstrated in philosophical thinking about reality. This is why, in the discussions about the separation between intellect and imagination, observations concerning the adequate thinking of the essences of things will be complemented by discussions concerning true thinking expressing things as to their existence (see Spinoza's discussion of fiction and falsehood concerning essences as well as concerning existences in §§ 52–76).

As is explicitly stated in § 69 and in letter 9, geometrical ideas and other well-formed thought constructions—for example, the well-formed plan of a machine or building or certain assumptions made in order to solve certain problems, such as the principle of inertia (§ 57n. y)—are, without hesitation, called true.[14] Yet a true idea, if it is to be the idea of real, "physical" things, should also correspond to reality and not simply be a well-formed construction. This is why the definition of a geometrical figure needs no further proof: constructibility is enough. But a definition of a real thing does need a proof as to its being the definition of a *real* thing. For things whose essence involves existence, this proof can be given a priori (§ 97); but for things whose essence does not involve existence, existence can only be affirmed if we take care to think this essence adequately and if "at the same time [we] attend to the order of Nature" (§ 65), which means (as we will see when discussing §§ 99, 102) that we have to think it through its first cause *and* that we rely on experience. Spinoza's conception of truth as an intrinsic characteristic of ideas, being the formation of objective essences in their intrinsic interconnections, is seen here to be compatible with, and complemented by, a view of truth as requiring — when it concerns the thought of "physical" things — not simply constructibility but a proof of the existence in reality of what is constructed in the mind. This activity of construction and demonstration of existence is precisely what is happening in metaphysics and physics. To have true ideas about finite things also requires correspondence established through experience. However, as we will see, this experience is fully embedded in the constructive process, in the process of the formation of objective essences as *"causally" interdependent* (§ 99). The order of thinking is as important as — almost more important than — reliance on experience, since it is this order that indicates how things, as to their essence as well as to their existence, depend on God.

Spinoza's ontologically based epistemology escapes contemporary tags. It is by possessing adequate ideas or "objective essences" that we are in the truth. Since the true idea is an objective essence (the thought expression of a formal essence of a thing), it also refers to those elements that presuppose the thing and are presupposed by it. This is why "its *objective* effects proceed *in the soul* according to the formal nature of its object. This is the same as what the ancients said, i.e., that true knowledge proceeds from cause to effect — except that so far as I know they never conceived the soul (as we do here) as acting according to certain laws, like a spiritual automaton" (§ 85; emphasis added). This spontaneous activity is none other than the one we find in geometry and in the new science, and that Spinoza hopes will prolong itself in a new metaphysics and ethics.

I The Idea and the Idea of Itself

Now that we know the nature of a true idea, we can investigate its relation to the idea of itself as a true idea. A true idea or real *essentia objectiva* is not only the expression in thought of something (for example, a body), it also is itself a real thing that can be expressed in an idea: it is something different from its object (presented as different in the idea itself) and, as such, the idea can be understood in its turn. Like every real, intelligible thing, it has an *essentia formalis,* which can be expressed in an *essentia objec-*

tiva—the idea of the idea (§ 33). The *idea* of a real thing—say, Peter—is "the object of a second idea, which will have in itself, objectively, whatever the [first] idea of Peter has formally [i.e., really, as a real idea]" (§ 34). And this idea, or *essentia objectiva,* of the first idea will, as *essentia formalis,* itself be the object of a third idea, or *essentia objectiva;* and so on (§ 34).

Is this an infinite regress? No, says Spinoza, because "to know that I know, I must first know," and "in order . . . to know, it is not necessary to know that I know, much less necessary to know that I know that I know—no more than it is necessary to understand the essence of a circle in order to understand the essence of a triangle" (§ 34). In other words, reflection presupposes the idea or understanding of an object.[15] Certainty (or knowing that one knows something) is "nothing but the objective essence itself," that is, "the mode by which we are aware of the formal essence [of a thing]" ("modus, quo sentimus essentiam formalem" [§ 35]). To have an idea or objective essence is to be *acquainted* with the formal or real essence of a thing. This expression of a thing in thought *in principle* includes reflection and certainty. "Certainty and an objective essence are the same thing" (§ 35). Spinoza thus concludes that "for the certainty of the truth [knowing that one knows], no other sign is needed than having a true idea" (§ 35).[16] Spinoza is saying that certainty is not to be obtained from an external correspondence or from "another sign" than the idea itself.[17] To have an idea—the expression of an object in thought—is to have awareness of it as being such an expression, is to be certain of one's knowing. It is clear that Spinoza is talking about "real" objective essences or ideas.

In the *Ethics* Spinoza also investigates the relation between an idea and the idea of an idea. As there is always an idea of a body, so there is always an idea of an idea. But the relation between an idea of an idea and an idea is not exactly like the relation between idea and body, which are modes of a different nature. The relation between an idea of an idea and an idea is such that an idea of an idea constitutes "the form of the idea insofar as this is considered as a mode of thinking without relation to the object" (*E* II, P. 21, Sch.). The form (*forma*) constitutes the peculiar reality of an idea, so each idea in principle contains an idea of itself or its self-awareness; otherwise, it would not be an idea.

All this is not to say that each idea that one has is certain in actuality. But to truly have it is to have an idea that is an *essentia objectiva,* intrinsically capable of reflection and certainty, as understood by Spinoza. Certainty about the truth of an idea is not secured simply by an external sign (empiricism) or by the guarantee given to our clear and distinct ideas by God's veracity (Cartesianism). It is secured in really having ideas, or *essentiae objectivae,* and in the knowing about knowing involved in them. The fundamental question for Spinoza does not concern the existence of an epistemological guarantee outside our ideas but rather the ontological possibility condition of our epistemological certainty, which is to be investigated in the *Philosophia.* Spinoza's views can be considered not only as a critique of empiricism but also as a critique and radicalization of Descartes.[18] This critique of Descartes will be made explicit in the next chapter, in Spinoza's discussion of doubt.

At this point, we can come back to our problem about method and how we can know what is the good method. All we need is a true idea that contains in itself its own sign of truth or certainty and allows us to eliminate all doubt. So "the true Method is not to seek a sign of truth after the acquisition of ideas, but the true Method is the way that truth itself, or the objective essences of things, or the ideas (all those signify the same) should be sought in the proper order" (§ 36). The idea, which is the sign (*index*) of its own truth, functions through the reflection on it as a guiding norm (*norma*) from which can be gathered rules of methodical thinking (*regulae*) (see chapter 7).

To make himself very clear, Spinoza stresses the difference between method and reasoning and intellection itself: "Method must speak about Reasoning, or [and] about the intellection; i.e., Method is not the reasoning itself by [through] which we understand the causes of things; much less the understanding of the causes of things" (§ 37). Indeed, reasoning (*ratiocinari*) is the deductive process geared toward the understanding of things according to their "causes"; the understanding of things is the result of this process. Method, although closely linked with these activities, should not be confused with them: they are the actual formation of the *essentiae objectivae* in their interconnection; method is the reflection on truth, understanding, and reasoning, which secures the *orderly* pursuit of truths.

It is obvious that Spinoza's conception of method lies between two extremes: method as an external device or no method at all (but pure presence of ideas). Method as reflection on a true idea, on intellection and reasoning, presupposes all these, but it can, as reflection, become aware of what truth, intellection, and good reasoning really mean, and so give guidance in further intellection and reasoning. This is even necessary because, although our mind is "like a spiritual automaton" (§ 85), we are not immediately and fully pure intellect, either. Method is important for minds that are in the *interim position* we talked about earlier.

What then is method itself? It is *reflexive* knowledge; "it is understanding what a true idea is by distinguishing it from the rest of the perceptions; by investigating its nature, so that from it we may come to know our power of understanding and so restrain the mind that it understands, according to that standard, everything that is to be understood; and finally by teaching and constructing certain rules as aids, so that the mind does not weary itself in useless things" (§ 37). In a word, it is an emendation of the intellect, both negatively (separating it from the *imaginatio*), and positively, by *self-consciously* organizing our knowledge, which is its regulative function. Here is the reason that, as Rousset puts it, before any *Traité du monde* a *Discours de la méthode* is necessary.[19]

The peculiar relationship between idea and *ideatum* (between *essentia objectiva* and *essentia formalis*), and between idea and the idea of this idea, makes method possible both as reflexive knowledge of the standard of true, intellectual thinking and as a self-conscious, rule-guided process in which ideas are linked together according to the real order of things. All this is further elaborated and confirmed in the next paragraphs. As Rousset puts it, the method is the expression of the *autonomy* of our intellectual thinking and reflectivity.[20] On the other hand, it is in methodical thinking that this autonomy is fully conquered, that we become self-conscious about our own activity as being the thinking of reality as it is.[21] It is this self-conscious activity that will constitute our happiness.

▌ Further Confirmation and Elaboration (§§ 38–42)

How can reflexive knowledge or method lead to the sort of knowledge we need for our happiness? To understand this, we have to grasp what is involved in the description of the method as specified in § 37: we have to understand the link between the good method and the perfection of this method. The good method is one based on our reflection on a given true idea. But "the most perfect Method will be the one that shows how the mind is to be directed according to the standard of the given idea of the most perfect Being" (§ 38). The method *in its completion* ("the whole of the Method," § 40) requires reflection not simply on a given true idea but on the idea of God, thus providing us with tools for proceeding methodically in our investigation of the things we have to know in view of our ultimate end. The relation between the good and the best method is explained in the following paragraphs.

One part of the method is to understand, on the basis of a reflection on a given true idea, what the standard of truth is; at the same time, we can perform the required separation between imagination and intellect (§§ 38, 39). In this way we obtain a certain understanding of the intellect as such. Yet the self-understanding of the intellect can and must be completed. To see this, it is enough to attend to the fact that "the relation between . . . two ideas is the same as the relation between the formal essences of those ideas" (this follows from our understanding of what an idea really is). In other words, truth has to do with a linkage between ideas—expressing the interaction of formal essences (this is explained in § 41)—and with the discovery of the idea of "the source and origin of the whole of Nature" (explained in § 42), which is "the source of the other ideas" we can have about reality.

Since method is obtained in reflection upon the intellect, and since the intellect is this perfect linkage of objective essences, the full or perfect method will require a reflection on the linkage of objective essences, and especially on the idea of God (§§ 38, 39). In general, the more the mind understands, the better it understands both its own powers and the order of Nature (§ 40). This is because reflection on the link between objective essences (discovered in reasoning) effectively teaches us how the intellect operates and, at the same time, leads to an understanding of "the order of Nature." The more we understand, the more our conscious "tools for proceeding further" will increase (§ 41). Our reflexive understanding of the intellect—and therefore our method —will be most perfect if we understand God; at the same time, this idea of God being the source of our other ideas will constitute a guarantee for a perfect understanding of the order of nature (§ 42). This constitutes the completion of the method, because reflexive knowledge of our idea of the most perfect being will lead to such an understanding of nature (and the elaboration of such rules) that the mind can restrain itself from useless pursuits (§ 40).

It turns out that our "completion" of the method cannot be separated from engagement in "the investigation of Nature," specifically from a discovery of the idea of God: we need reflection on the given idea of God. The whole problem will be how to reach that idea as soon as possible (§ 49). As it turns out, at the end of the *Treatise* (§§ 105ff.), where Spinoza performs this move, only knowledge of the intellect as a *real* activity gives us the platform to reach this idea of God.

It also is clear that the method is not something fixed, let alone something external to the actual understanding. On the contrary, it is a subtly developing and evolving tool, discovered in our reflection on the actual progress of understanding and giving direction to further understanding, in a kind of dialectical interplay. Logic must change itself into metaphysics to complete itself as logic: "the more the mind knows, the better it understands its own powers and the order of Nature. The better the mind understands its own powers, the more easily it can direct itself and propose rules to itself; the better it understands the order of Nature, the more easily it can restrain itself from useless pursuits. In these things, as we have said, the whole of the Method consists" (§ 40).

In §§ 38–42 Spinoza takes up again the essential elements of the method mentioned in §§ 36–37 and repeated in § 49. The advantage of the exposition at this point is that these elements are presented as nonfixed elements of a dynamic, ongoing reflection on a dynamic, ongoing process of understanding. The seeming passivity of the starting point (from a given inborn idea, which is the standard according to which the mind is to be directed; § 38) is changed into a situation in which the mind can *direct itself* more easily (§ 40).[22]

How can the reader at this stage even begin to trust all this talk of the master? This and other objections are dealt with in the following section.

| Objections and Answers
| (§§ 43–48)

The first objection (§ 43) has to do with the reasoning we have gone through in our discussion of the good method in order to show that the mind is to be directed according to the standard of a given true idea. The very fact that it was necessary to reason about this seems to indicate that this is not known through itself. But then the question arises, How do we know this reasoning is correct? In order to reason well, we have to start from a given, true idea; but this itself is shown in reasoning. How do we know this is itself correct reasoning? Does this not require another reasoning to show it is correct, and so on to infinity? The problem seems to be this: we have seen in our reasoning that the good method is to start from a given, true idea. But, instead of doing exactly that, we have been reasoning *about* doing it. How, then, do we know that this reasoning itself is correct?

The answer (§§ 44–45) consists in two parts. If somebody, by some chance (*fato quodam*), had proceeded in the way indicated (starting from a given, true idea and acquiring other ideas concerning nature in the proper order, according to the standard of the true idea), then "he would never have doubted the truth he possessed . . . and also everything would have flowed to him of its own accord."

But since this rarely happens, it is necessary *to deliberately acquire* what we cannot acquire by chance. This is why the master tells us about the way to acquire more truth, methodically starting from a true idea; this is why he shows that truth and good reasoning are self-sufficient and require no external justification. Although self-sufficient, good reasoning *can* be further corroborated by good reasoning.

The answer seems to come down to this: the problem is not the vicious regress in showing correctness of reasoning; the problem is getting started on the basis of a true idea and the reasonings related to it (reasonings that can be corroborated by reasoning; see footnote g). In order to get pupils to do this, if they do not already do it by chance, the master can engage in reasoning—especially since this accustoms readers "to their own internal meditations."

If someone should ask "why Nature is rarely investigated in the proper order," one can give many reasons: prejudices, the difficulty of the task (which "requires a considerable capacity for making accurate distinctions . . . and much effort"), the changeable condition of man, and other factors (perhaps Spinoza thinks here of superstition and the like, discussed in his *Tractatus Theologico-Politicus*[23]). The real problem, again, seems to be the transition from a situation in which man is dominated by imagination into one in which the intellect can develop itself through its inborn force. This is the problem of the realization of this inborn force *in time,* of the conscious self-possession of it *in time.*[24] How this transition from one level to another operates is not clarified here. The transition looks like a leap, which can be promoted by listening to the master, even though the real work (to really think through a given true idea in the right way) must be done by the pupil. Furthermore, once one is *in* adequate thinking, one can become aware that the self-possession and self-development of the truth is really the work of our own inborn power.

The second objection (§ 46) has to do with this question of "why I did[25] immediately, before anything else, display the truths of Nature in that [the right] order?" Spinoza replies that we should not reject these investigations as false because of paradoxes that occur here and there; rather, we should consider the order in which they are proven, and then we will become certain of their truth.

Whereas the first objection dealt with the demonstrations that went before and established the right method, this objection concerns the demonstrations to come in the *Philosophia* or in the investigation of nature itself. Here, again, the reply rests on the self-revealing character of the truth. The paradoxes that Spinoza is talking about may be ones such as freedom and determinism and Spinoza's conception of the relation God-man.[26] At the end of the *Short Treatise,* Spinoza warns his friends and readers of certain difficulties that may arise, but to which they should first give much of reflection before deciding to reject his ideas.

The answers Spinoza gives to the objections reveal a deep trust in the uncorrupted nature of our inborn force of thinking. Unfortunately, this inborn force is hindered by prejudices and the striving for false goods. The prejudices can be broken down by attentive meditation on given truths and their development and by the separation between the intellect and the imagination (see the first part of the method, §§ 50–90).

The third objection (§§ 47–48) is not to previous or future reasoning, but is a skepticism as to "the first truth itself and [to] everything we shall deduce according to the standard of the first truth." Spinoza's response to this skepticism is one of almost pure irritation. Spinoza repeats traditional objections within his own framework: either the skeptic speaks "contrary to his own consciousness" or "there are men whose minds also are completely blinded, either from birth, or from prejudices, i.e., because of some external [circumstance]." (In *Ethics* III, P. 3; and IV, App. 2, Spinoza explains the power of the imagination as an expression of our being under the influence of other factors, our not being determined by our own force.) A skeptic, though inevitably knowing something (at least that he or she doubts) or affirming and denying something (at least in everyday life), will deny that he or she knows anything or affirms or denies. If we would take skeptics seriously, we would have to regard them "as automata, completely lacking a mind," the opposite of an intellect, which is like an *automaton spirituale.*

In fact, what is needed to counter skepticism—which should not be confused with real doubt—is not a better method but a therapy for stubbornness (§ 77). Real doubt is like a play of forces between two ideas, neither of which is capable of allowing an affirmation (or negation) in one or other direction; this arises because of the absence of real cognition, which would put an end to this doubt (§ 78).

I Conclusion (§ 49)

The way to reach our end (by means of the fourth kind of perception) requires a method that proceeds according to the norm of one or other given, true idea. This method must allow us to do three things: to separate true ideas from others, to give us rules for knowing things still unknown according to the norm, and to establish an order to prevent us from spending our forces in the search for what is useless. Like some other commentators,[27] Curley wrongly thinks there is a fourth part to the method.[28] However, the fourth point mentioned in § 49 is not part of the enumeration of the elements of the method (described from § 50 onward) but belongs to the enumeration of what we have already seen in the previous paragraphs: (1) we have discussed our end (§§ 1–17); (2) we have learned the means to reach this end—that is, the fourth kind of perception (§§ 18–29); (3) we have learned about the real[29] way and the method (in general) to walk the way (§§ 30–48); and (4) we *have* seen in § 39 that this method "will be most perfect when we have the idea of the most perfect Being." This last point certainly does not indicate an *alternative* method;[30] neither is it a fourth element of the method to be developed. It recapitulates an important point already discovered (§ 39) precisely in our elucidation of the notion of method in general as reflection: that the correct method will be most perfect if we can reflect on the idea of God. So Spinoza can add, "in the beginning [of methodical thinking] we must take the greatest care that we arrive at knowledge of such a Being as quickly as possible" (§ 49). This care must be taken in performing some or all of the *three* tasks now assigned to methodical thinking.

I NOTES

1. See, for example, *TEI* 38: "vera Methodus est via."
2. Rousset notes that this answer is also to be found, *mutatis mutandis,* in Descartes, Bacon, and Geulincx; see Spinoza 1992, 210.
3. This and related concepts also are found in Bacon's *De dignitate et augmentis scientiarum* V, 5; see Bartuschat's introduction to Spinoza 1993, xxxiii, which also points to the difference between Bacon and Spinoza.

4. There are subtle differences in § 31 between *vis* (inborn power) and *potestas* (power); *vis* being the same as *potentia,* which is differentiated from *potestas* or the effective operation of *potentia* (for this distinction, see also *E* I, P. 35, 36).

5. About the *notiones communes,* see the second section of chapter 10.

6. This will be discussed in more detail in chapters 9 and 11.

7. Gueroult 1974, appendix 2; Mason 1986.

8. Mark 1978.

9. Cf. Wittgenstein 1977, § 676: "Someone who, dreaming, says, 'I am dreaming,' even if he speaks audibly in doing so, is no more right than if he said in his dream, 'it is raining,' while it was in fact raining. Even if his dream were actually connected with the noise of the rain" (Klever's reference in Spinoza 1986a, 156).

10. Garrett 1990, 17–18.

11. This argues against Walker 1985, 4, and agrees with Allison 1987, 102.

12. Walker 1985, 5.

13. Walker (1985, 5) holds this to be the case.

14. This argues against Curley in Spinoza 1985, 26n. 44, 31n. 51.

15. About reflection, see Bartuschat's comment in Spinoza 1993, 109; Matheron 1989.

16. Cf. *E* II, P. 43, Sch.: "truth is its own standard."

17. This goes against Bacon, who looks for *"indicia vera de interpretatione naturae"* (true signs for the interpretation of nature) (an expression used in the subtitle of Bacon's *Novum Organon;* see Klever's comment in Spinoza 1986a, 142).

18. Bartuschat's introduction to Spinoza 1993, xxxiv–xxxv. See further explicit criticism of Descartes and Bacon in letter 2 (of 1662) to Oldenburg.

19. Spinoza 1992, 238.

20. Spinoza 1992, 242–43.

21. See Bartuschat's introduction to Spinoza 1993, xv.

22. As Bartuschat puts it in Spinoza 1993, 110–11.

23. As Rousset notes in Spinoza 1992, 258.

24. Boss 1986.

25. The "[not]" added by Curley in his translation should be dropped; see Rousset's and Bartuschat's versions in Spinoza 1992, 258; 1993, 112, respectively.

26. See Rousset in Spinoza 1992, 260–61; and Bartuschat in Spinoza 1993, xxi–xxiii.

27. For example, Klever in Spinoza 1986a, 153–54 (criticized in De Dijn 1987, 423–24).

28. Spinoza 1985, 23n. 38.

29. The word *prima* in the expression *prima via* used here should not be understood as opposed to *secunda* but as meaning "chief," "most important"; see De Dijn 1987, 424.

30. As Klever thinks (Spinoza 1986a, 154; criticized in De Dijn 1987, 423–24).

First Part of the Method (§§ 50–90): The Separation between Intellect and Imagination

I Text

[50]   Incipiamus itaque a prima parte Methodi, quae est, uti diximus, distinguere, & separare ideam veram a caeteris perceptionibus, & cohibere mentem, ne falsas, fictas, & dubias cum veris confundat: quod utcunque fuse hic explicare animus est, ut Lectores detineam in cogitatione rei adeo necessariae, & etiam, quia multi sunt, qui vel de veris dubitant ex eo, quod non attenderunt ad distinctionem, quae est inter veram perceptionem, & alias omnes. Adeo ut sint veluti homines, qui, cum vigilarent, non dubitabant se vigilare; sed postquam semel in somniis, ut saepe fit, putarunt se certo vigilare, quod postea falsum esse reperiebant, etiam de suis vigiliis dubitarunt: quod contingit, quia nunquam distinxerunt inter somnum, & vigiliam.

[51]   Interim moneo, me hic essentiam uniuscujusque perceptionis, eamque per proximam suam causam non explicaturum, quia hoc ad Philosophiam pertinet, sed tantum traditurum id, quod Methodus postulat, id est, circa quae perceptio ficta, falsa, & dubia versetur, & quomodo ab unaquaque liberabimur. Sit itaque prima inquisitio circa ideam fictam.

[50] Let us begin, therefore, from the first part of the Method, which is, as we have said, to distinguish and separate true ideas from all other perceptions, and to restrain the mind from confusing false, fictitious, and doubtful ideas with true ones. It is my intention to explain this fully here, so as to engage my Readers in the thought of a thing so necessary, and also because there are many who doubt even true ideas, from not attending to the distinction between a true perception and all others. So they are like men, who, when they were awake, used not to doubt that they were awake, but who, after they once thought in a dream that they were certainly awake (as often happens), and later found that to be false, doubted even of their waking states. This happens because they have never distinguished between the dream and the waking state.

[51] In the meantime, I warn the reader that I shall not discuss the essence of each perception, and explain it by its proximate cause, because that pertains to Philosophy, but shall discuss only what the Method demands, i.e., what false, fictitious and doubtful ideas are concerned with, and how we shall be freed from each of them. Let the first inquiry, therefore, be about the fictitious idea.

[52] Cum omnis perceptio sit vel rei, tanquam existentis consideratae, vel solius essentiae, & frequentiores fictiones contingant circa res, tanquam existentes, consideratas, ideo prius de hac loquar; scilicet ubi sola existentia fingitur, & res, quae in tali actu fingitur, intelligitur, sive supponitur intelligi. Ex. gr. fingo Petrum, quem novi, ire domum, eum me invisere, &[r] similia. Hic quaero, circa quae talis idea versetur? Video eam tantum versari circa possibilia, non vero circa necessaria, neque circa impossibilia.

[53] Rem impossibilem voco, cujus natura [in existendo] implicat contradictionem, ut ea existat; necessariam, cujus natura implicat contradictionem, ut ea non existat; possibilem, cujus quidem existentia, ipsa sua natura, non implicat contradictionem, ut existat, aut non existat, sed cujus existentiae necessitas, aut impossibilitas pendet a causis nobis ignotis, quamdiu ipsius existentiam fingimus; ideoque si ipsius necessitas, aut impossibilitas, quae a causis externis pendet, nobis esset nota, nihil etiam de ea potuissemus fingere.

[54] Unde sequitur, si detur aliquis Deus, aut omniscium quid, nihil prorsus eum posse fingere. Nam, quod ad Nos attinet, postquam[s] novi me existere, non possum fingere me existere, aut non existere; nec etiam possum fingere elephantem, qui transeat per acus foramen; nec possum, postquam[t] naturam Dei novi, fingere eum existentem, aut non existentem: idem intelligendum est de Chimaera, cujus natura existere implicat. Ex quibus patet id, quod dixi, scilicet quod fictio, de qua hic loquimur, non contingit circa aeternas[u] veritates. Statim etiam ostendam, quod nulla fictio versetur circa aeternas veritates.

---

r. Vide ulterius id, quod de hypothesibus notabimus, quae a nobis clare intelliguntur; sed in eo est fictio, quod dicamus, eas tales in corporibus caelestibus existere.

s. Quia res, modo ea intelligatur, se ipsam manifestat, ideo tantum egemus exemplo sine alia demonstratione. Idemque erit hujus contradictoria, quae ut appareat esse falsa, tantum opus recenseri, uti statim apparebit, quum de fictione circa essentiam loquemur.

t. Nota. Quamvis multi dicant se dubitare, an Deus existat, illos tamen nihil praeter nomen habere, vel aliquid fingere, quod Deum vocant: id quod cum Dei natura non convenit, ut postea suo loco ostendam.

u. Per aeternam veritatem talem intelligo, quae, si est affirmativa, nunquam poterit esse negativa. Sic prima, & aeterna veritas est, *Deum esse,* non autem est aeterna veritas, *Adamum cogitare. Chimaeram non esse,* est aeterna veritas, non autem, *Adamum non cogitare.*

[52] Since every perception is either of a thing considered as existing, or of an essence alone, and since fictions occur more frequently concerning things considered as existing, I shall speak first of them—i.e., where existence alone is feigned, and the thing which is feigned in such an act is understood, or assumed to be understood. E.g., I feign that Peter, whom I know, is going home, that he is coming to visit me, and the like.[r] Here I ask, what does such an idea concern? I see that it concerns only possible, and not necessary or impossible things.

[53] I call a thing impossible whose nature implies that it would be contradictory for it to exist; necessary whose nature implies that it would be contradictory for it not to exist; and possible whose existence, by its very nature, does not imply a contradiction—either for it to exist or for it not to exist—but whose necessity or impossibility of existence depends on causes unknown to us, so long as we feign its existence. So if its necessity or impossibility, which depends on external causes, were known to us, we would have been able to feign nothing concerning it.

[54] From this it follows that, if there is a God, or something omniscient, he can feign nothing at all. For as far as We are concerned, after I know that I exist,[s] I cannot feign either that I exist or that I do not exist; nor can I feign an elephant which passes through the eye of a needle; nor, after I know the nature of God, can I feign either that he exists or that he does not exist.[t] The same must be understood of the Chimera, whose nature implies that it would be contradictory for it to exist. From this what I have said is evident: that the fiction of which we are speaking here does not occur concerning eternal truths.[u] I shall also show immediately that no fiction is concerned with eternal truths.

---

r. See further what we shall note concerning hypotheses that we clearly understand; but the fiction consists in our saying that such as these exist in the heavenly bodies.

s. Because the thing makes itself evident, provided it is understood, we require only an example, without other proof. The same is true of its contradictory—it need only be examined for its falsity to be clear. This will be plain immediately, when we speak of fictions concerning essence.

t. Note. Although many say that they doubt whether God exists, nevertheless they have nothing but the name, or they feign something which they call God; this does not agree with the nature of God, as I shall show later in the proper place.

u. By an eternal truth I mean one, which, if it is affirmative, will never be able to be negative. Thus it is a first and eternal truth *that God is;* but *that Adam thinks* is not an eternal truth. *That there is no Chimera* is an eternal truth; but not *that Adam does not think.*

[55]   Sed antequam ulterius pergam, hic obiter notandum est, quod illa differentia, quae est inter essentiam unius rei, & essentiam alterius, ea ipsa sit inter actualitatem, aut existentiam ejusdem rei, & inter actualitatem, aut existentiam alterius rei. Adeo ut si existentiam ex. gr. Adami tantum per generalem existentiam concipere velimus, idem futurum sit, ac si, ad concipiendam ipsius essentiam, ad naturam entis attendamus, ut tandem definiamus, Adamum esse ens. Itaque quo existentia generalius concipitur, eo etiam confusius concipitur, faciliusque unicuique rei potest affingi: econtra, ubi particularius concipitur, clarius tum intelligitur, & difficilius alicui, nisi rei ipsi, ubi non attendimus ad Naturae ordinem, affingitur. Quod notatu dignum est.

[56]   Veniunt jam hic ea consideranda, quae vulgo dicuntur fingi, quamvis clare intelligamus, rem ita sese non habere, uti eam fingimus. Ex. gr. quamvis sciam terram esse rotundam, nihil tamen vetat, quominus alicui dicam terram medium globum esse, & tanquam medium pomum auriacum in scutella, aut solem circum terram moveri, & similia. Ad haec si attendamus, nihil videbimus, quod non cohaereat cum jam dictis, modo prius advertamus, nos aliquando potuisse errare, & jam errorum nostrorum esse conscios; deinde quod possumus fingere, aut ad minimum putare, alios homines in eodem esse errore, aut in eum, ut nos antehac, posse incidere. Hoc, inquam, fingere possumus, quamdiu nullam videmus impossibilitatem, nullamque necessitatem: Quando itaque alicui dico, terram non esse rotundam, &c., nihil aliud ago, quam in memoriam revoco errorem, quem forte habui, aut in quem labi potui, & postea fingo, aut puto eum, cui hoc dico, adhuc esse, aut posse labi in eundem errorem. Quod, ut dixi, fingo, quamdiu nullam video impossibilitatem, nullamque necessitatem: hanc vero si intellexissem, nihil prorsus fingere potuissem, & tantum dicendum fuisset, me aliquid operatum esse.

[55]   But before proceeding further, I must note here in passing that the same difference that exists between the essence of one thing and the essence of another also exists between the actuality or existence of the one thing and the actuality or existence of the other. So if we wished to conceive the existence of Adam, for example, through existence in general, it would be the same as if, to conceive his essence, we attended to the nature of being, so that in the end we defined him by saying that Adam is a being. Therefore, the more generally existence is conceived, the more confusedly also it is conceived, and the more easily it can be ascribed fictitiously to anything. Conversely, the more particularly it is conceived, then the more clearly it is understood, and the more difficult it is for us, [even] when we do not attend to the order of Nature, to ascribe it fictitiously to anything other than the thing itself. This is worth noting.

[56]   Now we must consider those things that are commonly said to be feigned, although we understood clearly that the thing is not really as we feign it. E.g., although I know that the earth is round, nothing prevents me from saying to someone that the earth is a hemisphere and like half an orange on a plate, or that the sun moves around the earth, and the like. If we attend to these things, we shall see nothing that is not compatible with what we have already said, provided we note first that we have sometimes been able to err, and now are conscious of our errors; and then, we can feign, or at least allow, that other men are in the same error, or can fall into it, as we did previously.

We can feign this, I say, so long as we see no impossibility and no necessity. Therefore, when I say to someone that the earth is not round, etc., I am doing nothing but recalling the error which I, perhaps, made, or into which I could have fallen, and afterwards feigning, or allowing, that he to whom I say this is still in the same error, or can fall into it. As I have said, I feign this so long as I see no impossibility and no necessity. For if I had understood this, I could have feigned nothing at all, and it would have had to be said only that I had done something.

[57]   Superest jam, ut ea etiam notemus, quae in
Quaestionibus supponuntur; id quod passim etiam contingit
circa impossibilia. Ex. gr. quum dicimus: supponamus hanc
candelam ardentem jam non ardere, aut supponamus eam
ardere in aliquo spatio imaginario, sive ubi nulla dantur corpora: Quorum similia passim supponuntur, quamvis hoc ultimum clare intelligatur impossibile esse; sed quando hoc fit, nil
prorsus fingitur. Nam primo nihil aliud egi, quam quod^x in
memoriam revocavi aliam candelam non ardentem (aut hanc
eandem concepi sine flamma), &, quod cogito de ea candela, id
ipsum de hac intelligo, quamdiu ad flammam non attendo. In
secundo nihil aliud fit, quam abstrahere cogitationes a corporibus circumjacentibus, ut mens se convertat ad solam candelae,
in se sola spectatae, contemplationem, ut postea concludat
candelam nullam habere causam ad sui ipsius destructionem.
Adeo ut si nulla essent corpora circumjacentia, candela haec, ac
etiam flamma manerent immutabiles, aut similia: Nulla igitur
datur hic fictio, sed^y verae, ac merae assertiones.

---

x. Postea cum de fictione, quae versatur circa essentias, loquemur, clare apparebit, quod fictio nunquam aliquid novi facit, aut menti
praebet: sed quod tantum ea, quae sunt in cerebro, aut in imaginatione, revocantur ad memoriam, & quod confuse ad omnia simul mens
attendit. Revocantur ex. gr. in memoriam loquela, & arbor; & cum
mens confuse attendit sine distinctione, putat arborem loqui. Idem de
existentia intelligitur, praesertim, uti diximus, cum adeo generaliter,
ac ens, concipitur: quia tum facile applicatur omnibus, quae simul in
memoria occurrunt. Quod notatu valde dignum est.

y. Idem etiam de hypothesibus intelligendum, quae fiunt ad certos motus explicandum, qui conveniunt cum caelorum phaenomenis,
nisi quod ex iis, si motibus caelestibus applicentur, naturam caelorum
concludant, quae tamen alia potest esse, praesertim cum ad explicandum tales motus multae aliae causae possint concipi.

[57]   It remains now to note also those things that are supposed in Problems. This sometimes happens even concerning impossible things. E.g., when we say "Let us suppose that this burning candle is not now burning, or let us suppose that it is burning in some imaginary space, or where there are no bodies." Things like this are sometimes supposed, although this last is clearly understood to be impossible. But when this happens, nothing at all is feigned. For in the first case I have done nothing but recall to memory^x another candle that was not burning (or I have conceived this candle without the flame), and what I think about that candle, I understand concerning this one, so long as I do not attend to the flame.

In the second case, nothing is done except to abstract the thoughts from the surrounding bodies so that the mind directs itself toward the sole contemplation of the candle, considered in itself alone, so that afterwards it infers that the candle has no cause for its destruction. So if there were no surrounding bodies, this candle, and its flame, would remain immutable, or the like. Here, then, there is no fiction, but^y true and sheer assertions.

---

x. Afterwards, when we speak of fiction that concerns essences, it will be clear that the fiction never makes, or presents to the mind, anything new, but that only things which are in the brain or the imagination are recalled to memory, and that the mind attends confusedly to all of them at once. Speech and a tree, for example are recalled to memory, and since the mind attends confusedly, without distinction, it allows that the tree speaks. The same is understood concerning existence, especially, as we have said, when it is conceived so generally, as being. Then it is easily applied to all things which occur in the mind together. This is very much worth noting.

y. The same must also be understood concerning the hypotheses that are made to explain certain motions, which agree with the phenomena of the heavens; except that when people apply them to the celestial motions, they infer the nature of the heavens from them. But that nature can be different, especially since many other causes can be conceived to explain such motions.

[58]   Transeamus jam ad fictiones, quae versantur circa essentias solas, vel cum aliqua actualitate, sive existentia simul. Circa quas hoc maxime venit considerandum: quod, quo mens minus intelligit, & tamen plura percipit, eo majorem habeat potentiam fingendi, & quo plura intelligit, eo magis illa potentia diminuatur. Eodem ex. gr. modo, quo supra vidimus, nos non posse fingere, quamdiu cogitamus, nos cogitare, & non cogitare, sic etiam, postquam novimus naturam corporis, non possumus fingere muscam infinitam; sive postquam novimus naturam^z animae, non possumus fingere eam esse quadratam, quamvis omnia verbis possimus effari. Sed, uti diximus, quo minus homines norunt Naturam, eo facilius multa possunt fingere; veluti, arbores loqui, homines in momento mutari in lapides, in fontes, apparere in speculis spectra, nihil fieri aliquid, etiam Deos in bestias, & homines mutari, ac infinita ejus generis alia.

[59]   Aliquis forte putabit, quod fictio fictionem terminat, sed non intellectio; hoc est, postquam finxi aliquid, & quadam libertate volui assentiri, id sic in rerum natura existere, hoc efficit, ut postea non possimus id alio modo cogitare. Ex. gr. postquam finxi (ut cum iis loquar) naturam corporis talem, mihique ex mea libertate persuadere volui, eam sic realiter existere, non amplius licet muscam v.g. infinitam fingere, & postquam finxi essentiam animae, eam quadrare non possum, &c.

---

z. Saepe contingit, hominem hanc vocem *anima* ad suam memoriam revocare, & simul aliquam corpoream imaginem formare. Cum vero haec duo simul repraesentantur, facile putat se imaginari, & fingere animam corpoream: quia nomen a re ipsa non distinguit. Hic postulo, ut lectores non sint praecipites ad hoc refutandum, quod, ut spero, non facient, modo ad exempla quam accurate attendant, & simul ad ea, quae sequuntur.

[58]   Let us pass now to fictions that concern either essences alone or essences together with some actuality or existence. The most important consideration regarding them is that the less the mind understands and the more things it perceives, the greater its power of feigning is; and the more things it understands, the more that power is diminished.

For example, as we have seen above, we cannot feign, so long as we are thinking, that we are thinking and are not thinking; in the same way, after we know the nature of body, we cannot feign an infinite fly, or after we know the nature of the soul,^{z} we cannot feign that it is square, though there is nothing that cannot be put into words.

But as we have said, the less men know Nature, the more easily they can feign many things, such as, that trees speak, that men are changed in a moment into stones and into springs, that nothing becomes something, that even Gods are changed into beasts and into men, and infinitely many other things of that kind.

[59]   Someone, perhaps, will think that fiction is limited by fiction, but not by intellection. That is, after I have feigned something, and willed by a certain freedom to assent that it exists in nature in this way, this has the consequence that I cannot afterwards think it in any other way. For example, after I have feigned (to speak as they do) that body has such a nature, and willed, from my freedom, to be convinced that it really exists in this way, I can no longer feign an infinite fly; and after I have feigned the essence of the soul, I can no longer feign that it is square.

---

z.   It often happens that a man recalls this term *soul* to his memory, and at the same time forms some corporeal image. But since these two things are represented together, he easily allows that he imagines and feigns a corporeal soul: because he does not distinguish the name from the thing itself. Here I ask my readers not to hasten to refute this, which, as I hope, they will not do, provided that they attend as accurately as possible to the examples, and at the same time, to the things that follow.

[60]   Sed hoc examinandum. Primo: vel negant, vel concedunt nos aliquid posse intelligere. Si concedunt, necessario id
ipsum, quod de fictione dicunt, etiam de intellectione dicendum
erit. Si vero hoc negant, videamus nos, qui scimus, nos aliquid
scire, quid dicant. Hoc scilicet dicunt, animam posse sentire, &
multis modis percipere non se ipsam, neque res, quae existunt,
sed tantum ea, quae nec in se, nec ullibi sunt, hoc est, animam
posse sola sua vi creare sensationes, aut ideas, quae non sunt
rerum; adeo ut ex parte eam, tanquam Deum, considerent.
Porro dicunt, nos, aut animam nostram talem habere libertatem, ut nosmet, aut se, imo suam ipsam libertatem cogat: Nam
postquam ea aliquid finxit, & assensum ei praebuit, non potest
id alio modo cogitare, aut fingere, & etiam ea fictione cogitur, ut
etiam alia tali modo cogitentur, ut prima fictio non oppugnetur;
sicut hic etiam coguntur absurda, quae hic recenseo, admittere
propter suam fictionem; ad quae explodenda non defatigabimur
ullis demonstrationibus.

[61]   Sed eos in suis deliriis linquendo, curabimus, ut ex
verbis, quae cum ipsis fecimus, aliquid veri ad nostram rem
hauriamus, nempe hoc[a]: Mens, cum ad rem fictam, & sua
natura falsam attendit, ut eam pensitet, & intelligat, bonoque
ordine ex ea deducat, quae sunt deducenda, facile falsitatem
patefaciet; & si res ficta sua natura sit vera, cum mens ad eam
attendit, ut eam intelligat, & ex ea bono ordine incipit deducere,
quae inde sequuntur, feliciter perget sine ulla interruptione,
sicut vidimus, quod ex falsa fictione, modo allata, statim ad
ostendendam ejus absurditatem, & alias inde deductas, praebuit se intellectus.

------

a. Quamvis hoc experientia videar concludere, & quis dicat id nil
esse, quia deficit demonstratio, eam, si quis desiderat, sic habeat. Cum
in natura nihil possit dari, quod ejus leges oppugnet, sed cum omnia
secundum certas ejus leges fiant, ut certos, certis legibus, suos produ-
cant effectus irrefragabili concatenatione: hinc sequitur, quod anima,
ubi rem vere concipit, perget objective eosdem effectus formare. Vide
infra, ubi de idea falsa loquor.

[60]   But this needs to be examined. First, either they deny or they grant that we can understand something. If they grant it, then necessarily what they say about fiction will also have to be said about intellection. But if they deny it, let us—who know that we know something—see what they say.

Evidently, they say that the soul can sense and perceive in many ways, not itself, nor the things that exist, but only those things that are neither in itself nor anywhere; that is, the soul can, by its own force alone, create sensations or ideas, which are not of things; so they consider it, to some extent, as like God.

Next, they say that we, or our soul, has such a freedom that it compels us, or itself, indeed its own freedom. For after it has feigned something, and offered its assent to it, it cannot think or feign it in any other way, and is also compelled by that fiction so that even other things are thought in such a way as not to conflict with the first fiction. As they are here forced to admit the absurdities which I review here, because of their own fiction, we shall not bother to refute them with any demonstrations.

[61]   Rather, leaving them to their madness, we shall take care to draw from the words we have exchanged with them something true and to our purpose, *viz.*:[a] when the mind attends to a fictitious thing which is false by its very nature, so that it considers it carefully, and understands it, and deduces from it in good order the things to be deduced, it will easily bring its falsity to light. And if the fictitious thing is true by its nature, then when the mind attends to it, so that it understands it, and begins to deduce from it in good order the things that follow from it, it will proceed successfully, without any interruption—just as we have seen that, from the false fiction just mentioned, the intellect immediately applies itself to show its absurdity, and the other things deduced from that.

---

a. Although I seem to infer this from experience, and someone may say that this is nothing, because a demonstration is lacking, he may have one, if he wishes; since there can be nothing in nature that is contrary to its laws, but since all things happen according to certain laws of nature, so that they produce their certain effects, by certain laws, in an unbreakable connection, it follows from this that when the soul conceives a thing truly, it proceeds to form the same effects objectively. See below, where I speak of the false idea.

[62]   Nullo ergo modo timendum erit, nos aliquid fingere, si modo clare, & distincte rem percipiamus: nam si forte dicamus homines in momento mutari in bestias, id valde generaliter dicitur; adeo ut nullus detur conceptus, id est, idea, sive cohaerentia subjecti, & praedicati in mente: si enim daretur, simul videret medium, & causas, quo, & cur tale quid factum sit. Deinde nec ad naturam subjecti, & praedicati attenditur.

[63]   Porro, modo prima idea non sit ficta, & ex ea caeterae omnes ideae deducantur, paulatim praecipitantia fingendi evanescet; deinde cum idea ficta non possit esse clara, & distincta, sed solummodo confusa, & omnis confusio inde procedat, quod mens rem integram, aut ex multis compositam, tantum ex parte noscat, & notum ab ignoto non distinguat: praeterea quod ad multa, quae continentur in unaquaque re, simul attendat sine ulla distinctione, inde sequitur primo, quod si idea sit alicujus rei simplicissimae, ea non nisi clara, & distincta poterit esse: Nam res illa non ex parte, sed tota, aut nihil ejus innotescere debebit.

[64]   Sequitur secundo, quod si res, quae componitur ex multis, in partes omnes simplicissimas cogitatione dividatur, & ad unamquamque seorsim attendatur, omnis tum confusio evanescet. Sequitur tertio, quod fictio non possit esse simplex, sed quod fiat ex compositione diversarum idearum confusarum, quae sunt diversarum rerum, atque actionum, in Natura existentium; vel melius ex attentione[b] simul sine assensu ad tales diversas ideas: Nam si esset simplex, esset clara, & distincta, & per consequens vera. Si ex compositione idearum distinctarum, esset etiam earum compositio clara, & distincta, ac proinde vera. Ex. gr. postquam novimus naturam circuli, ac etiam naturam quadrati, jam non possumus ea duo componere, & circulum facere quadratum, aut animam quadratam, & similia.

---

b. NB. Quod fictio in se spectata non multum differat a somnio, nisi quod in somniis non offerantur causae, quae vigilantibus ope sensuum offeruntur: ex quibus colligunt illa repraesentamina illo tempore non repraesentari a rebus extra se constitutis. Error autem, ut statim apparebit, est vigilando somniare; &, si sit admodum manifestus, delirium vocatur.

[62]   So we ought not to fear in any way that we are feigning something, if only we perceive the thing clearly and distinctly. For if by chance we should say that men are changed in a moment into beasts, that is said very generally, so that there is in the mind no concept, i.e., idea, or connection of subject and predicate. For if there were any concept, the mind would see together the means and causes, how and why such a thing was done. And one does not attend to the nature of the subject and of the predicate.

[63]   Next, provided the first idea is not fictitious, and all the other ideas are deduced from it, the haste to feign things will gradually disappear. And since a fictitious idea cannot be clear and distinct, but only confused, and since all confusion results from the fact that the mind knows only in part a thing that is a whole, or composed of many things, and does not distinguish the known from the unknown (and besides, attends at once, without making any distinction, to the many things that are contained in each thing), from this it follows, first, that if an idea is of some most simple thing, it can only be clear and distinct. For that thing will have to become known, not in part, but either as a whole or not at all.

[64]   Secondly, it follows that if, in thought, we divide a thing that is composed of many things into all its most simple parts, and attend to each of these separately, all confusion will disappear.

Thirdly, it follows that a fiction cannot be simple, but that it is made from the composition of different confused ideas, which are different things and actions existing in nature; or rather, from attending at once,[b] without assent, to such different ideas. For if it were simple, it would be clear and distinct, and consequently true. And if it were made from the composition of distinct ideas, their composition would also be clear and distinct, and therefore true. For example, once we know the nature of the circle, and also the nature of the square, we cannot then compound these two and make a square circle, or a square soul, and the like.

---

b. Note that the fiction, considered in itself, does not differ much from the dream, except that the causes which appear to the waking by the aid of the senses, and from which they infer that those presentations are not presented at that time by things placed outside them, do not appear in dreams. But error, as will be evident immediately, is dreaming while awake. And if it is very obvious, it is called madness.

[65]   Concludamus iterum breviter, & videamus, quomodo fictio nullo modo sit timenda, ut ea cum veris ideis confundatur. Nam quoad primam, de qua prius locuti sumus, ubi scilicet res clare concipitur, vidimus, quod si ea res, quae clare concipitur, & etiam ipsius existentia sit per se aeterna veritas, nihil circa talem rem poterimus fingere; sed si existentia rei conceptae non sit aeterna veritas, tantum est curandum, ut existentia rei cum ejus essentia conferatur, & simul ad ordinem Naturae attendatur. Quoad secundam fictionem, quam diximus esse simul attentionem sine assensu ad diversas ideas confusas, quae sunt diversarum rerum, atque actionum, in Natura existentium; vidimus etiam rem simplicissimam non posse fingi, sed intelligi, & etiam rem compositam, modo ad partes simplicissimas, ex quibus componitur, attendamus; imo nec ex ipsis ullas actiones, quae verae non sunt, nos posse fingere: Nam simul cogemur contemplari, quomodo, & cur tale quid fiat.

[66]   His sic intellectis, transeamus jam ad inquisitionem ideae falsae, ut videamus, circa quae versetur, & quomodo nobis possimus cavere, ne in falsas perceptiones incidamus. Quod utrumque non erit nobis jam difficile post inquisitionem ideae fictae: Nam inter ipsas nulla alia datur differentia, nisi quod haec supponat assensum, hoc est (uti jam notavimus), quod nullae offeruntur causae, dum repraesentamina ipsi offeruntur, quibus, sicut fingens, possit colligere, ea non oriri a rebus extra se, & quod fere nihil aliud sit, quam oculis apertis, sive dum vigilamus, somniare. Versatur itaque idea falsa, vel (ut melius loquar) refertur ad existentiam rei, cujus essentia cognoscitur, sive circa essentiam eodem modo, ac idea ficta.

[67]   Quae ad existentiam refertur, emendatur eodem modo, ac fictio: nam si natura rei notae supponat existentiam necessariam, impossibile est, ut circa existentiam illius rei fallamur; sed si existentia rei non sit aeterna veritas, uti est ejus essentia, sed quod necessitas, aut impossibilitas existendi pendeat a causis externis, tum cape omnia eodem modo, quo diximus, cum de fictione sermo esset: nam eodem modo emendatur.

[65]   Let us sum up again briefly, and see why we do not need to fear that the fiction will in any way be confused with true ideas. For as for the first [fiction] of which we spoke before, *viz.* where the thing is clearly conceived, we saw that if that thing that is clearly conceived (and also its existence) is, through itself, an eternal truth, we can feign nothing concerning such a thing. But if the existence of the thing conceived is not an eternal truth, we need only to take care to compare the existence of the thing with its essence, and at the same time attend to the order of Nature.

As for the second fiction, we said that it consists in attending at once, without assent, to different confused ideas, which are of different things and actions existing in Nature. We saw also that a most simple thing cannot be feigned, but [only] understood, and also that a composite thing can be understood, provided that we attend to the most simple parts of which it is composed. Indeed we also cannot feign from them any actions that are not true; for at the same time we will be forced to consider how and why such a thing happened.

[66]   With these matters thus understood, let us pass now to the investigation of the false idea so that we may see what it is concerned with, and how we can take care not to fall into false perceptions. Neither of these will be difficult for us now, after our investigation of the fictitious idea. For between fictitious and false ideas there is no other difference except that the latter suppose assent; i.e. (as we have already noted), while the presentations appear to him [who has the false idea], there appear no causes from which we can infer (as he who is feigning can) that they do not arise from things outside him. And this is hardly anything but dreaming with open eyes, or while we are awake. Therefore the false idea is concerned with, or (to put it better) is related to the existence of a thing whose essence is known, or to an essence, in the same way as a fictitious idea.

[67]   [The false idea] that is related to existence is emended in the same way as the fiction. For if the nature of the thing known presupposes necessary existence, it is impossible for us to be deceived concerning the existence of that thing. But if the existence of the thing is not an eternal truth (as its essence is), so that its necessity or impossibility of existing depends on external causes, then take everything in the same way as we said when we were speaking of fictions. For it may be emended in the same way.

[68]   Quod attinet ad alteram, quae ad essentias refertur, vel etiam ad actiones, tales perceptiones necessario semper sunt confusae, compositae ex diversis confusis perceptionibus rerum in Natura existentium, ut cum hominibus persuadetur, in silvis, in imaginibus, in brutis, & caeteris adesse numina; dari corpora, ex quorum sola compositione fiat intellectus; cadavera ratiocinari, ambulare, loqui; Deum decipi, & similia; sed ideae, quae sunt clarae, & distinctae, nunquam possunt esse falsae: Nam ideae rerum, quae clare, & distincte concipiuntur, sunt vel simplicissimae, vel compositae ex ideis simplicissimis, id est, a simplicissimis ideis deductae. Quod vero idea simplicissima non queat esse falsa, poterit unusquisque videre, modo sciat, quid sit verum, sive intellectus, & simul quid falsum.

[69]   Nam, quod id spectat, quod formam veri constituit, certum est, cogitationem veram a falsa non tantum per denominationem extrinsecam, sed maxime per intrinsecam distingui. Nam si quis faber ordine concepit fabricam aliquam, quamvis talis fabrica nunquam exstiterit, nec etiam unquam exstitura sit, ejus nihilominus cogitatio vera est, & cogitatio eadem est, sive fabrica existat, sive minus; & contra si aliquis dicit, Petrum ex. gr. existere, nec tamen scit, Petrum existere, illa cogitatio respectu illius falsa est, vel, si mavis, non est vera, quamvis Petrus revera existat. Nec haec enunciatio, Petrus existit, vera est, nisi respectu illius, qui certo scit, Petrum existere.

[70]   Unde sequitur in ideis dari aliquid reale, per quod verae a falsis distinguuntur: quod quidem jam investigandum erit, ut optimam veritatis normam habeamus (ex data enim verae ideae norma nos nostras cogitationes debere determinare diximus, methodumque cognitionem esse reflexivam), & proprietates intellectus noscamus; nec dicendum hanc differentiam ex eo oriri, quod cogitatio vera est res cognoscere per primas suas causas, in quo quidem a falsa valde differret, prout eandem supra explicui: Cogitatio enim vera etiam dicitur, quae essentiam alicujus principii objective involvit, quod causam non habet, & per se, & in se cognoscitur.

[68]   As for the other kind of false idea, which is related to essences, or also to actions, such perceptions must always be confused, composed of different confused perceptions of things existing in nature—as when men are persuaded that there are divinities in the woods, in images, in animals, etc.; or that there are bodies from whose composition alone the intellect is made; or that corpses reason, walk, and speak; or that God is deceived, and the like. But ideas that are clear and distinct can never be false. For the ideas of things that are conceived clearly and distinctly, are either most simple, or composed of most simple ideas, i.e., deduced from most simple ideas. But that a most simple idea cannot be false, anyone can see—provided that he knows what the true is, or the intellect, and at the same time, what the false is.

[69]   As for what constitutes the form of the true, it is certain that a true thought is distinguished from a false one not only by an extrinsic, but chiefly by an intrinsic denomination. For if some architect conceives a building in an orderly fashion, then although such a building never existed, and even never will exist, still the thought of it is true, and the thought is the same, whether the building exists or not. On the other hand, if someone says, for example, that Peter exists, and nevertheless does not know that Peter exists, that thought, in respect to him is false, or, if you prefer, is not true, even though Peter really exists. Nor is this statement, Peter exists, true, except in respect to him who knows certainly that Peter exists.

[70]   From this it follows that there is something real in ideas, through which the true are distinguished from the false. This will now have to be investigated, so that we may have the best standard of truth (for we have said that we must determine our thoughts from the given standard of a true idea, and that method is reflexive knowledge), and may know the properties of the intellect. Nor must we say that this difference arises from the fact that the true thought is knowing things through their first causes. In this, indeed, it differs greatly from the false, as I have explained it above. For that Thought is also called true which involves objectively the essence of some principle that does not have a cause, and is known through itself and in itself.

[71]   Quare forma verae cogitationis in eadem ipsa cogitatione sine relatione ad alias debet esse sita; nec objectum tanquam causam agnoscit, sed ab ipsa intellectus potentia, & natura pendere debet. Nam si supponamus, intellectum ens aliquod novum percepisse, quod nunquam exstitit, sicut aliqui Dei intellectum concipiunt, antequam res crearet (quae sane perceptio a nullo objecto oriri potuit), & ex tali perceptione alias legitime deducere, omnes illae cogitationes verae essent, & a nullo objecto externo determinatae, sed a sola intellectus potentia, & natura dependerent. Quare id, quod formam verae cogitationis constituit, in ipsa eadem cogitatione est quaerendum, & ab intellectus natura deducendum.

[72]   Hoc igitur ut investigetur, ideam aliquam veram ob oculos ponamus, cujus objectum maxime certo scimus a vi nostra cogitandi pendere, nec objectum aliquod in Natura habere: in tali enim idea, ut ex jam dictis patet, facilius id, quod volumus, investigare poterimus. Ex. gr. ad formandum conceptum globi fingo ad libitum causam, nempe semicirculum circa centrum rotari, & ex rotatione globum quasi oriri. Haec sane idea vera est, & quamvis sciamus nullum in Natura globum sic unquam ortum fuisse, est haec tamen vera perceptio, & facillimus modus formandi globi conceptum. Jam notandum hanc perceptionem affirmare semicirculum rotari, quae affirmatio falsa esset, si non esset juncta conceptui globi, vel causae talem motum determinantis, sive absolute, si haec affirmatio nuda esset. Nam tum mens tantum tenderet ad affirmandum solum semicirculi motum, qui nec in semicirculi conceptu continetur, nec ex conceptu causae motum determinantis oritur. Quare falsitas in hoc solo consistit, quod aliquid de aliqua re affirmetur, quod in ipsius, quem formavimus, conceptu, non continetur, ut motus, vel quies de semicirculo. Unde sequitur simplices cogitationes non posse non esse veras, ut simplex semicirculi, motus, quantitatis, &c. idea. Quicquid hae affirmationis continent, earum adaequat conceptum, nec ultra se extendit; quare nobis licet ad libitum sine ullo erroris scrupulo ideas simplices formare.

[71]   So the form of the true thought must be placed in the same thought itself without relation to other things, nor does it recognize the object as its cause, but must depend on the very power and nature of the intellect. For if we should suppose that the intellect had perceived some new being, which has never existed (as some conceive God's intellect, before he created things—for that perception, of course, could not have arisen from any object), and that from such a perception it deduced others legitimately, all those thoughts would be true, and determined by no external object, but would depend only on the power and nature of the intellect. So what constitutes the form of the true thought must be sought in the same thought itself, and must be deduced from the nature of the intellect.

[72]   To investigate this, therefore, let us consider some true idea, of which we know most certainly that its object depends on our power of thinking, and that it has no object in nature. For it is clear from what has already been said that we shall be able more easily to investigate what we wish to in such an idea. E.g., to form the concept of a sphere, I feign a cause at will, say that a semicircle is rotated around a center, and that the sphere is, as it were, produced by this rotation. This idea, of course, is true, and even though we may know that no sphere in nature was ever produced in this way, nevertheless, this perception is true, and a very easy way of forming the concept of a sphere.

Now it must be noted that this perception affirms that the semicircle is rotated, which affirmation would be false if it were not joined to the concept of a sphere, or to a cause determining such a motion, or absolutely, if this affirmation were isolated. For then the mind would only tend to affirm of the semicircle nothing but motion, which neither is contained in the concept of the semicircle nor arises from the concept of the cause determining the motion. So falsity consists only in this: that something is affirmed of a thing that is not contained in the concept we have formed of the thing, as motion or rest of the semicircle.

From this it follows that simple thought cannot but be true; for example, the simple idea of a semicircle, or of motion, or of quantity, etc. Whatever they contain of affirmation matches their concept, and does not extend itself beyond [the concept]. So we may form simple ideas at will, without fear of error.

[73]   Superest igitur tantum quaerere, qua potentia mens
nostra eas formare possit, & quousque ea potentia se extendat:
hoc enim invento facile videbimus summam, ad quam possumus
pervenire, cognitionem. Certum enim est hanc ejus potentiam
se non extendere in infinitum: Nam cum aliquid de aliqua re
affirmamus, quod in conceptu, quem de ea formamus, non
continetur, id defectum nostrae perceptionis indicat, sive quod
mutilatas quasi, & truncatas habemus cogitationes, sive ideas.
Motum enim semicirculi falsum esse vidimus, ubi nudus in
mente est, eum ipsum autem verum, si conceptui globi junga-
tur, vel conceptui alicujus causae talem motum determinantis.
Quod si de natura entis cogitantis sit, uti prima fronte videtur,
cogitationes veras, sive adaequatas formare, certum est, ideas
inadaequatas ex eo tantum in nobis oriri, quod pars sumus
alicujus entis cogitantis, cujus quaedam cogitationes ex toto,
quaedam ex parte tantum nostram mentem constituunt.

[74]   Sed quod adhuc venit considerandum, & quod circa
fictionem non fuit operae pretium notare, & ubi maxima datur
deceptio, est, quando contingit, ut quaedam, quae in imaginatione offeruntur, sint etiam in intellectu, hoc est, quod clare, &
distincte concipiantur, quod tum, quamdiu distinctum a confuso
non distinguitur, certitudo, hoc est, idea vera cum non distinctis
commiscetur. Ex. gr. quidam Stoicorum forte audiverunt nomen
animae, & etiam quod sit immortalis, quae tantum confuse imaginabantur; imaginabantur etiam, & simul intelligebant corpora subtilissima caetera omnia penetrare, & a nullis penetrari.
Cum haec omnia simul imaginabantur, concomitante certudine
hujus axiomatis, statim certi reddebantur, mentem esse subtilissima illa corpora, & subtilissima illa corpora non dividi, &c.

[73]   It only remains, then, to ask by what power our mind can form these [simple ideas] and how far this power extends. For once this is discovered, we shall easily see the highest knowledge we can reach. It is certain that this power does not extend to infinity. For when we affirm of a things something not contained in the concept we form of it, that indicates a defect of our perception, *or* that we have thoughts, *or* ideas, which are, as it were, mutilated and maimed. For we saw that the motion of a semicircle is false when it is in the mind in isolation, but true if it is joined to the concept of a sphere, or to the concept of some cause determining such a motion. But if it is—as it seems at first—of the nature of a thinking being to form true, *or* adequate, thoughts, it is certain that inadequate ideas arise in us only from the fact that we are a part of a thinking being, of which some thoughts wholly constitute our mind, while others do so only in part.

[74]   But we still need to consider something which was not worth the trouble of noting concerning fictions, and which gives rise to the greatest deception—*viz.* when it happens that certain things that appear in the imagination are also in the intellect, i.e., that they are conceived clearly and distinctly. For then, so long as the distinct is not distinguished from the confused, certainty, i.e., a true idea, is mixed up with what is not distinct.

For example, some of the Stoics heard, perhaps, the word *soul,* and also that the soul is immortal, which they only imagined confusedly; they also both imagined and at the same time understood that the most subtle bodies penetrate all others, and are not penetrated by any. Since they imagined all these things at once—while remaining certain of this axiom—they immediately became certain that the mind was those most subtle bodies and that those most subtle bodies were not divided, etc.

[75]   Sed ab hoc etiam liberamur, dum conamur ad normam datae verae ideae omnes nostras perceptiones examinare cavendo, uti initio diximus, ab iis, quas ex auditu, aut ab experientia vaga habemus. Adde quod talis deceptio ex eo oritur, quod res nimis abstracte concipiunt: nam per se satis clarum est, me illud, quod in suo vero objecto concipio, alteri non posse applicare. Oritur denique etiam ex eo, quod prima elementa totius Naturae non intelligunt; unde sine ordine procedendo, & Naturam cum abstractis, quamvis sint vera axiomata, confundendo, se ipsos confundunt, ordinemque Naturae pervertunt. Nobis autem, si quam minime abstracte procedamus, & a primis elementis, hoc est, a fonte, & origine Naturae, quam primum fieri potest, incipiamus, nullo modo talis deceptio erit metuenda.

[76]   Quod autem attinet ad cognitionem originis Naturae, minime est timendum, ne eam cum abstractis confundamus: nam cum aliquid abstracte concipitur, uti sunt omnia universalia, semper latius comprehenduntur in intellectu, quam revera in Natura existere possunt eorum particularia. Deinde cum in natura dentur multa, quorum differentia adeo est exigua, ut fere intellectum effugiat, tum facile (si abstracte concipiantur) potest contingere, ut confundantur; at cum origo Naturae, ut postea videbimus, nec abstracte, sive universaliter concipi possit, nec latius possit extendi in intellectu, quam revera est, nec ullam habeat similitudinem cum mutabilibus, nulla circa ejus ideam metuenda est confusio, modo normam veritatis (quam jam ostendimus) habeamus: est nimirum hoc ens, unicum,[z] infinitum, hoc est, est omne esse, & praeter quod[a] nullum datur esse.

---

z.   Haec non sunt attributa Dei, quae ostendunt ipsius essentiam, ut in Philosophia ostendam.

a.   Hoc supra jam demonstratum est. Si enim tale ens non existeret, nunquam posset produci; adeoque mens plus posset intelligere, quam Natura praestare, quod supra falsum esse constitit.

[75]   But we are freed from this also, as long as we strive to consider all our perceptions according to the standard of a given true idea, being on guard, as we said in the beginning, against those we have from report or from random experience. Moreover, such a deception arises from the fact that they conceive things too abstractly. For it is sufficiently clear through itself that I cannot apply what I conceive in its true object to something else. Finally, it arises also from the fact that they do not understand the first elements of the whole of Nature; so proceeding without order, and confusing Nature with abstractions (although they are true axioms), they confuse themselves and overturn the order of Nature. But we shall not need to fear any such deception, if we proceed as far as we can in a manner that is not abstract, and begin as soon as possible from the first elements, i.e., from the source and origin of Nature.

[76]   But as for knowledge of the origin of Nature, we need not have any fear of confusing it with abstractions. For when things are conceived abstractly (as all universals are), they always have a wider extension in our intellect than their particulars can really have in nature. And then, since there are many things in nature whose difference is so slight that it almost escapes the intellect, it can easily happen, if they are conceived abstractly, that they are confused. But since, as we shall see later, the origin of Nature can neither be conceived abstractly, or universally, nor be extended more widely in the intellect than it really is, and since it has no likeness to changeable things, we need fear no confusion concerning its idea, provided that we have the standard of truth (which we have already shown). For it is a unique and infinite[z] being, beyond which there is no being.[a]

---

z.   These are not attributes of God that show his essence, as I shall show in [my] Philosophy.

a.   This has already been demonstrated above. For if such a being did not exist, it could never be produced; and therefore the mind would be able to understand more things than Nature could bring about—which we have shown above to be false.

[77] Hucusque de idea falsa. Superest, ut de idea dubia inquiramus, hoc est, ut inquiramus, quaenam sint ea, quae nos possunt in dubium pertrahere, & simul quomodo dubitatio tollatur. Loquor de vera dubitatione in mente, & non de ea, quam passim videmus contingere, ubi scilicet verbis, quamvis animus non dubitet, dicit quis se dubitare: non est enim Methodi hoc emendare; sed potius pertinet ad inquisitionem pertinaciae, & ejus emendationem.

[78] Dubitatio itaque in anima nulla datur per rem ipsam, de qua dubitatur, hoc est, si tantum unica sit idea in anima, sive ea sit vera, sive falsa, nulla dabitur dubitatio, neque etiam certitudo: Sed tantum talis sensatio. Est enim in se nihil aliud nisi talis sensatio; sed dabitur per aliam ideam, quae non adeo clara, ac distincta est, ut possimus ex ea aliquid certi circa rem, de qua dubitatur, concludere, hoc est, idea, quae nos in dubium conjicit, non est clara, & distincta. Ex. gr. siquis nunquam cogitaverit de sensuum fallacia, sive experientia, sive quomodocunque sit, nunquam dubitabit, an sol major, aut minor sit, quam apparet. Inde Rustici passim mirantur, cum audiunt solem multo majorem esse, quam globum terrae, sed cogitando de fallacia sensuum oritur dubitatio. Id est, scit sensus aliquando se decepisse; sed hoc tantum confuse scit: Nam nescit, quomodo sensus fallant, & si quis post dubitationem acquisiverit veram cognitionem sensuum, & quomodo per eorum instrumenta res ad distantiam repraesententur, tum dubitatio iterum tollitur.

[77]   So far we have been speaking of the false idea. It remains now to investigate the doubtful idea—i.e., to ask what are the things that can lead us into doubt, and at the same time, how doubt is removed. I am speaking of true doubt in the mind, and not of what we commonly see happen, when someone says in words that he doubts, although his mind does not doubt. For it is not the business of the Method to emend that. That belongs rather to the investigation of stubbornness, and its emendation.

[78]   There is no doubt in the soul, therefore, through the thing itself concerning which one doubts. That is, if there should be only one idea in the soul, then, whether it is true or false, there will be neither doubt nor certainty, but only a sensation of a certain sort. For in itself [this idea] is nothing but a sensation of a certain sort.

But doubt will arise through another idea which is not so clear and distinct that we can infer from it something certain about the thing concerning which there is doubt. That is, the idea that puts us in doubt is not clear and distinct. For example, if someone has never been led, either by experience or by anything else, to think about the deceptiveness of the senses, he will never doubt whether the sun is larger or smaller than it appears to be. So Country People are generally surprised when they hear that the sun is much larger than the earth. But in thinking about the deceptiveness of the senses, doubt arises. I.e., [the person] knows that his senses have sometimes deceived him, but he knows this only confusedly; for he does not know how the senses deceive. And if someone, after doubting, acquires a true knowledge of the senses and of how, by their means, things at a distance are presented, then the doubt is again removed.

[79] Unde sequitur, nos non posse veras ideas in dubium vocare ex eo, quod forte aliquis Deus deceptor existat, qui vel in maxime certis nos fallit, nisi quamdiu nullam habemus claram, & distinctam Dei ideam; hoc est, si attendamus ad cognitionem, quam de origine omnium rerum habemus, & nihil inveniamus, quod nos doceat, eum non esse deceptorem eadem illa cognitione, qua, cum attendimus ad naturam trianguli, invenimus ejus tres angulos aequales esse duobus rectis [, zo blijft de twijffeling]; sed si talem cognitionem Dei habemus, qualem habemus trianguli, tum omnis dubitatio tollitur. Et eodem modo, quo possumus pervenire ad talem cognitionem trianguli, quamvis non certo sciamus, an aliquis summus deceptor nos fallat, eodem etiam modo possumus pervenire ad talem Dei cognitionem, quamvis non certo sciamus, an detur quis summus deceptor, &, modo eam habeamus, sufficiet ad tollendam, uti dixi, omnem dubitationem, quam de ideis claris, & distinctis habere possumus.

[80] Porro si quis recte procedat investigando, quae prius sunt investiganda, nulla interrupta concatenatione rerum, & sciat, quomodo quaestiones sint determinandae, antequam ad earum cognitionem accingamur, nunquam nisi certissimas ideas, id est, claras, & distinctas habebit: Nam dubitatio nihil aliud est, quam suspensio animi circa aliquam affirmationem, aut negationem, quam affirmaret, aut negaret, nisi occurreret aliquid, quo ignoto cognitio ejus rei debet esse imperfecta. Unde colligitur, quod dubitatio semper oritur ex eo, quod res absque ordine investigentur.

[81] Haec sunt, quae promisi tradere in hac prima parte Methodi. Sed ut nihil omittam eorum, quae ad cognitionem intellectus, & ejus vires possunt conducere, tradam etiam pauca de memoria, & oblivione; ubi hoc maxime venit considerandum, quod memoria corroboretur ope intellectus, & etiam absque ope intellectus. Nam quoad primum, quo res magis est intelligibilis, eo facilius retinetur, & contra, quo minus, eo facilius eam obliviscimur. Ex. gr. si tradam alicui copiam verborum solutorum, ea multo difficilius retinebit, quam si eadem verba in forma narrationis tradam.

[79] From this it follows that, only so long as we have no clear and distinct idea of God, can we call true ideas in doubt by supposing that perhaps some deceiving God exists, who misleads us even in the things most certain. I.e., if we attend to the knowledge we have concerning the origin of all things and do not discover—by the same knowledge we have when, attending to the nature of the triangle, we discover that its three angles equal two right angles—anything that teaches us that he is not a deceiver [, then the doubt remains]. But if we have the kind of knowledge of God that we have of the triangle, then all doubt is removed. And just as we can arrive at such a knowledge of the triangle, even though we may not know certainly whether some supreme deceiver misleads us, so we can arrive at such a knowledge of God, even though we may not know whether there is some supreme deceiver. Provided we have that knowledge, it will suffice, as I have said, to remove every doubt that we can have concerning clear and distinct ideas.

[80] Further, if someone proceeds rightly, by investigating [first] those things which ought to be investigated first, with no interruption in the connection of things, and knows how to define problems precisely, before striving for knowledge of them, he will never have anything but the most certain ideas—i.e., clear and distinct ideas. For doubt is nothing but the suspension of the mind concerning some affirmation or negation, which it would affirm or deny if something did not occur to it, the ignorance of which must render its knowledge of the thing imperfect. From this it is [to be] inferred that doubt always arises from the fact that things are investigated without order.

[81] These are the matters I promised to discuss in this first part of the Method. But to omit nothing that can lead to knowledge of the intellect and its powers, I shall say a few words about memory and forgetting. The most important consideration is that memory is strengthened both with the aid of the intellect and also without its aid. For regarding the first, the more intelligible a thing is, the more easily it is retained; and conversely, the less intelligible, the more easily forgotten. E.g., if I give someone a large number of disconnected words, he will retain them with much more difficulty than if I give him the same words in the form of a story.

[82]   Corroboratur etiam absque ope intellectus, scilicet a vi, qua imaginatio, aut sensus, quem vocant communem, afficitur ab aliqua re singulare corporea. Dico *singularem:* imaginatio enim tantum a singularibus afficitur: Nam si quis legerit ex. gr. unam tantum Fabulam amatoriam, eam optime retinebit, quamdiu non legerit plures alias ejus generis, quia tum sola viget in imaginatione: sed si plures sint ejusdem generis, simul omnes imaginamur, & facile confunduntur. Dico etiam *corpoream:* nam a solis corporibus afficitur imaginatio. Cum itaque memoria ab intellectu corroboretur, & etiam sine intellectu, inde concluditur, eam quid diversum esse ab intellectu, & circa intellectum in se spectatum nullam dari memoriam, neque oblivionem.

[83]   Quid ergo erit memoria? Nihil aliud, quam sensatio impressionum cerebri, simul cum cogitatione ad determinatam durationem^d sensationis; quod etiam ostendit reminiscentia. Nam ibi anima cogitat de illa sensatione; sed non sub continua duratione; & sic idea istius sensationis non est ipsa duratio sensationis, id est, ipsa memoria. An vero ideae ipsae aliquam patiantur corruptionem, videbimus in Philosophia. Et si hoc alicui valde absurdum videatur, sufficiet ad nostrum propositum, ut cogitet, quod, quo res est singularior, eo facilius retineatur, sicut ex exemplo Comoediae modo allato patet. Porro quo res intelligibilior, eo etiam facilius retinetur. Unde maxime singularem, & tantummodo intelligibilem non poterimus non retinere.

---

d. Si vero duratio sit indeterminata, memoria ejus rei est imperfecta, quod quisque etiam videtur a natura didicisse. Saepe enim, ut alicui melius credamus in eo, quod dicit, rogamus, quando, & ubi id contigerit. Quamvis etiam ideae ipsae suam habeant durationem in mente, tamen cum assueti simus durationem determinare ope alicujus mensurae motus, quod etiam ope imaginationis fit, ideo nullam adhuc memoriam observamus, quae sit purae mentis.

[82]   It is also strengthened without the aid [of] the intellect, by the force with which the imagination, or what they call the common sense, is affected by some singular corporeal thing. I say *singular*, for the imagination is affected only by singular things. If someone, e.g., has read only one Comedy, he will retain it best so long as he does not read several others of that kind, for then it will flourish in isolation in the imagination. But if there are several of the same kind, we imagine them all together and they are easily confused. I say also *corporeal*, for the imagination is affected only by bodies. Therefore since the memory is strengthened both by the intellect and also without the intellect, we may infer that it is something different from the intellect, and that concerning the intellect considered in itself there is neither memory nor forgetting.

[83]   What, then, will memory be? Nothing but a sensation of impressions on the brain, together with the thought of a determinate duration[d] of the sensation, which recollection also shows. For there the soul thinks of that sensation, but not under a continuous duration. And so the idea of that sensation is not the duration itself of the sensation, i.e., the memory itself. But whether the ideas themselves undergo some corruption, we shall seen in [my] Philosophy.

If this seems quite absurd to anyone, it will suffice for our purpose if he thinks that the more singular a thing is, the more easily it may be retained, as the example of the Comedy just mentioned makes clear. Further, the more intelligible a thing is, the more easily it too is retained. So we cannot but retain a thing that is most singular if only it is also intelligible.

---

d. But if the duration is indeterminate, the memory of the things is imperfect, as each of us also seems to have learned from nature. For often, to believe someone better in what he says, we ask when and where it happened. Although the ideas themselves also have their own duration in the mind, nevertheless, since we have become accustomed to determine duration with the aid of some measure of motion, which is also done with the aid of the imagination, we still observe no memory that belongs to the pure mind.

[84]   Sic itaque distinximus inter ideam veram, & caeteras perceptiones, ostendimusque, quod ideae fictae, falsae, &
caeterae habeant suam originem ab imaginatione, hoc est, a
quibusdam sensationibus fortuitis, atque (ut sic loquar) solutis,
quae non oriuntur ab ipsa mentis potentia, sed a causis externis, prout corpus, sive somniando, sive vigilando varios accipit
motus. Vel si placet, hic per imaginationem, quicquid velis,
cape, modo sit quid diversum ab intellectu, & unde anima
habeat rationem patientis; perinde enim est, quicquid capias,
postquam novimus eandem quid vagum esse, & a quo anima
patitur, & simul etiam novimus, quomodo ope intellectus ab
eadem liberamur. Quare etiam nemo miretur, me hic nondum
probare, dari corpus, & alia necessaria, & tamen loqui de
imaginatione, de corpore, & ejus constitutione. Nempe, ut dixi,
est perinde, quid capiam, postquam novi esse quid vagum, &c.

[85]   At ideam veram simplicem esse ostendimus, aut ex
simplicibus compositam, & quae ostendit, quomodo, & cur
aliquid sit, aut factum sit, & quod ipsius effectus objectivi in
anima procedunt ad rationem formalitatis ipsius objecti; id,
quod idem est, quod veteres dixerunt, nempe veram scientiam
procedere a causa ad effectus; nisi quod nunquam, quod sciam,
conceperunt, uti nos hic, animam secundum certas leges agen-
tem, & quasi aliquod automa spirituale.

[86]   Unde, quantum in initio licuit, acquisivimus noti-
tiam nostri intellectus, & talem normam verae ideae, ut jam
non vereamur, ne vera cum falsis, aut fictis confundamus; nec
etiam mirabimur, cur quaedam intelligamus, quae nullo modo
sub imaginationem cadunt, & alia sint in imaginatione, quae
prorsus oppugnant intellectum; alia denique cum intellectu
conveniant; quandoquidem novimus operationes illas, a quibus
imaginationes producuntur, fieri secundum alias leges, prorsus
diversas a legibus intellectus, & animam circa imaginationem
tantum habere rationem patientis.

[84]   In this way, then, we have distinguished between a true idea and other perceptions, and shown that the fictitious, the false, and the other ideas have their origin in the imagination, i.e., in certain sensations that are fortuitous, and (as it were) disconnected; since they do not arise from the very power of the mind, but from external causes, as the body (whether waking or dreaming) receives various motions.

But if you wish, take imagination any way you like here, provided it is something different from the intellect, and in which the soul has the nature of something acted on. For it is all the same, however you take it, after we know that it is something random, by which the soul is acted on, and at the same time know how we are freed from it with the help of the intellect. So let no one be surprised that here, where I have not yet proved that there is a body, and other necessary things, I speak of the imagination, the body and its constitution. For as I have said, it does not matter what I take it to be, after I know that it is something random, etc.

[85]   We have shown that a true idea is simple, or composed of simple ideas; that it shows how and why something is, or has been done; and that its objective effects proceed in the soul according to the formal nature of its object. This is the same as what the ancients said, i.e., that true knowledge proceeds from cause to effect—except that so far as I know they never conceived the soul (as we do here) as acting according to certain laws, like a spiritual automaton.

[86]   From this we have acquired as much knowledge of our intellect as was possible in the beginning, and such a standard of the true idea that now we do not fear confusing true ideas with false or fictitious ones. Nor will we wonder why we understand certain things that do not fall in any way under the imagination, why there are some things in the imagination which are completely opposed to the intellect, and finally why there are others that agree with the intellect; for we know that those activities by which imaginations are produced happen according to other laws, wholly different from the laws of the intellect, and that in imagination the soul only has the nature of something acted on.

[87]   Ex quo etiam constat, quam facile ii in magnos errores possunt delabi, qui non accurate distinxerunt inter imaginationem, & intellectionem. In hos ex. gr. quod extensio debeat esse in loco, debeat esse finita, cujus partes ab invicem distinguuntur realiter, quod sit primum, & unicum fundamentum omnium rerum, & uno tempore majus spatium occupet, quam alio, multaque ejusmodi alia, quae omnia prorsus oppugnant veritatem, ut suo loco ostendemus.

[88]   Deinde cum verba sint pars imaginationis, hoc est, quod, prout vage ex aliqua dispositione corporis componuntur in memoria, multos conceptus fingamus, ideo non dubitandum, quin etiam verba aeque, ac imaginatio, possint esse causa multorum, magnorumque errorum, nisi magnopere ab ipsis caveamus.

[89]   Adde quod sint constituta ad libitum, & captum vulgi; adeo ut non sint nisi signa rerum, prout sunt in imaginatione, non autem prout sunt in intellectu; quod clare patet ex eo, quod omnibus iis, quae tantum sunt in intellectu, & non in imaginatione, nomina imposuerunt saepe negativa, uti sunt, incorporeum, infinitum, &c. & etiam multa, quae sunt revera affirmativa, negative exprimunt, & contra, uti sunt increatum, independens, infinitum, immortale, &c. quia nimirum horum contraria multo facilius imaginamur; ideoque prius primis hominibus occurrerunt, & nomina positiva usurparunt. Multa affirmamus, & negamus, quia natura verborum id affirmare, & negare patitur, non vero rerum natura; adeoque hac ignorata facile aliquid falsum pro vero sumeremus.

[90]   Vitamus praetera aliam magnam causam confusionis, & quae facit, quominus intellectus ad se reflectat: nempe, cum non distinguimus inter imaginationem, & intellectionem, putamus ea, quae facilius imaginamur, nobis esse clariora, & id, quod imaginamur, putamus intelligere. Unde quae sunt postponenda, anteponimus, & sic verus ordo progrediendi pervertitur, nec aliquid legitime concluditur.

[87]   From this it is also established how easily they can fall into great errors, who have not accurately distinguished between imagination and intellection. Such errors as: that extension must be in a place, that it must be finite, that its parts must be really distinguished from one another, that it is the first and only foundation of all things, that it occupies more space at one time than at another, and many other things of the same kind, all of which are completely opposed to the truth, as we shall show in the proper place.

[88]   Next, since words are part of the imagination, i.e., since we feign many concepts, in accordance with the random composition of words in the memory from some disposition of the body, it is not to be doubted that words, as much as the imagination, can be the cause of many and great errors, unless we are very wary of them.

[89]   Moreover, they are established according to the pleasure and power of understanding of ordinary people, so that they are only signs of things as they are in the imagination, but not as they are in the intellect. This is clear from the fact that the names given to things that are only in the intellect, and not in the imagination, are often negative (for example, infinite, incorporeal, etc.), and also from the fact that they express negatively many things that are really affirmative, and conversely (for example, uncreated, independent, infinite, immortal). Because the contraries of these are much more easily imagined, they occurred first to the earliest men, and they used positive names. We affirm and deny many things because the nature of words—not the nature of things—allows us to affirm them. And in our ignorance of this, we easily take something false to be true.

[90]   We avoid, moreover, another great cause of confusion which prevents the intellect from reflecting on itself—*viz.* when we do not distinguish between imagination and intellection, we think that the things we more easily imagine are clearer to us, and think we understand what we imagine. Hence, what should be put later we put first, and so the true order of making progress is overturned, and no conclusion is arrived at legitimately.

I Commentary

Spinoza begins by reminding us of the content of the method's first part: "to distinguish and separate true ideas from all other perceptions, and to restrain the mind from confusing false, fictitious, and doubtful ideas with true ones" (§ 50). This separation between true and untrue ideas is identified several times in what follows with the distinction between the intellect and the imagination (see, for example, § 84). The analysis that Spinoza gives here is not a full explanation "by its proximate cause" (§ 51); this will be given in the *Philosophia*. Here, we encounter something like a phenomenology quite sufficient for our purpose. The separation between imagination and intellect provides us with knowledge of the standard of a true idea, precisely what we need in order to engage in the second part of the method. At the same time, we arrive at knowledge of what we really are and of our real power: we are minds, we are like spiritual automata who, out of ourselves, can produce truth (§ 85) and who, in that (self-)production, can find a certain happiness.

I Getting Out of the Dream

The difference between imagination and intellect is presented as the difference between living steeped in dreams (or even madness) and living fully awake. The ideas or perceptions of the imagination—fictitious, false, and doubtful—are compared to different kinds of dreaming or to being under the influence of external forces.[1] Fictitious ideas are like dreams, without any real self-determination in thinking; they are characterized by purely accidental associations. False ideas (or error) are compared to dreaming with open eyes. Spinoza even adds in footnote b to § 64: "if it [error] is very obvious, it is called madness." Doubtful ideas are compared to the state of wondering whether one is dreaming or awake.

The real acquisition of intellectual ideas is compared to an awakening. It is particularly important for people to be fully aware of the difference between imagination and intellect, "because [otherwise] there are many who *doubt even true ideas.* . . . So they are like men, who, when they were awake, used not to doubt that they were awake, but who, after they once thought in a dream that they were certainly awake (as often happens), and later found that to be false, doubted even of their waking states. This happens because they have never distinguished between the dream and the waking state" (§ 50; emphasis added). So although truth is the sign of itself and of falsehood (§§ 35, 46), this "does not entail that we require no *labor* to isolate and appreciate the truth that already characterizes some of our ideas."[2] In fact, sometimes "it happens that certain things that appear in the imagination are also in the intellect. . . . [T]hen, so long as the distinct is not distinguished from the confused, certainty, i.e., a true idea, is mixed up with what is not distinct" (§ 74). The task of this first part of the method is not simply to reflect on (given) true ideas (we did this in §§ 33–36) but also and in particular to accustom us to *actively* distinguishing the intellect from the imagination, such that truth does not get mixed up with the confused thought of the latter. The task is to secure the working of the *pure* intellect according to the reflexive insight into true, intellectual thought.

The separation to be performed between intellect and imagination should not be understood as completely leaving the imagination behind. The relationship here is comparable to that between ordinary goods and the real good in the introduction to the *Treatise:* what is negative can become positive in a subordinate function. The separation between the intellect and the imagination will allow us to avoid confusing the two and even to use certain forms of the imagination in the service of the intellect. Indeed, certain elements of the imagination "agree with the intellect" (§ 86); this is the case with a careful usage of language in intellectual thinking (§ 88).

Some authors have rightly stressed that Spinoza does not have a Manichaean conception of the imagination.[3] In the first place, it is inevitable that the human mind will be characterized by the imagination: if we were without sensations altogether, we would be dead. As will be explained in the *Ethics,* the human mind can effectively *have* ideas only insofar as it *is* the idea of an actually existing body (*Ethics* II, P. 13, Sch.; *Ethics* V, P. 39, Sch.); to be this idea is for the mind automatically to have ideas of what happens to the human body: ideas of bodily sensations and whatever follows from such ideas (*Ethics* II, P. 14ff.). In some sense, this is even a prerequisite for *having* intellectual ideas. The mind can arrive at adequate ideas only if it first succeeds in perceiving bodies in a certain way (*Ethics* II, P. 13, Sch.; P. 29, Sch.; P. 37, Cor.; P. 38, Cor.). This supposes, of course, that bodies are first perceived in the ordinary way (through *imaginationes* or perceptions of bodily sensations).

That the imagination is a prerequisite for the life of the intellect is even clearer when we look at the importance of affective processes, which clearly belong to the imagination but are important for the development of the intellect and the attempt to reach real freedom (see *Ethics* IV). Finally, some forms of the imagination are quite compatible with, or even *part of,* the life of the intellect. We have mentioned language (if used with sufficient care). One also can refer to statements made by Spinoza that cannot be considered slips of the pen, such as, "the more men *imagine* to enjoy it (the intellectual love towards God), the more it must be encouraged" (*Ethics* V, P. 20, Dem.).

Although all of this is true—the imagination cannot be eliminated and is even part of intellectual life—it is crucial to separate the intellect and the imagination and to keep them separate (§ 74). This is the task of the first part of the method, which deals with the distinction and separation of true ideas from fictitious, false, and dubitable ideas, the intellect being the source of truth, the imagination of the rest.

It is striking how much time Spinoza spends discussing fictitious ideas. This probably is not accidental. Spinoza stresses the spontaneous and active character of intellection. Superficially, this looks like the spontaneity and activity of fiction. So it is not surprising that Spinoza spends time showing that fiction itself is not at all this spontaneous and creative power people sometimes take it to be. Real activity, spontaneity, and creativity in thinking are properties of the *intellect.* In imagination, especially in certain of its forms, we are rather like mindless automata (§ 48); it is the intellect that makes us look like spiritual automata (§ 85).

Anticipating Freud, Spinoza tries to show that the life of dreaming, especially in the form of fictitious ideas, is not creative but rather is fundamentally passive. In imagination the mind is acted upon, it undergoes things (§ 86). Fiction never produces anything new. What looks new is, in fact, nothing but the remains of "things which are in the brain or the imagination," recalled to memory and confusedly associated together (§ 57n. x). Spinoza even claims that "the less the mind understands and the more things it perceives, the greater its power of feigning is; and the more things it understands, the more that power is diminished" (§ 58). This is because, once things are understood "clearly and distinctly" (according to their internal constitution and relations), it is impossible to produce fictions (to think confusedly and without order about them). So fiction is limited also by the intellect, and not only, as some claim, by fiction itself (§ 59). The self-limitation of fiction by fiction is supposed to follow from the fact that the mind, although free in its fiction, has to operate in a consistent way. But, says Spinoza, if people claiming this accept that we can also understand clearly and distinctly, why would self-consistency not imply a limitation of fiction through the intellect? The idea of freedom that they use leads to absurdities (§§ 59–60).

In our reflection upon some *given* true idea (§§ 33, 38, 39, 43), we discover what constitutes real intellectual thinking: the formation of objective essences, with their intrinsic characteristic of truth (§§ 69–72). It is a form of thinking that contains *in itself* something distinguishing it from imaginative thinking (§ 70), from fiction and falsehood. It is the intellect that is the truly creative activity. One could almost say that it forms a purified "fictional" activity, a kind of "spiritual automaton": "For if we should suppose that the intellect had perceived some new being, which has never existed (as some conceive God's intellect, before he created things—for that perception, of course, could not have arisen from any object), and that from such perception it deduced others legitimately, all those thoughts would be true, and determined by no external object, but would depend only on the power and nature of the intellect" (§ 71). Of course, this conception of God is wrong, and the creativity of the intellect should correspond to "external objects." Yet it is clear that Spinoza is stressing the autonomous, constructive power of the intellect, as opposed to the passivity of the imagination. This constructive activity is observable not only in geometry but also in the formation of hypotheses (§ 57 and note y), thought experiments (§ 57), and philosophy. Constructive thought *about reality* must not only be constructive but also provide a proof of the existence of what is thought (see the next section of the commentary and §§ 99ff.). But this does not contradict the insight into the fundamental character of intellectual thinking stressed so strongly here by Spinoza: its constructivity.

In view of this, it is not surprising that Spinoza gives as an example of intellectual thinking the constructive thought of an architect conceiving in orderly fashion a building that may never exist (§ 69). The other examples come from geometry (which is the basis of architecture). We have seen that geometry is the perfect bridge between logic and philosophy: it is precisely the sort of thinking in which the intellect displays its powers and in which the difference between intellect and imagination becomes most clear. Here we have a "fiction" ("I feign a cause at will," § 72) that is perfectly safe and teaches us the standard of true thinking as well as the power of the intellect. In the appendix to *Ethics* I, Spinoza will say that the standard of truth might forever have escaped mankind if mathematics had not been invented, which "is concerned not with ends, but only with the essences and properties of figures."[4]

For Cartesian readers of the *Treatise,* Spinoza's concept of the intellect as a creative force for constructing objective essences may be acceptable as a way out of the dreaming life of the imagination; but it still leaves room for Cartesian doubt. How do we know that our intellectual constructions express reality? Perhaps even the life of the intellect is only a dream: "can we [not] call true ideas in doubt by supposing that perhaps some deceiving God exists, who misleads us even in the things most certain[?]" (§ 79).

In his answer (§ 79),[5] Spinoza first appeals to an insight with which Descartes also agrees: "we can arrive at [clear and distinct] knowledge of the triangle, even though we may not know certainly whether some supreme deceiver misleads us"; that is, even though we do not know whether we are deceived by a supreme being, we can come to know for certain that the three angles of a triangle equal two right angles. This truth is indubitable as long as we attend to the nature of the triangle. And even though we do not know whether there is a supreme deceiver, we can progress in our thinking and discover the clear and distinct idea of God. Attending carefully to this idea, we must conclude that God cannot be a deceiver, in the same way that, once we have the idea of the triangle, we must conclude its three angles to be equal to two right angles. This conclusion eliminates all doubt. So "[p]rovided we have that knowledge [of God], it will suffice . . . to remove every doubt that we can have concerning clear and distinct ideas." In § 80 Spinoza adds that doubt only arises if things are investigated without order. So if someone would, by any chance, begin by investigating the most basic things, and knew how to proceed properly in the investigation of the connection of things, he would never have but the most certain ideas.

Spinoza's solution to the Cartesian doubt is not simply an answer to a difficult objection. It highlights his conception of the fundamental characteristics of intellectual thinking: its active construction of objective essences, performed in such a way that things are understood as effects of the ultimate and necessary origin of all reality. It is reflexive awareness of these characteristics that will constitute not only the good, but even the perfect, method.

I The Imagination and the Intellect

If we carefully attend to given true ideas, such as the ones of geometry, we cannot but notice the difference between the creative and orderly form of thinking in that domain and the domain of the imagination, which consists of fictitious, false, and dubitable ideas.[6]

We know that fiction, falsehood, and doubt are not expressions of man's freedom (as Descartes and others would have it). This is denied even by careful observation, in which the passivity of these ideas comes to the fore (furthermore, there is no free will). Even without a theoretical explanation (which will only be given in the *Philosophia*), we can see that the mind is "acted upon" in these ideas (§ 86), that it is "under the influence." This is evident from the "fortuitous, and (as it were) disconnected" character of these ideas,[7] which shows the imagination to be a form of thinking that is "random" (§ 84). This is a clear reference to the second kind of perception, that "from random experience," which was rejected for our purpose. The link between imagination and the first kind of perception ("from report or from some conventional sign") is discussed explicitly in §§ 88–89. The fortuitous character of the ideas of the imagination shows itself also in the way they affirm or deny. We know that all ideas inherently contain an affirmation (or negation). The affirmation (or negation) contained in false ideas, their absence in fictitious ideas, and the wavering in dubitable ideas are all the result of fortuitous factors. For example, doubt arises because of the fortuitous arrival of an idea of which the affirmation (or negation) conflicts with the affirmation (or negation) of a first idea (or belief) (§ 78).

In a paragraph clearly referring to the explanation of the imagination in the *Philosophia,* the ideas of the imagination are called *inadequate* ideas (§ 73). Whereas in the *Treatise* Spinoza usually characterizes ideas in a rather Cartesian vocabulary — stressing the importance of attention and calling true, intellectual ideas "clear and distinct" (§§ 63, 91) and ideas of the imagination "confused" — in the *Ethics* he will consistently call the former adequate and the latter inadequate. In this way Spinoza stresses that intellectual ideas are ideas in which the intrinsic force of thinking, of forming objective essences, is at play; these ideas guarantee truth by themselves, whereas the opposite is true of ideas of the imagination.

As we have seen, the domain of the intellect contains ideas that are clear and distinct, true in virtue of their "intrinsic" characteristics, and well ordered. Since our aim is to obtain knowledge of *real* things (and not simply of geometrical constructions), we should investigate what characterizes false, fictitious, and dubitable ideas about *real things* — that is, things considered both under the aspect of their essence and of their existence: "every perception is either of a thing considered as existing, or of an essence alone" (§ 52). This description of fiction, falsehood, and doubt should be contrasted with the description of true intellectual thinking, as found clearly in geometry. In this way, we will come to know *reflexively* the difference between imagination and intellect, and what would constitute intellectual thinking about reality. This reflexive insight will lead (§§ 91ff.; second part of the method) to a formulation of the conditions for forming a true idea (a good definition) of real things, and of the way to *find* such ideas (or definitions, and what follows from them).

What is characteristic of inadequate thought concerning *the existence of things?* What are the remedies against confusing this kind of thought with true ideas? When the existence of a thing is seen to be either necessary or impossible—that is, when we have to do with "eternal truths"—there is no occasion for (and therefore also no danger of) inadequate thought (§§ 53–54, 66–67). Spinoza defines an eternal truth as "one, which, if it is affirmative, will never be able to be negative" (footnote u to § 54). Spinoza's examples are "that God is" or "[t]hat there is no Chimera." "That Adam thinks" or "that Adam does not think" are not eternal truths (they are not a priori but rather a posteriori truths). Again "after I know that I exist, I cannot feign either that I exist or that I do not exist" (§ 54), "[b]ecause the thing makes itself evident, provided it is understood" (§ 54n. s). In other words, there can be no problems with ideas about the existence of things if these ideas come down to immediately evident or necessary truths (comparable to the truths of geometry). A problem will arise with a thing "whose existence, by its very nature, does not imply a contradiction—either for it to exist or for it not to exist—but whose necessity or impossibility of existence depends on causes unknown to us"; Spinoza calls such a thing "possible" (§ 53).[8]

Inadequate thought arises when we conceive existence too "generally" and do not attend to the order of nature (§ 55). The existence of a thing is something as concrete and particular as its essence and is bound up with the concrete order of nature. The use of general words like "existence" in connection with excessive trust in report and random experience (perception of the first and second kinds) leads to all sorts of fiction and falsehood, easily disturbed by new "information" and therefore easily leading to doubt. The remedy to inadequate thought concerning the existence of things is "to take care to compare the existence of the thing with its essence, and at the same time attend to the order of

Nature" (§ 65). To compare the existence of a thing with its essence means, admittedly, that we check the affirmation of existence with what we know about the nature of the thing. (For example, "I [cannot] feign [that] an elephant . . . passes through the eye of a needle," § 54.) At the same time, we should attend to the order of nature—to what we know on the basis of carefully checked experience and to our knowledge of the unbreakable laws of nature. What is stressed in this remedy is not the need of experience on its own but the intelligible link between the way things are and the ultimate determinants (laws of nature, ultimate causes) of their being (see § 75).

What is characteristic of inadequate thought concerning the essence of things? What are the remedies against confusing intellect with imagination in this domain? Here the confusion of our inadequate thought (§§ 62, 68) is characteristic, as well as its disorderly development (§§ 61, 75).

Fiction, falsehood, and doubt do not consist of clear and distinct ideas (§§ 63, 68, 78); on the contrary, they are all confused or compounded of confused ideas (Spinoza gives many examples of this; see § 58n. 2; §§ 68, 74, 78). Confusion means that objects are thought together, without attention to their fine distinctions and even though they cannot belong together (§ 57n. x). In other words, objects are correlated, without one attending carefully to their nature, such that one cannot understand the linkage of subject and predicate (For example, when it is said that men are suddenly changed into beasts in § 62). Here the mind produces only thoughts "which are, as it were, mutilated and maimed" (§ 73); things are known here only in part, without any distinction between the known and the unknown (§ 63).

It is not surprising that such ideas are vulnerable to abstractions and universals and to the deleterious influence of language,[9] which, in turn, leads to even more confusion (§ 76; see also *Ethics* II, P. 40, Sch. 1). Confusion and mutilation are closely related to abstraction and the formation of universals. To think abstractly is to think things incompletely and then to extend the thought inappropriately to other things, disregarding their subtle differences; this process leads to universals (§§ 55, 76).[10] Abstractions and universals are particularly dangerous because they prevent us from thinking things according to their particular nature and character. Language exacerbates this process because words are randomly assigned to combinations of confused ideas (§ 74), producing even more abstractions and universals that are without any ground in things (objective essences), thus being "the cause of many and great errors" (§ 88). According to Spinoza, the very origin of words in the imagination makes language a difficult tool for expressing intellectual ideas (§ 89).[11]

How can one escape this randomness, confusion, and abstraction in thought? In the context of his description of fictitious, false, and dubitable ideas, Spinoza indicates a number of remedies. The chief remedies correspond to characteristics of the true ideas of the intellect: paying careful *attention* such that things are thought *clearly* and *distinctly* according to their essential (simple) elements, and such that we proceed *in good (intelligible) order*. This sort of thinking automatically eliminates falsehood and doubt and makes fiction into something that need not be feared (§ 61).[12]

First, Spinoza highlights the importance of *attention* (§ 61). This focus on attention looks very Cartesian. Some authors claim that we have here a deepening of Cartesian ideas about thinking:[13] thinking, for Spinoza, is not just mirroring (it is not "something mute, like a picture on a tablet [but] a mode of thinking, *viz.* the very [act of] understanding," *Ethics* II, P 43, Sch.). Thinking is a real *activity* of the mind, in which the mind is immediately aware of this very activity of constructing an objective essence in thought. Yet if this is a deepening of Cartesian ideas about thinking, there also is a fundamental difference.[14]

For Descartes, an idea and its affirmation (which is a mode of willing) are something different. For Spinoza, idea, affirmation, and attention are all one. This means that the mind's progress from a state of being unaware of its inborn instruments to a fully attentive awareness of them could not be brought about by attention alone. Somehow, the presence of the inborn instruments must make itself felt in the mind—must, as it were, impose itself on the mind—for the attention in which the difference between imagination and intellect can be noticed to be possible. As Koyré said, this requires something like a leap, like a conversion—in Koyré's expressive formula, "the conversion precedes the meditation."[15] This leap is equally present in the *Ethics,* as is perhaps most clear from an intriguing passage in *Ethics* II, P. 28, Sch.: "so long as it [the mind] is determined externally, from fortuitous encounters with things, to regard this or that [then it has not an adequate, but only a confused knowledge], and not so long as it is determined internally, from the fact that it regards a number of things at once, to understand their agreements, differences, and oppositions." What triggers attention to such "internal determination?" It is the actual operation of constructive thought, the reflection upon which will strengthen this thinking in its purity.

The requirement to think *clearly and distinctly*[16] the internal cohesion of a thing means to check whether the thing is "true" or "false by its very nature" (§ 61)—that is, whether we succeed in really thinking "objective essences," as we do in the constructive thinking of geometry. This requirement sometimes is expressed in a Scholastic way: we have to think the connection between subject and predicate of a proposition, but in such a way that this connection is understood through the middle term (indicating the "cause" of the connection, § 62).[17] Real understanding of a proposition requires penetration of the link between subject and predicate: it is seeing the proposition as the conclusion of a syllogism in which the middle term shows how this linkage is possible, by giving the "cause" of this linkage. At other moments, Spinoza expresses the same requirement in terms of the necessity of thinking things in function of their *simple parts:* "all confusion results from the fact that the mind knows only in part a thing that is a whole, or composed of many things, and does not distinguish the known from the unknown (and besides, attends at once, without making any distinction, to the many things that are contained in each thing)" (§ 63). Confusion prevents us from really thinking an objective essence. The remedy is to "divide a thing that is composed of many things into all its most simple parts, and attend to each of these separately" and to think their composition on the basis of such simple ideas. "For example, once we know the nature of the circle, and also the nature of the square, we cannot then compound these two and make a square circle, or a square soul, and the like" (§ 64).

We do not have to fear fiction or falsehood, provided we accurately think objective essences as we do in mathematics: thinking things on the basis of their essential "parts" (or "causes" or "intrinsic denominations").[18] In order to do this, we have to divide the objects of thought into their simple parts (§§ 63–64, 68) and, after we have penetrated their internal constitution, infer the right consequences from this (§ 61). To think objective essences according to their simple parts does not mean thinking their literal (observable or imaginable) parts. Like the notion of "cause," that of "part" must be understood as referring to our "intrinsic denomination"—to intelligible data that allow us to understand the thing adequately. Thinking things in terms of whole and parts is really no different from thinking things in terms of causes and effects ("true knowledge proceeds from cause to effect," § 85) or in terms of principles and consequences.

All this becomes clearer if, like Spinoza, we concentrate on, attend to, the geometrical example of thinking a sphere. To think the sphere as an objective essence is to penetrate the internal constitution of the object by understanding it as the integration of intelligible parts—for example, a semicircle and rotation (of the semicircle around a center). This perception, says Spinoza, is true "even though we may know that no sphere in nature was ever produced in this way" (§ 72). This reminds us that intellectual thinking is not to be characterized intrinsically as correspondence; it is rather like the "creation" of an object in thought. To really think the sphere is to think it in terms of its intelligible parts, which are themselves wholes with respect to their parts and simple with respect to the whole they are part of. The ideas that express "simple natures" cannot be anything but true (real objective essences, true "by [their] nature," § 61). Fiction or falsehood arise only when they are combined with other ideas that do not intrinsically belong to them—for example, if, without reason, the idea of motion is added to the idea of semicircle. In other words, to really think things, it is not sufficient to heap together ideas accidentally; the parts must be understood in their intrinsic relation to the whole. Otherwise, we think something that is "false by its very nature" (§ 61): "the motion of a semicircle is false when it is in the mind in isolation, but true if it is joined to the concept of sphere, or to the concept of some cause determining such motion" (§ 73).

To understand a thing in function of its parts is, then, to understand the "rationale" (or "cause") that holds the parts together and differentiates the whole from a pure juxtaposition of parts (the thought of which would be "false"): it is the same as understanding *why* a thing is *what* it is; it is comprehension of its "proximate cause" (§ 92), which is the law of integration of the parts. From such an insight into the internal constitution of a thing we can derive all the essential properties of the thing (§ 95). For example, from an insight into the constitution of a triangle in terms of its intelligible parts, one can conclude that a triangle is necessarily constituted of three angles that together form 180 degrees. In this way truth or falsity will be brought to light (§ 61).

The parts that constitute a whole are not all of the same level or category. There are parts (such as semicircle, rotation, angle) that are the constitutive elements of an objective essence. But there also are parts (let us call them "constituting parts") that are the possibility condition of any construction of an objective essence (of a certain kind). For example, geometrical space is the possibility condition of any geometrical figure. These constituting elements are called simple in the sense that they are understood either fully or not at all (§ 63). They are a kind of first cause of all objective essences. Full understanding of an objective essence is not to be had if these first elements are not taken into account. The *order* requires that somehow these elements are understood *first*. This is why Spinoza writes that "we shall not need to fear any . . . deception, if we proceed as far as we can in a manner that is not abstract, and begin as soon as possible from the first elements, i.e., from the source and origin of Nature" (§ 75). Concerning this origin of nature, Spinoza adds that "we need not have any fear of confusing it with abstractions" (§ 76), since it cannot even be imagined. Abstractions or universals extend beyond the particulars that are confused in them. Concerning the origin of nature, no such confusion is possible, because it is totally unlike changeable things given in experience.

In order to understand the constitution of any objective essence of a thing, one needs to understand the proximate cause (or the whole of the constitutive parts) *and* the first elements or constituting part(s). This is one reason why it is necessary to begin "as soon as possible from the first elements, i.e., from the source and origin of Nature" (§ 75). But there is another reason. If, in order to possess the standard of truth, we have to have a true idea to reflect upon; and if, in order to have a true idea, we also have to have the idea of the origin of all things, it seems absolutely important that we arrive at the idea of the first cause as soon as possible. But here we seem to be involved in a paradox, if not a vicious circle: if, to have the standard of truth, we have to have a true idea—for which we need the idea of the first cause—how can we ever arrive methodically at this idea of the first cause through the possession of the standard of truth?

Spinoza has already given his answer and repeats it in the context of our discussion of imaginative ideas. If we have a true idea—and we do have it (for example, in the idea of a triangle or sphere)—we have an inborn instrument for becoming aware of what it is to have a true idea, and thus for searching for the idea of the origin of all things; and the reflexive possession of this idea will help us to penetrate the truth even further and develop it fully (§ 79). To become aware of the truth, it is not necessary to have from the beginning the *whole* truth. It is sufficient to become aware, in the thinking of an objective essence, of what true thinking is all about—of what, in other words, the intellect is. Nevertheless, through the awareness of the standard of true thinking, we must proceed further and acquire "new instruments."

Fortunately, the mind, as the formative process of objective essences, is like a spiritual automaton, that is, "its objective effects proceed in the soul according to the formal nature of its object" (§ 85; compare *Ethics* II, P. 7: "The order and connection of ideas is the same as the order and connection of things"; P. 7, Sch.: "one and the same order, or one and the same connection of causes"). This means that in our intellectual thinking we will try to proceed from causes to effects; we will try to "begin as soon as possible from the first elements [of all thinking], i.e., from the source and origin of Nature" (§ 75). And then, "if someone proceeds rightly, by investigating [first] those things which ought to be investigated first, with no interruption in the connection of things, and knows how to define problems precisely, before striving for knowledge of them, he will never have anything but the most certain ideas— i.e., clear and distinct ideas" (§ 80; see also § 104). In this way it does not happen that "what should be put later we put first, and so the true order of making progress is overturned, and no conclusion is arrived at legitimately" (§ 90). As we see in the final paragraphs of the *Treatise,* "as soon as possible" will be very soon, because to understand the nature of true thinking of something or to understand the intellect requires us to think "the source and origin of Nature" itself. Next, it is important to know "how to define problems" so as to continue the intellectual train of thought. It is not clear what Spinoza had in mind here. Rousset remarks that this is an obvious reference to the title of the fifth part of Descartes's *Discours de la méthode:*[19] Descartes claims here that precisely determining the order of questions has the result that we continue to have very certain ideas that escape doubt. Spinoza will have more to say about the right order in the rest of his methodology, which we will discuss in chapter 8.

As it turns out, the first characteristic of intellectual thinking—clearness and distinctness—is closely related to the second, which is proceeding in the right order. To understand clearly and distinctly is to think things according to their intrinsic constitution. But to understand things in terms of their constitutive elements ultimately requires also understanding their constituting parts or fundamental possibility conditions as soon as possible. In other words, our thinking should proceed in an orderly way such that our ideas concerning the essence and the existence of things objectively represent the fundamental order of nature itself.

In the previous paragraphs, we have encountered many elements that will play an important role in the rest of the method:

1. We must start from a given, true idea, in which we actively think an objective essence on the basis of its constitutive parts or "intrinsic denominations."
2. This will give us an idea of this idea, or reflexive understanding of the intellect as power of thinking, allowing us to actively separate the intellect from the imagination: "From [all] this we have acquired as much knowledge of our intellect *as was possible in the beginning,* and such a standard of the true idea that now we do not fear confusing true ideas with false or fictitious [or dubitable] ones" (§ 86; emphasis added).
3. *As soon as possible* we must link this reflexive knowledge of the intellect with the ideas concerning the origin of nature.
4. From there, knowing how to proceed in the right order (of causes and effects), we must come to know other things as far as this is necessary in order to obtain our final aim.

I Logic Is Not the Same as Theory

Spinoza explicitly states that in the logic he is not giving an explanation of the imagination "by its proximate cause"; this will be given in the *Philosophia* (§ 51). Explaining things by their proximate cause means giving an insight into the nature or essence of the thing, so that we can understand all its properties. To do this with respect to the imagination, which itself is a property of the human mind, would require developing a theory of the mind as the actually existing idea of a really existing human body—the sort of theory we find in *Ethics* II (P. 11–16). The imagination refers not to the mind as an eternal idea of the essence of the body but to the mind only insofar as it is an idea of an actually existing body in which there are other ideas or which has other ideas expressing and corresponding to sense-impressions brought about by the encounter of an actually existing body with other surrounding bodies (see the first section of chapter 10). These ideas that the mind has are *imaginationes,* which are the starting point for a whole range of fictitious, false, and dubious ideas about all sorts of things. These *imaginationes* and the ideas derived from them are, strictly speaking, not produced in the mind by the body: as we will see later, there is no causal relation possible between modifications of *different* attributes of substance. But since there must be an idea of every body in the attribute of thought, every happening to this body must also automatically be expressed in the mind, being the idea of that body. The mind, being the idea of an actually existing body, cannot have ideas except as expressions in the mind of changes to the body: the actual affections of the body are expressed in the mind as actual sense-experiences of the mind proliferating into all sorts of ideas (as explained in *Ethics* II, P. 17ff.). The *actual having* of adequate ideas can only be triggered by the mind's *having* actual experiences (see the first section of chapter 10). In the *Treatise,* Spinoza gives a few clues to a real theory of the imagination: he says that fictitious, false, and dubitable ideas "have their origin in the imagination, i.e., in certain sensations that are fortuitous, and (as it were) disconnected;[20] since they do not arise from the very power of the mind, but from external causes, as the body (whether waking or dreaming) receives various motions" (§ 84). In § 83 he relates memory to "a sensation of impressions on the brain" and adds that he will discuss the problem of a possible corruption of ideas in his *Philosophia.*[21] But he realizes that he cannot at this time make such assertions. This is why he adds: "But if you wish, take imagination any way you like here, provided it is something different from the intellect, and in which the soul has the nature of something acted on. . . . So let no one be surprised that here, where I have not yet proved that there is a body, and other necessary things, I speak of the imagination, the body and its constitution" (§ 84).

Concerning both the intellect and the imagination there are some announcements of a theoretical, ontological treatment that correspond with ideas developed in the *Ethics.* In § 73 Spinoza says that if it belongs to the nature of intellection to form true or adequate thoughts, this must be explained "from the fact that we are a part of a thinking being, of which some thoughts wholly constitute our mind"; correspondingly, "inadequate ideas arise in us only from the fact that we are a part of a thinking being, of which . . . others [other thoughts] do so only in part [i.e., constitute our mind]." In § 86 the passivity of the imagination is related to the fact that "in imagination the soul only has the nature of something acted upon [habere rationem patentis]." In the *Ethics,* Spinoza explains our having adequate and inadequate ideas precisely as a function of our mind being "a part of the infinite intellect of God" (*Ethics* II, P. 11, Cor.).

As we will discuss in chapter 9, section 3, the infinite intellect of God is the infinite mode of the attribute thought (*Cogitatio*) of the divine substance. It is the infinite effect of God's power as thought, an effect in which all things—all effects of God's power in all its forms or attributes—are expressed as objective essences. The infinite intellect is the way God (as thought) *effectively* thinks everything there is. It is the unique, infinite whole of all ideas (or objective essences) that are its parts. The human mind is said to think inadequately, or only partially, "when we say that God has this or that idea, not only insofar as he constitutes the nature of the human Mind (as part of the infinite intellect), but insofar as he also has the idea of another thing (another part) together with the human Mind" (*Ethics* II, P. 11, Cor.). The mind is said to perceive adequately when we say that God has this or that idea "insofar as he has ideas that are in the human Mind" (*Ethics* II, P. 38, Dem.), or when we say "that (by E P 11 C) in the Divine intellect there is an idea of which God is the cause, not insofar as he is infinite, nor insofar as he is affected with the ideas of a great many singular things, but insofar as he constitutes only the essence of the human Mind" (*Ethics* II, P. 40, Dem.). The difference between adequacy and inadequacy of ideas in the mind is explained as the difference between the divine intellect understanding something fully by simply containing the human mind as its part and the divine intellect not fully understanding something through the ideas that the human mind has and needing other parts, other ideas of something, to comprehend the object fully. All human thinking is explained here as an *effect* of the ontological *cause* (God under his attribute of thought), and as part of the infinite mode of thought, the divine intellect.

At this stage in the *Treatise,* we do not need a full explanation of the imagination in order to understand what we have to understand: the difference between intellectual and nonintellectual ideas. We do not come to understand what intellectual ideas are on the basis of an explanation of the imagination (let alone on the basis of the imagination itself). On the contrary, it is through our awareness of intellectual ideas and their standard that we separate imagination and intellection. Ideas that do not correspond to the standard of truth cannot have their origin in the pure intellect; and thus if they belong to the mind, they must find their origin in causes (whatever they are) external to the mind's pure intellectual power.

Although the *Ethics* gives us an ontological explanation of the mind as imagination and as intellection, and of the difference between the two, the problem of the transition from "a life of dreaming" to a life of intellection is not really explored; this is done in the *Treatise.* On the other hand, in the *Treatise* the problem of weakness of the mind is not attacked. This is the problem of the emotional hindrances to intellectual progress. To tackle this problem, the development of a theory of the emotions and their relation to thinking is necessary. This theory is provided in *Ethics* III and applied in *Ethics* IV–V: in *Ethics* IV the weakness of *ratio*[22] is analyzed; in *Ethics* V Spinoza discusses the power of the intellect vis-à-vis the emotions. Since the treatment of this specific problem requires the development of a theory of motivation (*conatus*) and of the emotions, which itself requires the elaboration of a theory of man as part of nature, this problem is not approached here (except in a very provisional way in the introduction of the *Treatise*). The urgent problem of the logic is precisely to arrive fully at the stage of intellectual thinking. Of course, the "ethical" problematic is part of the program of the sciences that must be developed after the logic and that will help us reach our ultimate end (§§ 14–16). In a sense, the emendation of the intellect is found even more in the *Ethics* than in the *Treatise*:[23] that is, as the fight against emotional hindrances to the intellectual life.

| N O T E S

1. Garrett 1986, 76 (and n. 13).
2. Garrett 1986, 70.
3. See especially De Deugd 1966.
4. Spinoza 1985, 441.
5. There are similar ideas in *PPC* (G 1:147–48).
6. For an elaborate discussion of these different sorts of ideas belonging to the imagination, see Joachim 1940; and Parkinson 1954 (which discusses Joachim's views extensively).
7. They are not *really* disconnected, of course: the order of inadequate ideas is rigorously determined (*E* II, P. 36).
8. See also *E* I, P. 33, Sch.
9. Donagan 1988, 49–53.
10. See also *E* II, P. 40, Sch. 1.
11. Abstraction can also be part of intellectual thinking when this uses axioms that, in principle, extend to infinitely many things (§§ 76, 93). Spinoza does not reject them but warns us not to confuse them with the thought of real particulars or to use them in total abstraction from the thought concerning these particulars.
12. One seeks to eliminate the inadequate character of the idea, not necessarily the idea itself; see *TEI* § 86 and *E* II, P. 35, Sch. (See also the second section of chapter 10.)
13. Bartuschat's introduction to Spinoza 1993, xi.
14. Van Peursen, 519–22.
15. Spinoza 1990, xxi, xx.
16. Rousset repeats here the Cartesian definition of clearness and distinctness (from the *Principes* 1:45): "I call clear [the idea] that is present and manifest to an attentive mind" and "distinct that which is so precise and different from all the others that it comprehends in itself

only what manifestly appears to everybody considering it in the proper way" (Spinoza 1992, 302).

17. Curley translates "medium" as "means." Spinoza refers, however, to the middle term (of a syllogism). See Rousset's comment in Spinoza 1992, 302ff.

18. In the *Ethics,* all things are seen as modifications of some attribute of substance, which has to be understood first and which is the ultimate or first cause of their essences as well as of their existence (*E* I, P. 25). The notion of "intrinsic denomination" is used in *TEI* § 69 and *E* II, Def. 4.

19. Spinoza 1992, 350.

20. See note 7 above.

21. Spinoza refers here to the Neoplatonic problem of intellectual memory; see Rousset's comment in Spinoza 1992, 356.

22. See chapter 11, section 3 (and De Dijn 1992a).

23. See Bartuschat's introduction to Spinoza 1993, xxv.

Second Part of the Method
(§§ 91–98): The Rules of Definition

Text

[91]^e   Porro, ut tandem ad Secundam Partem hujus Methodi perveniamus, proponam primo nostrum scopum in hac Methodo, ac deinde media, ut eum attingamus. Scopus itaque est claras, & distinctas habere ideas, tales videlicet, quae ex pura mente, & non ex fortuitis motibus corporis factae sint. Deinde, omnes ideae ad unam ut redigantur, conabimur eas tali modo concatenare, & ordinare, ut mens nostra, quoad ejus fieri potest, referat objective formalitatem naturae, quoad totam, & quoad ejus partes.

[92]   Quoad primum, ut jam tradidimus, requiritur ad nostrum ultimum finem, ut res concipiatur vel per solam suam essentiam, vel per proximam suam causam. Scilicet si res sit in se, sive, ut vulgo dicitur, causa sui, tum per solam suam essentiam debebit intelligi; si vero res non sit in se, sed requirat causam, ut existat, tum per proximam suam causam debet intelligi: Nam revera^f cognitio effectus nihil aliud est, quam perfectiorem causae cognitionem acquirere.

---

e.   Praecipua hujus partis Regula est, ut ex prima parte sequitur, recensere omnes ideas, quas ex puro intellectu in nobis invenimus, ut eae ab iis, quas imaginamur, distinguantur; quod ex proprietatibus uniuscujusque, nempe imaginationis et intellectionis, erit eliciendum.

f.   Nota, quod hinc appareat nihil nos de Natura posse [wettelijk, of behorelijk] intelligere, quin simul cognitionem primae causae, sive Dei ampliorem reddamus.

[91]ᵉ To arrive finally at the second part of this Method, I shall set forth first our aim in this Method, and then the means to attain it. The aim, then, is to have clear and distinct ideas, i.e., such as have been made from the pure mind, and not from fortuitous motions of the body. And then, so that all ideas may be led back to one, we shall strive to connect and order them so that our mind, as far as possible, reproduces objectively the formal character of nature, both as to the whole and as to the parts.

[92] As for the first, our ultimate end requires (as we have already said) that the thing be conceived either through its essence alone or through its proximate cause. If the thing is in itself, or, as is commonly said, is the cause of itself, then it must be understood through its essence alone; but if it is not in itself, but requires a cause to exist, then it must be understood through its proximate cause. For really, knowledgeᶠ of the effect is nothing but acquiring a more perfect knowledge of its cause.

---

e. The principal Rule of this part (as follows from the first part) is to review all the ideas we discover in us from the pure intellect, so that they are distinguished from those we imagine. This will have to be elicited from the properties of each, i.e., of the imagination and the intellection.

f. Note that it is evident from this that we cannot [legitimately or properly] understand anything of Nature without at the same time rendering our knowledge of the first cause, *or* God, more ample.

[93]   Unde nunquam nobis licebit, quamdiu de Inquisitione rerum agimus, ex abstractis aliquid concludere, & magnopere cavebimus, ne misceamus ea, quae tantum sunt in
intellectu, cum iis, quae sunt in re. Sed optima conclusio erit
depromenda ab essentia aliqua particulari affirmativa, sive a
vera & legitima definitione. Nam ab axiomatibus solis universa-
libus non potest intellectus ad singularia descendere, quandoquidem axiomata ad infinita se extendunt, nec intellectum
magis ad unum, quam ad aliud singulare contemplandum,
determinant.

[94]   Quare recta inveniendi via est ex data aliqua definitione cogitationes formare: quod eo felicius & facilius procedet,
quo rem aliquam melius definiverimus. Quare cardo totius
hujus secundae Methodi partis in hoc solo versatur, nempe in
conditionibus bonae definitionis cognoscendis, & deinde in modo
eas inveniendi. Primo itaque de conditionibus definitionis agam.

[95]   Definitio ut dicatur perfecta, debebit intimam essentiam rei explicare, & cavere, ne ejus loco propria quaedam
usurpemus; ad quod explicandum, ut alia exempla omittam, ne
videar aliorum errores velle detegere, adferam tantum exem-
plum alicujus rei abstractae, quae perinde est, quomodocunque
definiatur, circuli scilicet: quod si definiatur, esse figuram
aliquam, cujus lineae, a centro ad circumferentiam ductae, sunt
aequales, nemo non videt talem definitionem minime explicare
essentiam circuli; sed tantum ejus aliquam proprietatem. Et
quamvis, ut dixi, circa figuras, & caetera entia rationis hoc
parum referat, multum tamen refert circa entia Physica, &
realia: nimirum, quia proprietates rerum non intelliguntur,
quamdiu earum essentiae ignorantur; si autem has praetermit-
timus, necessario concatenationem intellectus, quae Naturae
concatenationem referre debet, pervertemus, & a nostro scopo
prorsus aberrabimus.

[96]   Ut itaque hoc vitio liberemur, erunt haec observanda
in Definitione.

I.   Si res sit creata, definitio debebit, uti diximus, compre-
    hendere causam proximam. Ex. gr. circulus secundum
    hanc legem sic esset definiendus: eum esse figuram,
    quae describitur a linea quacunque, cujus alia extremi-
    tas est fixa, alia mobilis, quae definitio clare compre-
    hendit causam proximam.

[93]   Therefore, so long as we are dealing with the Investigation of things, we must never infer anything from abstractions, and we shall take very great care not to mix up the things that are only in the intellect with those that are real. But the best conclusion will have to be drawn from some particular affirmative essence, or, from a true and legitimate definition. For from universal axioms alone the intellect cannot descend to singulars, since axioms extend to infinity, and do not determine the intellect to the contemplation of one singular thing rather than another.

[94]   So the right way of discovery is to form thoughts from some given definition. This will proceed the more successfully and easily, the better we have defined a thing. So the chief point of this second part of the Method is concerned solely with this: knowing the conditions of a good definition, and then, the way of finding good definitions. First, therefore, I shall deal with the conditions of definition.

[95]   To be called perfect, a definition will have to explain the inmost essence of the thing, and to take care not to use certain *propria* in its place. So as not to seem bent on uncovering the errors of others, I shall use only the example of an abstract thing to explain this. For it is the same however it is defined. If a circle, for example, is defined as a figure in which the lines drawn from the center to the circumference are equal, no one fails to see that such a definition does not at all explain the essence of the circle, but only a property of it. And though, as I have said, this does not matter much concerning figures and other beings of reason, it matters a great deal concerning Physical and real beings, because the properties of things are not understood so long as their essences are not known. If we neglect them, we shall necessarily overturn the connection of the intellect, which ought to reproduce the connection of Nature, and we shall completely miss our goal.

[96]   These are the requirements which must be satisfied in Definition, if we are to be free of this fault:

1. If the thing is created, the definition, as we have said, will have to include the proximate cause. E.g., according to this law, a circle would have to be defined as follows: it is the figure that is described by any line of which one end is fixed and the other movable. This definition clearly includes the proximate cause.

II. Talis requiritur conceptus rei, sive definitio, ut omnes proprietates rei, dum sola, non autem cum aliis conjuncta, spectatur, ex ea concludi possint, uti in hac definitione circuli videre est. Nam ex ea clare concluditur omnes lineas a centro ad circumferentiam ductas aequales esse; quodque hoc sit necessarium requisitum definitionis, adeo per se est attendenti manifestum, ut non videatur operae pretium in ipsius demonstratione morari, nec etiam ostendere ex hoc secundo requisito omnem definitionem debere esse affirmativam. Loquor de affirmatione intellectiva, parum curando verbalem, quae propter verborum penuriam poterit fortasse aliquando negative exprimi, quamvis affirmative intelligatur.

[97]   Definitionis vero rei increatae haec sunt requisita.

I. Ut omnem causam secludat, hoc est, objectum nullo alio praeter suum esse egeat ad sui explicationem.

II. Ut data ejus rei definitione nullus maneat locus Quaestioni, An sit?

III. Ut nulla, quoad mentem, habeat substantiva, quae possint adjectivari, hoc est, ne per aliqua abstracta explicetur.

IV. Et ultimo (quamvis hoc notare non sit valde necessarium) requiritur, ut ab ejus definitione omnes ejus proprietates concludantur. Quae etiam omnia attendenti accurate fiunt manifesta.

[98]   Dixi etiam, quod optima conclusio erit depromenda ab essentia aliqua particulari affirmativa: Quo enim specialior est idea, eo distinctior, ac proinde clarior est. Unde cognitio particularium quam maxime nobis quaerenda est.

2. We require a concept, *or* definition, of the thing such that when it is considered alone, without any others conjoined, all the thing's properties can be deduced from it (as may be seen in this definition of the circle). For from it we clearly infer that all the lines drawn from the center to the circumference are equal.

That this is a necessary requirement of a definition is so plain through itself to the attentive that it does not seem worth taking time to demonstrate it, nor to show also, from this second requirement, that every definition must be affirmative.

I mean intellectual affirmation—it matters little whether the definition is verbally affirmative; because of the poverty of language it will sometimes, perhaps, [only] be able to be expressed negatively, although it is understood affirmatively.

[97]   These are the requirements for the definition of an uncreated thing:

1. That it should exclude every cause, i.e., that the object should require nothing else except its own being for its explanation.
2. That, given the definition of this thing, there should remain no room for the Question—does it exist?
3. That (as far as the mind is concerned) it should have no substantives that could be changed into adjectives, i.e., that it should not be explained through any abstractions.
4. Finally (though it is not very necessary to note this) it is required that all its properties be inferred from its definition.

All these things are evident to those who attend to them accurately.

[98]   I have also said that the best conclusion will have to be drawn from a particular affirmative essence. For the more particular an idea is, the more distinct, and therefore the clearer it is. So we ought to seek knowledge of particulars as much as possible.

I Commentary

In the previous part of the method, we distinguished and separated the intellect from the imagination, or the true idea from the fictitious, false, and dubitable idea. This distinction remains the principal rule of the second part (§ 91n. c), which shows the unity of these parts, the second part being a kind of reformulation of the results of the first. As we learned in § 49, the second part of the method must provide us with rules for coming to know new things according to the standard of truth we have discovered. In this part, Spinoza will give us the conditions of a good definition. These are nothing but an explication of the standard of truth and must help us in our search for new true ideas. In fact, these rules echo the remedies against the imagination we discovered in the first part of the method.

The first paragraph of this part (§ 91) reminds us of the aim (*scopus*) of the method as well as of the means to attain it. The aim is to have clear and distinct (that is, purely intellectual) ideas. The means to attain this aim is to order our ideas in such a way "that our mind, as far as possible, reproduces objectively the formal [i.e., real] character of nature, both as to the whole and as to the parts." Indeed, to really have clear and distinct ideas, involving a full awareness of them, requires knowledge of the source and origin of all things.

In §§ 92–93, Spinoza reformulates the information concerning the intellect in terms of the perception of the fourth kind, which we agreed upon as being the best means of attaining our final end (*finis*). In §§ 94–97, the reflexive insight into true perception, that of the fourth kind, is translated into observations concerning what is a good definition, again taking into account our reflexive knowledge of the intellect already gained.

I Knowledge of Real Things (§§ 92–93)

As we have seen, our ultimate end (*finis*) requires that we make use of the fourth kind of perception, which is conceiving a thing "either through its essence alone or through its proximate cause" (see also §§ 19, 29). "If a thing is in itself, *or*, as is commonly said, is the cause of itself, then it must be understood through its essence alone; but if it is not in itself, but requires a cause to exist, then it must be understood through its proximate cause. For really, knowledge of the effect is nothing but acquiring a more perfect knowledge of its cause" (§ 92).

Since existence and essence are different aspects of the same thing, we can expect that the mode of existence of a thing somehow expresses its essence. Therefore, the way a thing is to be understood (as to its essence, in a definition) is related to its mode of existence. If a thing is in itself or the cause of itself (*causa sui*), it must exclude all other things for its explanation; that is, it must be understood through its essence alone. Such an understanding leaves no room for the question, Does it exist? (§ 97). Its existence is affirmed as an "eternal truth" (§ 54), characterized by necessity: a thing is "necessary whose nature implies that it would be contradictory for it not to exist" (§ 53).

If a thing is not in itself or a cause of itself, or if a thing is "created" (§ 96), its existence has no necessary connection with its essence; its existence is not affirmed as an eternal truth (§ 100) because the existence of such a thing is neither necessary nor impossible (§ 53). The necessity or impossibility of the existence of such a thing depends on external causes; if we do not know whether these causes bring or do not bring about its existence, we call such a thing possible (§ 53; see also *Ethics* I, P. 33, Sch. 1).

To really know a thing that is in itself, it is sufficient to understand it through its essence alone (from which its existence follows, affirmed in an eternal truth). But how can we really know a thing that is not in itself, that is not a cause of itself? Of course, as an effect it must be understood through its proximate cause. This proximate cause cannot be the array of concrete causes of its existence, because they themselves require other concrete causes for their existence, and so on indefinitely. To try to explain something in this way would lead to a vicious regress. The proximate cause that can explain a created thing is the uncreated cause, which is the *first* cause, as is clear from § 92n. f: "Note that it is evident from this that we cannot understand anything of Nature without at the same time rendering our knowledge of the first cause *or* God, more ample." This is the only possibility, because such a cause can itself be understood "through its essence alone."

On the other hand, since the first, uncreated cause is, as proximate cause, the same for all created things, the differences among created things (as to their essence) cannot be obtained by reference to the first cause alone. These differences, expressed in their different definitions, will require a specification of the *peculiar* effects or modifications of the first cause that they constitute.[1] A full understanding of a created thing as to its essence therefore requires both a reference to its first cause and an understanding of why it is the peculiar effect (or modification) it is. Such an understanding of a finite thing is, in a sense, a "more ample" understanding of the first cause (§ 92n. f): it gives an insight into the ultimate cause as expressing itself concretely in a particular thing (see also *Ethics* V, P. 24).

In the terms used in our explanation of §§ 63, 75, the fourth kind of perception of created things requires an understanding both of the constituting part (the first cause) and of the constitutive parts of the thing. In other words, the understanding of a created thing "through its proximate cause" is the *complete* understanding of the sort of effect (or modification) of its first cause that the thing is (this will be discussed in more detail in chapter 8).

To understand a thing "through its proximate cause"— through the first cause as modified in a certain way—guarantees that we deal with real things, that we form real objective essences corresponding to reality. In this way we escape becoming involved only with abstractions, with things that "are only in the intellect" and not in reality (§ 93). This is a repetition of the critique of knowledge (or perception) of the third kind, which we encountered before (§§ 19, 21, 28). Spinoza warns us here not only against the abstractions and universals of the imagination but also against certain constructions of the intellect that "do not determine the intellect to the contemplation of one singular thing rather than another": universal axioms that "extend to infinity" should not be the basis of our thinking (§ 93). He does not reject axioms that "extend to infinity" (such as *Ethics* I, Ax. 1: that things are either in themselves or in something else). But unless axioms are combined with insight into the particular essences of real things—with "a true and legitimate definition" (§ 93)—we will not obtain the sort of knowledge required for our aim.[2]

This is not a rejection of earlier statements concerning the spontaneous and self-sufficient power of the intellect. On the contrary, it is an attempt to show that the constructive power present in the formation of objective essences should not be suspected of missing the target of reality, *provided* we can think things as necessary modifications of something we cannot understand except as existing necessarily.

Does this mean we can now derive the concrete existence of a thing simply from our understanding of it as being God insofar as modified (*Deus quatenus modificatus*), or from its definition through the proximate cause? Certainly not. Since a definition "expresses nothing other than the nature of the things defined . . .

there must be, for each existing thing, a certain cause on account of which it exists." Furthermore, "no definition involves or expresses any number of individuals"; so "the cause why [say] twenty men exist, and consequently, why each of them exists, must necessarily be outside each of them [outside their nature]" (*Ethics* I, P. 8, Sch. 2). To eliminate all fear of fiction, falsehood, and doubt concerning the existence of finite things, we have "to take care to relate[3] the existence to the essence, and at the same time to attend to the order of Nature" (§ 65). In other words, we have to rely on experience (of the "common order of Nature," as he sometimes says in the *Ethics*) and understand the existence of things as the existence of a real determination of nature, which, as such, *had* to come into existence at some point in the flux of things. In other words, in our search for knowledge of real things, we have to use experience (see §§ 102–3); but we also have to attend to the existence of things as necessarily belonging to their essence—not, of course, in view of this essence alone, but in view of the fact that this essence expresses divine nature and power (about this notion of existence, see also *Ethics* II, P. 45, Sch.; V, P. 39, Sch.).

I Theory of Definition (§§ 94–97)

The analysis of clear and distinct understanding, which turns out to be the same as the fourth kind of perception, continues in §§ 94–97 and is developed into a theory of the conditions of definition. Such a theory does not stand on its own but is inevitably related to the general methodological problem of the progress of knowledge, of the discovery of new knowledge.[4] As § 49 announced, the second part of the method must "teach rules so that we may perceive things unknown according to such a standard [of truth]." In other words, reflexive logic must teach us the right way (or method) of progressing in the knowledge of things, of looking for new clear and distinct ideas in the order required (*debito ordine*) (§ 36). Here (§ 94) it is said that the right way to discover (*recta inveniendi via*) is "to form thoughts from some given definition"; therefore, the core of the second part of the method is to know "the conditions of a good definition" before we learn "the way of finding good definitions."

Logic, we must remember, is not reducible to reasoning or intellection itself (§ 37); it is what we get in a reflection on intellection and reasoning. What is thus obtained is the right way or method to help us to discover the truth about things unknown. What is this method of discovery?

In methodological treatises of early modernity, a distinction often is made between the method of exposition of truths and the method of discovery of truths. A deductive (demonstrative) exposition of truths would, according to Descartes, be nothing more than an *ordering* of truths already discovered, adding no real insight to what has been discovered.[5] According to Hobbes, the true method of discovery is the method of demonstration (from principles) *itself*.[6] When Spinoza says that the right way of discovery is "to form thoughts from some given definition" (§ 94), he seems to take the side of Hobbes—that is, of an amended Euclidean conception of method.[7]

If the right method of discovery is to demonstratively deduce many truths from a definition, built up according to the conditions governing adequate, or true, ideas, the question still remains how to methodically discover new definitions. It is hardly likely that this could be the work of pure demonstration from one, already given definition, unless, of course, all new definitions of new things are somehow related to the definition of one fundamental thing (God or substance, of which everything else is a mode). This seems to be the solution of the *Ethica*. Even so, there is no obvious deductive passage from the definition of God and its subsequent demonstrations to the demonstrations concerning one or another mode. This problem—which is, again, the problem of a kind of leap, but now within adequate thinking itself—will crop up again in the first section of chapter 8.

The geometrical method or way of demonstration, which is the method of discovery, should not be confused with a purely formal deduction or with an axiomatic method. A purely formal method (in the contemporary sense) disregards content. The geometrical method is part of a general *reflexive* method, presupposing content or the presence of objective essences and their interrelations. It is a method of "causal" deduction in which it is indicated how, from definition or understanding "through the proximate cause," real properties can be deduced, and how we must proceed from one real essence to another, according to the intrinsic, causal relations between them.

Neither can the deduction be purely axiomatic: the essence of the geometrical order is *not* deducing propositions in a truth-preserving way from explicitly defined terms and principles considered or accepted provisionally as self-evident.[8] Rather it is the forming of *real* causal definitions and the linking of objective essences. Of course, to do this we also need axioms and demonstrations of propositions. But what is going on, thanks to all these demonstrations from axioms, is not simply a truth-preserving derivation of propositions but a "going from cause to effect." There is no opposition between axiomatic method and geometrical method, provided one starts from real definitions describing the proximate cause of something.[9]

The theory of definition is the cornerstone of the method of discovery. In this theory, Spinoza first investigates "the conditions of a good definition" (§ 94). He begins with two warnings (§ 95). First, "a [perfect] definition will have to explain the inmost essence of the thing, and [we should] take care not to use certain *propria* in its place." Second, definitions must be of "[p]hysical and real beings," and not of abstractions or universals (a requirement expressed in § 93).

From letter 9 (to de Vries) we know that Spinoza accepts two kinds of definitions: definitions of "physical" things and definitions of purely conceived things, as in architecture or geometry. We have stressed the peculiar character of geometrical thought: although the geometrical figures are "abstract," they are not the objects of imagination but of the intellect, and what is important in definitions of such objects is their conceivability or constructibility. (In the preface of *Ethics* IV, Spinoza distinguishes between *entia imaginationis,* beings of imagination, which are confused, and *entia rationis,* beings of reason. The latter should not be confused with real things, but they can be fruitful and necessary in intellectual thinking, not only in geometry, but also for example in *ethical* thought.) Since the method aims at helping us in our investigations of real things (as far as necessary for our ultimate aim, § 93), we will have to look for definitions of "physical and real beings," and not of abstractions, even though they are perfectly conceivable (§ 94). In the words of letter 9, we look for the conditions of *real* definitions—that is, descriptions of the essence of things that correspond to reality.

Real definitions are divided into two categories (§ 96): definitions of a created thing and definitions of an uncreated thing. Both must explain the inmost essence and not confuse essence and property (§ 95). Spinoza carefully lists the conditions for each sort of real definition. The definition of a created thing should exhibit "the proximate cause" (§ 96) that gives insight into the essence of the thing and should not be confused with the understanding of a property. Only such a definition "explain[s] the inmost essence of the thing" (§ 95). From it can be deduced the *propria,* or essential properties, of the thing, as effects of a cause, as consequences of principles. These properties "are not understood [really] so long as their [the things'] essences are not known." "If a circle, for example, is defined as a figure in which the lines drawn from the center to the circumference are equal, no one fails to see that such a definition does not at all explain the essence of the circle, but only a property of it" (§ 95). On the contrary, "a circle would have to be defined as . . . the figure that is described by any line of which one end is fixed and the other movable" (§ 96). The definition of the sphere given earlier (§ 72) also fulfills this requirement of being a definition through the proximate cause.

It is remarkable that Hobbes, in his *Examinatio et Emendatio Mathematicae Hodiernae* (1660),[10] gives exactly the same requirements for (and examples of) a causal definition of the circle, criticizing Euclid's definition, which is only through a property.[11] Hobbes calls this amended definition a *genetic* definition, which gives us an insight into the *generatio,* the production of the essence as a construction on the basis of essential parts (for example, for the circle it is a line and its rotation around one end, which is fixed; for the sphere it is semicircle and rotation). A definition, indicating the proximate cause or way of construction or genesis of a thing, is "such that when it [the thing] is considered alone, without any others conjoined, all the thing's properties can be deduced from it" (§ 96). Answering Tschirnhaus's doubt that from the definition of a thing, considered on its own, only one property can be deduced, Spinoza says that this is perhaps true for very simple things or things that exist only in the intellect (such as figures), but not for real things. As an example, he gives the deduction of many properties from the definition of God in the *Ethics* (letter 83). Euclid's definition, giving only a *proprium* (or essential property), can be deduced from the genetic definition.

A good definition is, of course, affirmative as far as the intellect (and not necessarily language) is concerned: it affirms a certain constitution as essential for the thing defined. In geometry the affirmation of constructibility (on the basis of essential parts) is all we need—the existence of geometrical figures is their constructibility or intelligibility.[12] In philosophy, which deals with real, "physical" things—things belonging to nature—constructibility does not imply actual existence, unless this is a necessary property appertaining to the essence defined (which is only true for God: see § 97); therefore, a proof of existence still is required for created things.

We now have the three requirements (or rules) for a good definition of a created thing: the definition includes the proximate cause; from it all properties can be deduced; it is affirmative.

If the thing defined is "an uncreated thing," the requirements or conditions are that (§ 97)

1. the definition "should exclude every cause, i.e., that the object should require nothing else except its own being for its explanation" (§97): "it must be understood through its essence alone" (§ 92). In letter 60, to Tschirnhaus, Spinoza seems to modify this requirement, saying that the definition of God in *Ethics* I is clearly a definition "through the [proximate] cause"—in this case, not an external but an internal cause. From this definition all the properties can be perfectly deduced (see fourth requirement). As Curley remarks, it is Martial Gueroult who first drew attention to this change.[13] The change does not really contradict the ideas of the *Treatise:* "It would still be true that God requires nothing else except his own being (i.e., the elements of his being, the attributes) for his explanation. But it would not be correct to say that a definition in terms of those elements excludes every cause. Whereas the notion of being *causa sui* is here treated as if equivalent to being without a cause, later it will be treated more positively."[14] The change indicates the parallel between God's existence and God's essence as highlighted in letter 60: God's being *causa sui* with respect to his existence is paralleled by his being intelligible on the level of his essence by a positive "cause or reason" (*causa sive ratio*)[15] explaining why he is what he is. This proximate cause explaining God's essence is that he is the integration of all attributes or infinities "in [their] own kind" (*Ethics* I, Def. 6, Expl., and passim) (see the first section of chapter 9). The advantage of this change is that *all* knowledge or understanding of things (as to their essence) can now be described as "through the [proximate] cause." In the case of God, this proximate cause is purely internal. In the case of finite, created things, the proximate cause is not really external (see I, P. 18: "God is the immanent, not the transient, cause of all things";[16] and I, P. 28, Sch.: "God cannot properly be called the remote cause of singular things") but immanent, *Deus quatenus modificatus.*

2. "given the definition of this thing, there should remain no room for the Question—does it exist?" Indeed, God is

a being "whose nature implies that it would be contradictory for it not to exist," he is a necessary being as to
his existence (§ 53; see also § 76).

3. "(as far as the mind is concerned) it should have no substantives that could be changed into adjectives, i.e., that
it should not be explained through any abstractions".
This requirement is an application of the general warn-
ing of § 93 with respect to the definition of an uncaused
thing. Substantives that can be changed into adjectives
are terms such as "goodness" and "infinity"; they are
easily changed into abstractions that "extend to infinity,
and do not determine the intellect to the contemplation
of one singular thing rather than another" (§ 93). Substantives that cannot be changed into adjectives refer to
parts of the divine nature, such as thought and extension, that Spinoza in his *Ethics* calls attributes (or essential elements of substance) and that are different
from properties (*propria*), however necessarily these
two may belong to God's being. These essential elements cannot be changed into adjectives that can be in-
discriminately applied to all sorts of things: thought and
extension are attributes that the intellect attributes to
the divine substance, and to it alone (*Ethics* I, Def. 4; letter 9). This requirement explicitly refers to the mind: "as
far as the mind is concerned." This does not mean that
there is access to things apart from the mind. The remark is intended to stress that the mind has its proper
ways to grasp what is real, and that we should be careful to use these proper ways, and none other, so as to
think through real, physical things. Things are neither
substantives nor adjectives; but it is "substantives" (like
extension or thought) that we must use to think the nature of real things that are uncaused or *causa sui*.

4. "all its properties be inferred from its definition."

I Conclusion (§ 98)

Spinoza concludes these paragraphs by stressing the importance
of thinking concrete reality: "the best conclusion will have to be
drawn from a particular affirmative[17] essence" (§ 98). Clearness
and distinctness of thought depend on whether or not our
thought is "specialior"—that is, closer to the idea of particular
things than other ideas. "So we ought to seek knowledge of par-

ticulars as much as possible." The most perfect example of such a clear and distinct thought of something particular is the idea of the divine being itself. Consequently, if we succeed in thinking the idea of God according to the requirements stipulated, we will be able to follow that most perfect method, which is none other than "the one that shows how the mind is to be directed according to the standard of the given idea of the most perfect Being" (§ 38).

In this second part of the method, we learned reflexively what it is to have clear and distinct, or adequate, ideas, what it is to be an intellect: it is to have knowledge consisting of definitions that obey certain rules (that are not external but internal to thinking properly, to having true ideas or objective essences). We learned what it is to have a good definition of "created" things, and what a good definition of an "uncreated" thing is.

But do we know by all this "the way of finding [new] good definitions" (§ 94)? Clearly not; Spinoza has not been able to teach this yet (see § 107, where he says literally: "But so far we have had no rules for discovering definitions"). Discovering new, adequate ideas or definitions (as far as this is a *methodological* problem) requires, first, reflection on the relationship between the objective essence of (some) created thing(s) and the objective essence of God; and, second, reflection on the relationship among objective essences themselves (this reflection expresses real causal relationships of formal essences). This is why Spinoza in previous paragraphs repeatedly stressed that "as soon as possible" we need to think the idea of the most perfect being or of the source of nature (§§ 38–39, 49). This problem of finding new definitions *is* the problem of order (the next part of the method). The solution to this problem seems to require a switch from logic to ontology and back again, since reflexive thinking demands that the idea of God is actually reached, that we can reflect upon it and then continue our understanding and reasoning in a reflexively guided way.

Some commentators see many flaws, hesitations, and unclarities in the *Treatise* — for example, in the paragraphs discussed in this chapter.[18] However, a careful reading of the text reveals how consistent and clear-headed Spinoza is: these paragraphs are a kind of repetition or elucidation of ideas from the previous chapter, on the separation of intellect and imagination. The same is true for the next chapter: our reflection or meditation penetrates ever more deeply into the nature of true knowledge or understanding.

▮ N O T E S

1. The term "modifications" is taken from the *Ethics* (passim).
2. See also letter 9, of 1663, to de Vries in Spinoza 1985, 194.
3. Curley has "to compare."
4. We could also say "the invention" or "constitution" of new knowledge.
5. See Descartes's *Secondes réponses* (Descartes 1953, 387). More about this in De Dijn 1973, 720ff.
6. See Hobbes's *De Corpore* I, 6, § 7. See also De Dijn 1973, 714–19.
7. Although there are strong similarities, it is not certain that Spinoza read Hobbes's ideas on this topic; for doubts about the possible influence of Hobbes on Spinoza's methodology, see Schuhmann 1987. The distinction between method of discovery and method of demonstration is often related to another methodological distinction: that between analytic and synthetic method. About this distinction in relation to Spinoza, see De Dijn 1973, 1986a; Koyré's comment in Spinoza 1990, 110; Kennington 1980.
8. This goes against the interpretation of the geometrical method as a purely axiomatic method given in Mark 1975 and Hubbeling 1964. About Spinoza's geometrical method, see also Gueroult 1968; Schneider 1981.
9. De Dijn 1986a, 68–69.
10. See Spinoza 1990, 108, where Koyré refers to Ernest Cassirer for this link made between Spinoza's and Hobbes's methodology.
11. De Dijn 1973, 716.
12. See Koyré's comment in Spinoza 1990, 107–8; De Dijn 1973, 727–32.
13. Gueroult 1968, 172–73.
14. Spinoza 1985, 40n. 64.
15. See *E* I, P. 11, Dem. 2.
16. Curley translates *transiens* as "transitive."
17. "Affirmative" is used in the sense of the essence as understood by what it is in itself, not through its external relation with other things (as in the third kind of knowledge); see Rousset's comment in Spinoza 1992, 392.
18. For example, Joachim 1940, 198.

The Order of Thinking (§§ 99–end)

I Text

[99]   Quoad ordinem vero, & ut omnes nostrae perceptiones ordinentur, & uniantur, requiritur, ut, quamprimum fieri potest, & ratio postulat, inquiramus, an detur quoddam ens, & simul quale, quod sit omnium rerum causa, ut ejus essentia objectiva sit etiam causa omnium nostrarum idearum, & tum mens nostra, uti diximus, quam maxime referet Naturam: Nam & ipsius essentiam, & ordinem, & unionem habebit objective. Unde possumus videre, apprime nobis esse necessarium, ut semper a rebus Physicis, sive ab entibus realibus omnes nostras ideas deducamus, progrediendo, quoad ejus fieri potest, secundum seriem causarum ab uno ente reali ad aliud ens reale, & ita quidem, ut ad abstracta, & universalia non transeamus, sive ut ab iis aliquid reale non concludamus, sive ut ea ab aliquo reali non concludantur: Utrumque enim verum progressum intellectus interrumpit.

[100]   Sed notandum, me hic per seriam causarum, & realium entium non intelligere seriem rerum singularium mutabilium, sed tantummodo seriem rerum fixarum, aeternarumque. Seriem enim rerum singularium mutabilium impossibile foret humanae imbecillitati assequi, cum propter earum omnem numerum superantem multitudinem, tum propter infinitas circumstantias in una & eadem re, quarum unaquaeque potest esse causa, ut res existat, aut non existat; quandoquidem earum existentia nullam habet connexionem cum earundem essentia, sive (ut jam diximus) non est aeterna veritas.

[99]   As for order, to unite and order all our perceptions, it is required, and reason demands, that we ask, as soon as possible, whether there is a certain being, and at the same time, what sort of being it is, which is the cause of all things, so that its objective essence may also be the cause of all our ideas, and then our mind will (as we have said) reproduce Nature as much as possible. For it will have Nature's essence, order, and unity objectively.

From this we can see that above all it is necessary for us always to deduce all our ideas from Physical things, *or* from the real beings, proceeding, as far as possible, according to the series of causes, from one real being to another real being, in such a way that we do not pass over to abstractions and universals, neither inferring something real from them, nor inferring them from something real. For to do either interferes with the true progress of the intellect.

[100]   But note that by the series of causes and of real beings I do not here understand the series of singular, changeable things, but only the series of fixed and eternal things. For it would be impossible for human weakness to grasp the series of singular, changeable things, not only because there are innumerably many of them, but also because of the infinite circumstances in one and the same thing, any of which can be the cause of its existence or nonexistence. For their existence has no connection with their essence, *or* (as we have already said) is not an eternal truth.

[101]   Verumenimvero neque etiam opus est, ut earum seriem intelligamus: siquidem rerum singularium mutabilium essentiae non sunt depromendae ab earum serie, sive ordine existendi; cum hic nihil aliud nobis praebeat praeter denominationes extrinsecas, relationes, aut ad summum circumstantias; quae omnia longe absunt ab intima essentia rerum. Haec vero tantum est petenda a fixis, atque aeternis rebus, & simul a legibus in iis rebus, tanquam in suis veris codicibus, inscriptis, secundum quas omnia singularia, & fiunt, & ordinantur; imo haec mutabilia singularia adeo intime, atque essentialiter (ut sic dicam) ab iis fixis pendent, ut sine iis nec esse, nec concipi possint. Unde haec fixa, & aeterna, quamvis sint singularia, tamen ob eorum ubique praesentiam, ac latissimam potentiam erunt nobis, tanquam universalia, sive genera definitionum rerum singularium mutabilium, & causae proximae omnium rerum.

[102]   Sed, cum hoc ita sit, non parum difficultatis videtur subesse, ut ad horum singularium cognitionem pervenire possimus: nam omnia simul concipere res est longe supra humani intellectus vires. Ordo autem, ut unum ante aliud intelligatur, uti diximus, non est petendus ab eorum existendi serie, neque etiam a rebus aeternis. Ibi enim omnia haec sunt simul natura. Unde alia auxilia necessario sunt quaerenda praeter illa, quibus utimur ad res aeternas, earumque leges intelligendum; attamen non est hujus loci ea tradere, neque etiam opus est, nisi postquam rerum aeternarum, earumque infallibilium legum sufficientem acquisiverimus cognitionem, sensuumque nostrorum natura nobis innotuerit.

[103]   Antequam ad rerum singularium cognitionem accingamur, tempus erit, ut ea auxilia tradamus, quae omnia eo tendent, ut nostris sensibus sciamus uti, & experimenta certis legibus, & ordine facere, quae sufficient ad rem, quae inquiritur, determinandam, ut tandem ex iis concludamus, secundum quasnam rerum aeternarum leges facta sit, & intima ejus natura nobis innotescat, ut suo loco ostendam. Hic, ut ad propositum revertar, tantum enitar tradere, quae videntur necessaria, ut ad cognitionem rerum aeternarum pervenire possimus, earumque definitiones formemus conditionibus supra traditis.

[101]   But there is also no need for us to understand their series. The essences of singular, changeable things are not to be drawn from their series, *or* order of existing, since it offers us nothing but extrinsic denominations, relations, or at most, circumstances, all of which are far from the inmost essence of things. That essence is to be sought only from the fixed and eternal things, and at the same time from the laws inscribed in these things, as in their true codes, according to which all singular things come to be, and are ordered. Indeed these singular, changeable things depend so intimately, and (so to speak) essentially, on the fixed things that they can neither be nor be conceived without them. So although these fixed and eternal things are singular, nevertheless, because of their presence everywhere, and most extensive power, they will be to us like universals, *or* genera of the definitions of singular, changeable things, and the proximate causes of all things.

[102]   But since this is so, there seems to be a considerable difficulty in our being able to arrive at knowledge of these singular things. For to conceive them all at once is a task far beyond the powers of the human intellect. But to understand one before the other, the order must be sought, as we have said, not from their series of existing, nor even from the eternal things. For there, by nature, all these things are at once. So other aids will have to be sought beyond those we use to understand the eternal things and their laws.

Nevertheless, this is not the place to treat them, nor is it necessary until after we have acquired a sufficient knowledge of the eternal things and their infallible laws, and the nature of our senses has become known to us.

[103]   Before we equip ourselves for knowledge of singular things, there will be time to treat those aids, all of which serve to help us know how to use our senses and to make, according to certain laws, and in order, the experiments that will suffice to determine the thing we are seeking, so that at last we may infer from them according to what laws of eternal things it was made, and its inmost nature may become known to us, as I shall show in its place.

Here, to return to our theme, I shall only try to treat those things that seem necessary for us to be able to arrive at knowledge of eternal things, and for us to form their definitions according to the conditions laid down above.

[104]   Quod ut fiat, revocandum in memoriam id, quod
supra diximus, nempe quod, ubi mens ad aliquam cogitationem
attendit, ut ipsam perpendat, bonoque ordine ex ea deducat,
quae legitime sunt deducenda, si ea falsa fuerit, falsitatem
deteget; sin autem vera, tum feliciter perget sine ulla interruptione res veras inde deducere; hoc, inquam, ad nostram rem
requiritur. Nam ex nullo alio fundamento cogitationes nostrae
determinari querunt.

[105]   Si igitur rem omnium primam investigare velimus,
necesse est dari aliquod fundamentum, quod nostras cogitationes eo dirigat. Deinde quia Methodus est ipsa cognitio reflexiva,
hoc fundamentum, quod nostras cogitationes dirigere debet,
nullum aliud potest esse, quam cognitio ejus, quod formam
veritatis constituit, & cognitio intellectus, ejusque proprieta-
tum, & virium: hac enim acquisita fundamentum habebimus, a
quo nostras cogitationes deducemus, & viam, qua intellectus,
prout ejus fert capacitas, pervenire poterit ad rerum aeternarum cognitionem, habita nimirum ratione virium intellectus.

[106]   Quod si vero ad naturam cogitationis pertineat
veras formare ideas, ut in prima parte ostensum, hic jam
inquirendum, quid per vires & potentiam intellectus intelligamus. Quoniam vero praecipua nostrae Methodi pars est vires
intellectus, ejusque naturam optime intelligere, cogimur necessario (per ea, quae in hac secunda parte Methodi tradidi) haec
deducere ex ipsa cogitationis, & intellectus definitione.

[107]   Sed hucusque nullas regulas inveniendi definitiones habuimus, & quia eas tradere non possumus, nisi cognita
natura, sive definitione intellectus, ejusque potentia, hinc
sequitur, quod vel definitio intellectus per se debet esse clare,
vel nihil intelligere possumus. Illa tamen per se absolute clara
non est; attamen quia ejus proprietates, ut omnia, quae ex
intellectu habemus, clare, & distincte percipi nequeunt, nisi
cognita earum natura: ergo definitio intellectus per se innotes-
cet, si ad ejus proprietates, quas clare, & distincte intelligimus,
attendamus. Intellectus igitur proprietates hic enumeremus,
easque perpendamus, deque nostris innatis[g] instrumentis agere
incipiamus.

[108]   Intellectus proprietates, quas praecipue notavi, &
clare intelligo, hae sunt.

I.   Quod certitudinem involvat, hoc est, quod sciat res
ita esse formaliter, ut in ipso objective contineantur.

---

g.   Vide supra § 31.

[104]   To do this, we must recall what we said above: when the mind attends to a thought—to weigh it, and deduce from it, in good order, the things legitimately to be deduced from it—if it is false, the mind will uncover the falsity; but if it is true, the mind will continue successfully, without any interruption, to deduce true things from it. This, I say, is required for our purpose. For our thoughts cannot be determined from any other foundation.

[105]   If, therefore, we wish to investigate the first thing of all, there must be some foundation that directs our thoughts to it.

Next, because Method is reflexive knowledge itself, this foundation, which must direct our thoughts, can be nothing other than knowledge of what constitutes the form of truth, and knowledge of the intellect, and its properties and powers. For once we have acquired this [knowledge], we shall have the foundation from which we shall deduce our thoughts and the way by which the intellect, according to its capacity, will be able to reach the knowledge of eternal things, with due regard, of course, to its own powers.

[106]   But if forming true ideas pertains to the nature of thought, as shown in the first part, here we must investigate what we understand by the powers of the intellect. Since the chief part of our Method is to understand as well as possible the powers of the intellect, and its nature, we are necessarily forced, by what I have taught in this second part of the Method, to deduce these from the very definition of thought and intellect.

[107]   But so far we have had no rules for discovering definitions. And because we cannot give them unless the nature, or definition, of the intellect, and its power are known, it follows that either the definition of the intellect must be clear through itself, or else we can understand nothing. It is not, however, absolutely clear through itself; but because its properties (like all the things we have from intellect) cannot be perceived clearly and distinctly unless their nature is known, if we attend to the properties of the intellect that we understand clearly and distinctly, its definition will become known through itself. We shall, therefore, enumerate the properties of the intellect here, and consider them, and begin to deal with our innate tools.[g]

[108]   The properties of the intellect which I have chiefly noted, and understand clearly, are these:

1. That it involves certainty, i.e., that the intellect knows that things are formally as they are contained objectively in itself.

---

g. Cf. above § 31.

II. Quod quaedam percipiat, sive quasdam formet ideas absolute, quasdam ex aliis. Nempe quantitatis ideam format absolute, nec ad alias attendit cogitationes; motus vero ideas non, nisi attendendo ad ideam quantitatis.

III. Quas absolute format, infinitatem exprimunt; at determinatas ex aliis format. Ideam enim quantitatis si per causam percipit, tum eam per quantitatem determinat, ut cum ex motu alicujus plani corpus, ex motu lineae vero planum, ex motu denique puncti lineam oriri percipit; quae quidem perceptiones non inserviunt ad intelligendam, sed tantum ad determinandam quantitatem. Quod inde apparet, quia eas quasi ex motu oriri concipimus, cum tamen motus non percipiatur, nisi percepta quantitate, & motum etiam ad formandam lineam in infinitum continuare possumus, quod minime possemus facere, si non haberemus ideam infinitae quantitatis.

IV. Ideas positivas prius format, quam negativas.

V. Res non tam sub duratione, quam sub quadam specie aeternitatis percipit, & numero infinito; vel potius ad res percipiendas, nec ad numerum, nec ad durationem attendit: cum autem res imaginatur, eas sub certo numero, determinata duratione, & quantitate percipit.

VI. Ideae, quas claras & distinctas formamus, ita ex sola necessitate nostrae naturae sequi videntur, ut absolute a sola nostra potentia pendere videantur; confusae autem contra. Nobis enim invitis saepe formantur.

VII. Ideas rerum, quas intellectus ex aliis format, multis modis mens determinare potest: ut ad determinandum ex. gr. planum ellipseos, fingit stylum chordae adhaerentem circa duo centra moveri, vel concipit infinita puncta eandem semper, & certam rationem ad datam aliquam rectam lineam habentia, vel conum plano aliquo obliquo sectum, ita ut angulus inclinationis major sit angulo verticis coni, vel aliis infinitis modis.

VIII. Ideae, quo plus perfectionis alicujus objecti exprimunt, eo perfectiores sunt. Nam fabrum, qui fanum aliquod excogitavit, non ita admiramur, ac illum, qui templum aliquod insigne excogitavit.

2. That it perceives certain things, *or* forms certain ideas, absolutely, and forms certain ideas from others. For it forms the idea of quantity absolutely, without attending to other thoughts, but it forms the ideas of motion only by attending to the idea of quantity.

3. Those that it forms absolutely express infinity, but determinate ideas it forms from others. For if it perceives the idea of a quantity through a cause, then it determines [that idea] through [the idea] of a quantity, as when it perceives that a body arises from the motion of some plane, a plane from the motion of a line, and finally, a line from the motion of a point. These perceptions do not help to understand the quantity, but only to determine it. This is evident from the fact that we conceive them as arising from the motion, although the motion is not perceived unless the quantity is perceived, and also because we can continue the motion to form a line to infinity, which we could not do at all, if we did not have the idea of infinite quantity.

4. It forms positive ideas before negative ones.

5. It perceives things not so much under duration as under a certain species of eternity, and in an infinite number— or rather, to perceive things, it attends neither to number nor to duration; but when it imagines things, it perceives them under a certain number, determinate duration and quantity.

6. The clear and distinct ideas that we form seem to follow so from the necessity of our nature alone that they seem to depend absolutely on our power alone. But with confused ideas it is quite the contrary—they are often formed against our will.

7. The mind can determine in many ways the ideas of things that the intellect forms from others—as, for example, to determine the plane of an ellipse, it feigns that a pen attached to a cord is moved around two centers, or conceives infinitely many points always having the same definite relation to some given straight line, or a cone cut by some oblique place, so that the angle of inclination is greater than the angle of the cone's vertex, or in infinite other ways.

8. The more ideas express of the perfection of some object, the more perfect they are. For we do not admire the architect who has designed a chapel so much as one who has designed a notable temple.

[109]   Reliqua, quae ad cogitationem referuntur, ut amor,
laetitia, &c. nihil moror: nam nec ad nostrum institutum
praesens faciunt, nec etiam possunt concipi, nisi percepto
intellectu. Nam perceptione omnino sublata ea omnia tolluntur.
    [110]   Ideae falsae, & fictae nihil positivum habent (ut
abunde ostendimus), per quod falsae, aut fictae dicuntur; sed ex
solo defectu cognitionis, ut tales considerantur. Ideae ergo
falsae, & fictae, quatenus tales, nihil nos de essentia cogitationis docere possunt; sed haec petenda ex modo recensitis proprietatibus positivis, hoc est, jam aliquid commune statuendum
est, ex quo hae proprietates necessario sequantur, sive quo dato
hae necessario dentur, & quo sublato haec omnia tollantur.
    Reliqua desiderantur.

[109]   I shall not linger over the other things that are referred to thought, such as love, joy, etc. For they contribute nothing to our present purpose, nor can they be conceived unless the intellect is perceived. For if perception is altogether taken away, then all these are taken away.

[110]   False and fictitious ideas have nothing positive (as we have shown abundantly) through which they are called false or fictitious, but they are considered as such only from a defect of our knowledge. So false and fictitious ideas, as such, can teach us nothing concerning the essence of thought. It is rather to be sought from the positive properties just surveyed, i.e., we must now establish something common from which these properties necessarily follow, or such that when it is given, they are necessarily given, and when it is taken away, they are taken away.

The rest is lacking.

| Commentary

Among commentators there is some debate as to whether the next group of paragraphs (§§ 99–end) corresponds to the third part of the method ("third, establish an order, so that we do not become weary with trifles" [§ 49])[1] or continues the problematic of the second part ("second, teach rules so that we may perceive things unknown according to such a standard" [§ 49]).[2]

Wolfgang Bartuschat claims that the order discussed in § 99 cannot be the order required in the third part of the method, which is an order established such that the intellect does not become involved with useless things—useless in terms of our ultimate end. The order talked about in §§ 99ff. is the order of real things insofar as this can be discovered by the intellect.[3] According to Bartuschat, to implement the program of the third part, as announced in § 49, would require that a train of thought be established that keeps the intellect from engaging in those realms where adequate thinking is impossible and that enables the intellect to effectively reach the ultimate goal. This program, which demands a study of the relative power of the intellect vis-à-vis the emotions, is not worked out in the *Treatise* but rather in *Ethics* IV and V.[4]

The reluctance of some commentators to consider §§ 99ff. as constituting the third part of the method is fueled by the way the content of part two is described in § 91, where Spinoza distinguishes the aim (*scopus*) of the method and the means to attain it and seems to comprehend both as belonging to the second part. The aim is to have clear and distinct ideas, appertaining to "the pure mind" and obeying the rules of definition. The means consist in connecting and ordering all ideas, "so that our mind, as far as possible, reproduces objectively the formal [i.e., real] character of nature, both as to the whole and as to the parts." What he calls here "the means" is clearly what is discussed from § 99 onward. This gives the impression that these paragraphs belong to the second part of the method, and that the third part is missing. Furthermore, in § 106, Spinoza explicitly speaks about "this second part of the Method," which shows that the paragraphs following § 99 are considered as part of the second part.

Thus Bartuschat is right in claiming that Spinoza must have had something else in mind with his third part of the method than what is given in §§ 99ff. The order talked about in relation to the third part ("establish an order, so that we do not become weary with trifles") must then be something other than the order discussed from § 99 onward ("to unite and order all our perceptions . . . [such that] our mind will . . . reproduce Nature as much as possible").[5] What could this order of the third part be? Is it, as Bartuschat suggests, an order of thinking that is adapted to the problem of the relationship between the intellect and the emotions (the problematic of *Ethics* IV and V)? I tend to agree; but we should attend more closely to the references to order in the *Ethics* as a whole, and in the introduction to the *Treatise,* where we read that, in function of our ultimate aim (happiness), it is necessary "to understand as much of Nature as suffices for acquiring such a [perfect] nature" (§ 14), and that "anything in the sciences [in general] which does nothing to advance us toward our goal must be rejected as useless" (§ 16). This is echoed in the *Ethics,* where Spinoza effectively concentrates not on all things that necessarily follow from the essence of God "but only [on] those that can lead us, by the hand, as it were, to the knowledge of the human Mind and its highest blessedness" (*Ethics* II, Pref.[6]); "those things" are discussed in a theory of man (*Ethics* II) and of the emotions (*Ethics* III) and in the ethics (*Ethics* IV, V). In the logic, we aim at reaching as soon as possible the idea of the source of nature so as to arrive at the *perfect* method. The aim is, in other words, through a reflection on the idea of God, to come to know how to deductively reach all the other knowledge necessary in function of our ultimate aim. The third part of the method, as conceived by Spinoza, could well correspond to this methodical procedure, present in the *Ethics* itself, of carefully steering our thoughts in such a way as to obtain our final aim. All this is quite consistent with what we stressed before: at a certain stage, the logic becomes one with a self-consciously developed metaphysics culminating in an ethics (Spinoza considered logic and philosophy as a unity).

Nevertheless, there is a reason why other commentators have thought that the third part of the method is contained in §§ 99ff. This is not surprising because, in the first place, each part of the method actually comes down to the same thing: understanding the standard of truth or what real thinking (or intellect) is. This unity of the three parts (mentioned in § 49) is anticipated in § 37: "the Method . . . is understanding what a true idea is . . . [which finally consists in] teaching and constructing certain rules as aids, and also making sure that the mind does not weary itself in useless things."[7] In the paragraphs following § 37, this unity of the different requirements of the method is stressed again: according to § 38 the *good* method is reflexive knowledge that indicates *how* the mind is to be directed according to the norm of the given true idea (that is, according to the conditions of a good definition); and according to § 40 adequate ideas hang together in the way formal realities hang together, so the *most perfect* method will teach the way to order and unite our ideas under the guidance of reflexive knowledge of the adequate idea of God—all of which results in the avoidance of useless efforts in thinking.

Although Spinoza formally distinguishes the second and the third part of the method as two successive phases, it is inevitable that the requirements of the third part somehow crop up in the second.[8] The problem of order in the second part (to obtain knowledge of God as soon as possible so as to possess the perfect method) clearly is an anticipation of the problem of order in the third (escaping useless efforts and difficulties). The major problem we will encounter in the following paragraphs is this: how can a reflection on the intellect—on the intellectual thinking present in the given true ideas of geometry—be transformed into methodical thinking about reality, into a methodologically appropriate thinking of the first cause of all reality?

▌ The Order of Our Intellectual Perceptions (§§ 99–103)

The order required by the method is not just any order; it is one that guarantees a *union* among our ideas. As Spinoza expressed it in § 91: "we shall strive to connect and order them [our ideas] so that our mind, as far as possible, reproduces objectively the formal character of nature, both as to the whole and as to the parts." To guarantee such a union methodically, "it is required, and reason demands, that we ask, as soon as possible, whether there is a certain being, and at the same time, what sort of being it is, which is the cause of all things, so that its objective essence may also be the cause of all our ideas, and then the mind will (as we have said[9]) reproduce Nature as much as possible. For it will have Nature's essence, order, and unity objectively" (§ 99).

In the following paragraphs, Spinoza investigates what this order (and unity) should take into account so that it is about reality. It should be an order of ideas concerning real or "physical" things: "proceeding, as far as possible, according to the series of causes, from one real being to another real being" (§ 99). However, the order should be an intelligible one: "But note that by the series of causes and of real beings I do not here understand the series of singular, changeable things, but only the series of fixed and eternal things" (§ 100). Real knowledge of things is causal knowledge, giving a description of their proximate cause. In other words, we are looking for knowledge of things as effects of a certain cause or series of causes. The series of causes looked for is not the series of singular, changeable things, which cannot be mastered by the human intellect, "not only because there are innumerably many of them, but also because of the infinite circumstances in one and the same thing, any of which can be the cause of its existence or nonexistence" (§ 100). The series of changeable things follows the order of their concrete existence, and there is no direct connection between their existence and their essence. That we cannot know this series is not important, since this order "offers us nothing but extrinsic denominations, relations, or at most, circumstances, all of which are far from the inmost essence of things" (§ 101). Rather, we are looking for the causal relations between things, which give us an insight into the "intrinsic denominations" constituting their essences; we are looking for causal relations that explain the *whatness* of the thing—*why* things are *what* they are. In other words, we have to attend to the series of *fixed and eternal things,* to which things belong according to their essence. "That essence [of things] is to be sought only from the fixed and eternal things, and at the same time from the laws inscribed in these things, as in their true codes, according to which all singular things come to be, and are ordered" (§ 101).

This notion of fixed and eternal things has been the subject of much speculation in the Spinoza literature.[10] Spinoza distinguishes them from the eternal laws that are "inscribed in [them], as in their true codes." On them depend "intimately, and (so to speak) essentially" all singular, changeable things, which cannot be, or be conceived, without them (§ 101). Although these fixed and eternal things are themselves singular, "nevertheless, because of their presence everywhere, and most extensive power, they will be to us like universals, *or* genera of the definitions of singular, changeable things, and the proximate causes of all things" (§ 101).

This is valuable information concerning the fixed and eternal things and their relation to singular, changeable things. The latter are said to depend intimately—"so to speak," essentially—upon the former. Singular, finite things cannot be, or be conceived, without the fixed and eternal things, so they depend upon these both for their existence and for their essence. The fixed and eternal things are present everywhere and have an extensive power through which they are immanent in finite things. They are like universals, or *genera,* of the definitions of singular things, and at the same time they are their proximate cause. The Scholastic definition of a thing indicates the genus and specific difference of the thing (for example, a human being is a rational animal); together these constitute the "formal cause" or the rationale of a thing (why the thing is what it is). The Spinozistic definition of a finite, singular thing also comprehends something like a genus and specific difference, with this crucial difference: the genus is not simply a universal term but is itself a *singular thing*.

Indeed, each finite thing, being a modification of some attribute(s) of the divine substance, is a specific modification of a certain genus, that is, of a certain attribute, which itself is a singular, if infinite, reality. (In the *Ethics*, Spinoza also calls the attribute of substance a kind of *genus* [I, P. 16, Dem.]; see the first section of chapter 9.) Substance under one or another of its attributes at the same time provides the first cause and something like a universal genus for all finite things, which are modifications of this attribute. The definition of a finite thing, if fully spelled out, provides us with the proximate cause, which is the *first* cause as modified in a certain way in one or another attribute of substance.

Understood in this way, the Spinozistic definition of a finite, singular thing resembles the Scholastic definition of an accident, which, as *accident of a substance,* must contain a reference to the substance and the substantial nature of which it is an accident.[11]

But in what sense can substance, under one or another of its attributes, be a *proximate* cause of finite things? In a passage of the *Ethics* (I, P. 28, Sch.), Spinoza clarifies what he means by this rather Scholastic terminology, clearly borrowed from the *Philosophia novantiqua:*[12] God is called the proximate cause of all finite things—not the *absolutely* proximate cause but the proximate cause *only in his own kind.* He is the absolutely proximate cause only of effects that are themselves infinite (the infinite modes that are wholes or totalities of all modes belonging to a certain attribute; see chapter 9, section 2). God is the proximate cause of finite things only in his own kind (of cause)—that is, as *first* cause, not as to other kinds of causal relation. The absolutely proximate cause of finite things as to their concrete existence is other, actually existing finite things. This does not mean, Spinoza hastens to say, that God is a *remote* cause (on the contrary, God is the immanent cause of finite things; see *Ethics* I, P. 18). The *absolutely* proximate cause of finite things, as to their essence, is not God as such but God as modified ("Deus quatenus modificatus"; *Ethics* I, P. 28, Dem.). In other words, the full definition of a finite thing must refer not simply to God as such but to one or another of God's attributes as modified into a mode with a particular essence that—together with the essences of all other modes also belonging to a certain attribute—forms an infinite mode of God's attribute (see *Ethics* V, P. 40, Sch.). It should be obvious that when Spinoza speaks of the essence of a thing, he does not mean a generic concept of whatness, but the principle that makes a concrete thing into what it is; this is why he talks about essence as *particular*.

After all this, can we decide for certain the fixed and eternal things and their series discussed in §§ 100–101? We can gather that the substantial attributes without doubt belong to them: they are at the same time fundamental causes (of essence and existence) and a kind of genera in the definitions of created things. A finite thing is truly nothing but substance modified in one of its attributes in a certain way—it is God or substance as affected in some way or mode (*Ethics* I, P. 15, Sch.) or as constituting some modification in one of its attributes (*Ethics* II, P. 11, Cor.). But are attributes also a kind of true code in which are inscribed "the laws . . . according to which all singular things come to be, and are ordered" (§ 101)? As some commentators remark, Spinoza seems unclear and insecure here.[13]

From letter 64, to G. H. Schuller, and from the *Tractatus Theologico-Politicus,* we learn that the things in which laws are inscribed (as in their *codices*) are not the attributes of substance but the infinite modes.[14] These infinite modes are totalities, or wholes of finite things, which through the laws inscribed in them determine the behavior of the parts with respect to one another. They cannot at the same time be the fundamental cause or origin of the essences of things. Nevertheless, Spinoza says that the intimate essence "is to be sought only from the fixed and eternal things, and at the same time from the laws" (§101). Furthermore, if we exclude infinite modes from the series of fixed and eternal things, there does not seem to be much of a series left.

Although infinite modes and their inscribed universal laws cannot be causes explaining essences, they play a role in the definition of these essences. This is not surprising: after all, they are wholes of the parts to be defined. So in the understanding of a thing's essence, we need not a reference to an indefinite series of changeable things but a reference to a *determined* series of "fixed and eternal" things: substantial attribute(s), infinite mode(s), finite eternal essence.

If the definition of singular, changeable things cannot be found by considering the chain in which they come to exist and pass out of existence, there is serious difficulty as to how we can arrive at knowledge of their particular essences. "For to conceive them all at once is a task far beyond the powers of the human intellect. But to understand one before the other, the order must be sought, as we have said, not from their series of existing, nor even from the eternal things. For there, by nature, all these things are at once" (§ 102). Indeed, according to their essences, all things are at the same time in the attribute as its effects and as parts in the infinite mode. Spinoza concludes that "other aids will have to be sought beyond those we use to understand the eternal things and their laws" (§ 102) in order to come to an understanding of exactly why the thing is what it is, of why it is this particular *Deus quatenus modificatus*.

At the end of § 102, Spinoza says that this is not the place to talk about these aids, because we need first "sufficient knowledge of the eternal things and their infallible laws" and sufficient knowledge of "the nature of our senses" (which is the subject of optics). In what is probably a digression originally added as a note,[15] Spinoza does mention those aids, "all of which serve to help us know how to use our senses and to make, according to certain laws, and in order, the experiments that will suffice to determine the thing we are seeking, so that at last we may infer from them according to what laws of eternal things it was made, and its inmost nature may become known to us, as I shall show in its place" (§ 103). As with his promise in note i to § 27 (to extensively examine experience and "the Method of proceeding of the Empiricists and of the new Philosophers"), Spinoza seems not to have executed this plan; there are indications about experience and experimentation in letter 6 (concerning Boyle) and in letters 2 (about Bacon and Descartes) and 10.

It is clear that the infinite modes and the laws inscribed in them play a role in the determination of the essence or intimate nature of things, although on their own they are insufficient to give this determination, since they are conditions of the definition of any mode whatsoever.[16] In addition to them, we need experience and experimentation, which in turn require a *theory* of experience (in order to know how they can help us to reach knowledge that is adequate).

It is equally clear that Spinoza does not simply reject experience but thinks it is a prerequisite for arriving at definitions of "singular, changeable things." A complete methodology of the discovery of new definitions cannot do without a theory of experimentation (and observation), and of how, together with knowledge of the fixed and eternal things and the laws inscribed in them, we gather the required insight in the nature of "real, physical things."

In chapter 7 of the *Tractatus Theologico-Politicus,* we find an interesting passage concerning the investigation of nature. Spinoza compares the method of interpreting Scripture with the method of interpreting nature, a comparison that reminds us of the well-known topos of the two books of learning, the Bible and the book of nature. "[T]he method of interpreting Nature consists essentially in composing a detailed study of Nature [*historia Naturae*] from which, as being the source of our assured data, we can deduce the definitions of the things of Nature"; "in examining natural phenomena we first of all try to discover those features that are most universal and common to the whole of Nature, to wit motion and rest and the rules and laws governing them which Nature always observes and through which she constantly acts; and then we advance gradually from these to other less universal features."[17]

The problem of finding definitions of physical things is presented here as a problem of interpretation: "definitions of the things of Nature must be inferred from the various operations of Nature."[18] This interpretation requires, on the one hand, knowledge of those features most universal and common to the whole of nature and, on the other, "assured data" gathered from "a detailed study of Nature," a "natural history" in which theoretically guided observation and experimentation play a crucial role. For the understanding of physical things, this means that definitions must be obtained from an interpretation of such "assured data" concerning various bodies and their operations in light of the most universal and common features—motion and rest—and the rules and laws inscribed in these. (In letter 64, to Schuller, motion and rest are called the infinite [immediate] mode of the substantial attribute extension.[19])

Spinoza has not shown how exactly such interpretation is to be performed (except perhaps in the letter to Boyle concerning the nature of niter[20]). Nevertheless, it at least is certain that we need "assured data" (in which the empiricists are right) and that we need an insight into the ultimate cause and the whole of nature, and into the ultimate laws governing all operations of nature, which cannot be got from experience and/or abstraction (in which the rationalists are right). It also is certain that the cause of the essence, which is discovered in the process of interpretation and expressed in the definition, can be conceived in many equivalent ways (see § 108, 7; and letter 6). The way that such a definition is formed can be called a kind of *extraction* or abduction, comparable, according to Zweerman,[21] to the way an essence is formed in the mind as that which is common to all the known properties (the expression *petere ex,* "to extract," "to abduct," is used in § 110). As letter 10 says, experience on its own cannot teach us the essences of things, certainly not of things whose essence includes existence (like the attributes); but experience is needed to determine our mind to think of certain essences of things rather than others.[22] As we will see in chapter 10, both these requirements are fulfilled in the study of the essence of man in *Ethics* II.

At this point, one may wonder how all this squares with Spinoza's conception of the mind as actively constructing definitions of objective essences? Is it not the case that the mind appears here as fundamentally dependent on experience? Of course. But for Spinoza, this dependence is not passivity, because experiential and experimental data are reinterpreted carefully within a framework of intellectual ideas concerning fixed and eternal things and the laws inscribed in them as in their codes. In this way an intellectual decoding of this experience is obtained that yields intellectual constructions of essences and their properties (and possible relations with other existing essences).

After all this, we can wonder again about the method we must use in the investigation of nature, which is a subproblem in our general logic or methodology. In the previous chapter, we discovered that this method, called "geometrical" in the *Ethics,* is not simply an axiomatic method, even though it takes the form of an axiomatic deduction. Rather, it is a method of causal deduction. Here we see that this deduction is not incompatible with input from experience. On the contrary, in order to discover new definitions of *particular* things (modifications of nature), an interpretation of experimental and carefully observed data is needed in the context of our knowledge of fixed and eternal things and the laws inscribed in them. In this sense, Spinoza's geometrical method is somehow closer to a hypothetical-deductive method than to a purely formal, axiomatic method[23] — with this proviso, of course: Spinoza thinks that the ultimate framework, in terms of which experiential data are interpreted, can be understood adequately, once and for all.

At this stage, the problem in the logic is not so much the right way of discovering new definitions of finite things, but that "as soon as possible" we must find a way to discover the definition of the ultimate cause (§ 99) and of the fixed and eternal things (§ 103). How do we get there methodically?

The Problem of the Foundation (§§ 104–5)

How do we methodically discover the definitions of fixed and eternal things, especially of the first cause? Spinoza reminds us here of ideas expressed earlier (§§ 59-61): "when the mind attends to a thought—to weigh it, and deduce from it, in good order, the things legitimately to be deduced from it—if it is false, the mind will uncover the falsity; but if it is true, the mind will continue successfully, without any interruption, to deduce true things from it." This reminder is precisely to the point, for, as the original text—changed unnecessarily by Gebhardt and Curley—says, "there is no foundation which can put a stop to our thoughts" ("Nam ex nullo fundamento cogitationes nostrae terminari queunt," § 104). If, therefore, we want to investigate the first cause, "there must be some foundation that directs our thoughts to it," and this foundation can be found only in thinking.

These observations are not easy to understand. Some commentators even suspect that the original text is corrupt.[24] But it is not impossible to make sense of what Spinoza says. Much clarity is gained from the introduction that Spinoza gives to his description of method or logic in letter 37 (to Bouwmeester). The mind as intellect is like a spiritual automaton: the clear and distinct ideas it forms come from other clear and distinct ideas and have no cause outside the intellect. Thus clear and distinct ideas depend exclusively on our own nature and its laws—not on fortune but on our own absolute (that is, separated from external causes) power. In other words, once we are in possession of clear and distinct ideas, we can—in an organized way (*arte*) not determined by external, accidental factors (*fortuna*)—deduce other clear and distinct ideas. The intellect is the only foundation for an active pursuit of the idea of the first cause. As Rousset explains, a foundation should not be confused with a principle.[25] The distinction between the two can be found in Spinoza's rendering of Descartes's *Principia Philosophiae*:[26] a principle is a premise allowing certain conclusions; a foundation is not a principle of a deductive chain of propositions but rather that platform which enables us to reach such principle(s) and to engage in a deduction of adequate ideas. Spinoza's move in the paragraphs at hand is similar to Descartes's, who wanted to gain knowledge of God as the principle of all scientific knowledge but thought that we need a foundation, the intrinsic certainty of the *Cogito,* in order to reach that principle. Spinoza's foundation is also reflexive thought itself (on the intellect, as pure construction of geometrical essences); in this reflection comes the realization that something *real* is being thought (the act of thinking or the intellect itself); in this reflexive awareness of the intellect we must discover our principle, the idea of the first cause.

First, then, Spinoza reminds us that once thinking gets going, there is nothing in intellectual thinking as such (nor, of course, outside thinking[27]) that can put a stop to it. On the other hand, if we wish to investigate the first cause and arrive at knowledge of it, "there must be some foundation that directs our thoughts to it." What could this foundation be—given that what we are engaged in is method, or logic, or reflexive knowledge itself—"other than knowledge of what constitutes the form of truth, and knowledge of the intellect, and its properties and powers" (§ 105)? In other words, it is in reflexive insight *itself*, in our awareness of intellectual thinking as a reality with specific properties and capacities, that the platform is given to us to proceed.

This reflexive knowledge will be the foundation from which we can produce (in a not strictly deductive way) other thoughts; it will be "the way by which the intellect, according to its capacity, will be able to reach the knowledge of eternal things, with due regard, of course, to its own powers" (§ 105). The whole question will be *how* we can reach our principle, the idea of the first cause, on the foundation of this reflexive knowledge. According to our own methodological rules (§ 94), a proper understanding of the intellect requires a definition through the proximate cause. Unfortunately, we have not yet discovered ways to discover definitions, neither of the intellect nor of the first cause. This is the problem tackled in the next section, which seems to end in deadlock.

From Foundation to Principle (§§ 106–end)

The business of the second part of the method was first to formulate the rules of a good definition and then to organize our ideas in such a way that we reflexively understand the unity of the things of nature. In order to do this, we must have a foundation to direct our thoughts to the first cause. This foundation can be nothing other than the intellect itself—or, better, the reflexive knowledge of the power of thinking. However, Spinoza seems saddled with a paradox: in order to understand the powers of the intellect, we are forced (§ 94) to derive this understanding from the definition of thought and intellect (§ 106). Unfortunately, "so far we have had no rules for discovering [new] definitions" (§ 107), not even of the fixed and eternal things we have to know first. On the contrary, the acquisition of these rules seems to depend on our knowledge of the power, and therefore the nature, of the intellect. But then either this nature is known or clear "through itself" or we can understand nothing. It is not, however, absolutely clear through itself.[28]

Is this the end of our endeavor? Many commentators think that at this point Spinoza has involved himself in a contradiction, and that this is why he interrupted the *Treatise* and began his *Ethics*.[29] But did he not get himself involved in a similar contradiction in § 40? And if he so obviously did in §§ 106–7, why did he continue for a few more paragraphs if the effort was doomed to failure?

Actually, Spinoza continues thus: "but because its properties (like all the things we have from the intellect) cannot be perceived clearly and distinctly unless their nature [i.e., the nature of the intellect] is known, if we attend to the properties of the intellect that we understand clearly and distinctly, its definition will become known through itself. We shall, therefore, enumerate the properties of the intellect here, and consider them, and begin to deal with our innate tools" (§ 107).

It is obvious that Spinoza thinks that the properties of the intellect *can* be understood clearly and distinctly, that from them we *can* discover the nature involved in them such that the definition of the intellect will become known through itself, and, finally, that from there we *will* obtain the necessary innate tools to begin the investigation of nature. That Spinoza continues his investigation *after* he has formulated the paradox points to everything *but* an awareness that he had arrived at a dead end. In a move comparable to Descartes's (but without accepting the necessity of a methodical doubt), Spinoza will try to understand the nature of the intellect on the basis of the mind's awareness of the intellect's properties and powers. This should enable him to reach the insight into the fixed and eternal things, especially the first cause, the principle of an investigation of nature leading us ultimately to our final aim.

In the following paragraphs (§§ 106–10) Spinoza lists the properties of the intellect. This list relies heavily on insights gathered in the previous part of the method (a reflection on given, true ideas—mainly of geometry, which is the basis of physics). This shows the intricate connection among the different parts. The properties of the intellect are (§ 108):

1. "That it involves certainty, i.e., that the intellect knows that things are formally as they are contained objectively in itself"; see §§ 35–36 (and Ethics II, P. 43 and Sch.);

2. "That it perceives certain things, *or* forms certain ideas, absolutely, and forms certain ideas from them"; see §§ 92ff.

and § 72 (and *Ethics* II, P. 45–47). The examples that Spinoza gives to clarify this are taken from geometry: "For it [the intellect] forms the idea of quantity absolutely, without attending to other thoughts, but it forms the ideas of motion [of a certain kind, e.g., of a semicircle] only by attending to the idea of quantity." In order to think quantity absolutely, we should not confuse it with what is given in the imagination, which leads to erroneous views (§ 87; see also *Ethics* I, P. 15, Sch.; and letter 12, to L. Meijer). In geometry, to think quantity absolutely means to think it as the ultimate, and therefore infinite, possibility condition of all geometrical constructions and problems, as the genus that enters into all definitions of geometrical constructions as constructions of or within geometrical space. This is clearly indicated by the fact that each geometrical figure is defined as "the figure which . . ."—that is, as a particular modification of infinite quantity or extension. This property of the intellect has consequences for the investigation of nature: it implies that we must try to think, before anything else, that which can be thought *absolutely,* as is shown in the next property.

3. "Those that it forms absolutely express infinity, but determinate ideas it forms from others. For if it perceives the idea of a quantity through a cause, then it determines quantity [I translate the Latin text, "Ideam enim quantitatis, si eam per causam percipit, tum quantitatem determinat"[30]], as when it perceives that a body arises from the motion of some plane, a plane from the motion of a line, and finally, a line from the motion of a point. These perceptions do not help to understand the quantity, but only to determine it." Spinoza clearly distinguishes here between absolute quantity and quantity as determined.[31] Determined quantity consists of parts that are distinguished not *realiter* (that is, as different substances), but *modaliter* (that is, as different modes of the same substance). To think something absolutely, then, is to think something infinite. The thinking of *determinations* of infinity or, as they are also called in the *Ethics, modifications* of infinity requires the conception of a cause determining infinity into a specific structure (such as point, line, plane, which are modifications of infinite quantity). The "perceptions" of point, line, figure, and body originate in a determination of infinite quantity by means of one or an-

other motion: a point is obtained by the cause or determination of infinitely small motion,[32] a line by motion of a point, and so on. Infinite quantity cannot be understood through its determinations. On the contrary, it is required first to understand all its determinations. "This is evident from the fact that we conceive them as arising from the motion, although the motion is not perceived unless the quantity is perceived, and also because we can continue the motion to form a line to infinity, which we could not do at all, if we did not have the idea of infinite quantity." This indicates that the notion of an *indefinite* extension (such as an infinite line) presupposes the notion of the infinite absolutely speaking.[33]

4. "It forms positive ideas before negative ones" (see also §§ 89, 98).

5. "It perceives things not so much under duration as under a certain species of eternity, and in an infinite number—or rather, to perceive things, it attends neither to numbers nor to duration; but when it imagines things, it perceives them under a certain number, determinate duration and quantity" (see also §§ 83, 100; and letter 10). Again, it is striking that geometry functions as the prototype of intellectual thinking from which we can learn what the intellect really is. Although it makes use of experience in order to express reality (§ 102), intellectual thinking is primarily interested in knowledge of the essences of things, of their essential properties, and of the intrinsic relations between things (expressed in "eternal truths"). A perception of things "under a certain . . . determinate duration and quantity" is said to belong to the imagination. Undoubtedly, the qualification of "a *certain* determinate duration" is important here—Spinoza does not reject the idea of duration altogether.[34] However, the imagination conceives duration and quantity as divisible and calculable through discrete numbers, whereas each "part" of space and time is infinitely divisible and not really intelligible in terms of discrete numeration (see *Ethics* I, P. 15, Sch.; and letter 12). The intellect is not such that it denies all duration, it only "attends neither to number nor to duration" but "perceives [things] . . . under a certain aspect of eternity [sub quadam specie aeternitatis]." To conceive things "under a certain aspect of eternity" is to conceive them according to their essence, as necessary effects of some attribute(s) of substance. (In

Ethics II the second kind of knowledge, reason [*ratio*], is said "to perceive things under a certain aspect of eternity," which means either that they are considered generally as a necessary effect of God, or under "common notions" that indicate properties necessarily belonging to all things of a certain kind.[35])

6. "The clear and distinct ideas that we form seem to follow so from the necessity of our nature alone that they seem to depend absolutely on our power alone. But with confused ideas it is quite the contrary—they are often formed against our will" (see also §§ 85–86, 104). This is not an acceptance of free will as distinct from intellect; it means that in the imagination the formation of inadequate ideas cannot be understood through the intrinsic order of the ideas themselves but must be understood in terms of the mind forming a sequence of ideas expressing the fortuitous encounters of the body (see § 84 and the explanation of the imagination in *Ethics* II). Our clear and distinct ideas, on the contrary, "seem to depend absolutely on our power alone"; we encounter here again the concept of the mind as the spontaneous power of forming objective essences. Of course, our clear and distinct ideas do not depend on our power alone (they only *"seem* to depend absolutely"), because we possess this power only insofar as we are modifications of God's power of thinking and parts of his infinite intellect (see also § 73; and *Ethics*: II, P. 10, Cor.; P. 11, Cor.; and V, P. 40, Sch.).

7. "The mind can determine in many ways the ideas of things that the intellect forms from others [which it forms absolutely]." To think the essence of something finite as a particular determination (or modification) of an infinite nature is to think a cause (or rationale) of this determination. This cause, which explains the internal structure or essence of the thing, can be conceived in many equivalent ways. This certainly is the case in geometry, as Spinoza shows in his example of the definition of an ellipse; but he seems to claim the same for definitions outside the realm of geometry (for example, in physics; see also letter 6).

8. "The more ideas express of the perfection of some object, the more perfect they are. For we do not admire the architect who has designed a chapel so much as one who has designed a notable temple" (see also § 38). At first reading

this may seem false: is not a true and adequate idea always a true and adequate idea, whatever its object? Yet ideas can be "richer" in consequences, and the most "perfect" idea in this respect is the idea of the infinite, or the source of everything.

The next two paragraphs deal negatively with elements that Spinoza does not plan to take into account. The mind as intellectual thinking also is characterized by affects or emotions, such as love and joy. It is not only for the sake of completeness that Spinoza mentions here the affects, particularly love and joy; the whole point of our endeavor is precisely to reach that joy and love in which real happiness consists. Nevertheless, at this moment, the relation between knowledge and joy and love does not have to be taken into account: first, because it contributes nothing to the present problematic (the logic); and second, because the affects presuppose thought, and not vice versa (see also *Ethics* II, Ax. 3). However, later in the *Philosophia,* a careful investigation of the affects—and of their relation to the imagination and to the intellect and its power—will play an essential role in the problematic of obtaining our final aim, happiness (*Ethics* III–V).

Spinoza next repeats something we know already: that false and fictitious ideas cannot teach us anything concerning the real essence of thought. Falsity and fiction do not indicate any positive properties of thinking (see also *Ethics* II, P. 35, and Sch.). The capacity to express falsehood and fiction is due not to a special creative power of the mind but to a defect of our knowledge.

After we have surveyed all positive qualities of the intellect, we return to the question of the definition of the intellect (§ 110): "we must now establish something common from which these properties necessarily follow, *or* such that when it is given, they are necessarily given, and when it is taken away, they are taken away." Then, as the editors of the *Treatise* say,[36] "The rest is lacking."

As Rousset rightly notes, it is remarkable how many ideas in *Ethics* II are anticipated here.[37] Yet they are not derived systematically from an insight into the essence of the human mind, as they are in *Ethics* II; on the contrary, they are set forth to establish "something common" from which all these properties follow. This "something" can be nothing other than the essence of the intellect itself. Somehow, in our reflexive thinking on given, true ideas, especially in geometry, we are capable of clearly and distinctly thinking fundamental properties of the intellect (in separation from the imagination). It is clear that Spinoza does not doubt any of this. On the other hand, it is necessary to penetrate the internal nature of the intellect, on the basis of the "something common" present in the properties. This presents an additional problem, since such a definition presupposes understanding of the fixed and eternal things, without which the intellect—the mind as having intellectual ideas—cannot be properly understood.

How can we solve this problem? Somehow, we must already possess the necessary "innate tools" to do this. In our knowledge of the properties, we must, as Spinoza says, somehow already know the essence of the intellect (this is particularly clear from properties 1 and 6 in § 108): an autonomous power to think things as they are. In our knowledge of the properties of the intellect, gathered in our reflection, we must also find the tools to define the first cause and to come, on this basis, to a genetic definition of the intellect, which completes our logical search and positions us to arrive at our final aim (the ethical problematic with which we started).

In other words, a solution to the problem with which the logic ends can be found only if we succeed in beginning the *Philosophia,* or investigation of nature, in the proper order (*Ethics* I) and if, reflexively guiding this investigation toward a theory of the human mind, we discover the cause for the properties of the intellect as *real* essence (*Ethics* II). This means that the enumeration of the properties of the intellect not only contains all sorts of elements to be explained in a "geometrical" order in *Ethics* II; it also must provide us with the essential elements or tools to establish an ontology and/or metaphysics.

In recapitulating the fundamental properties of thinking, inevitably we recapitulated essential features belonging to the intelligible structure of any objective essence: this recapitulation gives us the innate tools to begin the investigation of nature itself. We learned that there must be two sorts of objective essences: those that express an infinite nature (attribute) of things that are *causa sui* (substance) and those that express determinations of infinite natures, which therefore are "finite in their kind" and can be called modifications belonging to something that is *causa sui.*

That which is *causa sui* is always a substance. Substance is necessarily characterized not only as *causa sui* but also as eternal and free. In other words, in this reflection on the properties of the intellect, the main definitions and axioms of *Ethics* I can be easily discovered. Some of the axioms (for example, *Ethics* I, Ax. 2, 4, 6), which are epistemological in nature, are simply repetitions of insights into the nature of the intellect. The sixth definition, the definition of God, postulates the idea of a real first cause of everything—the postulation of which is related to the central axiom 4—which is explicated in terms of innate notions such as substance, attribute, infinite, and thing.

As Gueroult has rightly pointed out,[38] the central and only real definition of *Ethics* I is definition 6, the definition of the object investigated in *Ethics* I, "De Deo." All the other definitions are of innate *categories,* which express fundamental properties of the only two sorts of objective essences of things that are conceivable. We discover this idea of God in us as the idea of the first ultimate cause, which everybody calls "the absolutely infinite being." How it is that this idea can be in our mind will be explained once we come to an understanding of ourselves on the basis of an understanding of this very idea of God itself. Again, the idea of our thinking selves is an idea we cannot fail to have if we are thinking at all. This absolute certainty will be expressed in the most crucial, "existential" axiom of *Ethics* II, Axiom 2. Everything we need to solve the fundamental problems left over in the logic is now present.

During our reflection on geometrical ideas, we learned the standard of truth; we learned that we should not be afraid to construct objective essences as long as we think "clearly and distinctly." Paradoxically, in reflecting on a kind of intellectual fiction (geometrical ideas), we can come to know clearly and distinctly a real objective essence: the intellect itself. Even though we do not know it immediately according to its full proximate cause, nevertheless we know it sufficiently to use it as our foundation for thinking the first cause of the intellect and of everything else. We discover the tools to do this in our reflection on the properties of intellectual thinking itself, as they show themselves in the thinking of the amended Euclidean geometry.[39]

My interpretation of Spinoza here shows that, at the point the *Treatise* ends, we are at the brink of the *Philosophia* (as it is developed in the *Ethics*).[40] This is further confirmed if we look at the four points that, according to letter 37, are the task of the logic: (1) to adopt a provisional morals; (2) to establish a short "history of the mind" (the four kinds of perception); (3) to distinguish intellect and imagination; and (4) to come to know the nature and properties of the intellect. These four points are all met in the text of the *Treatise.*

▍ General Conclusion

The method presented in Spinoza's logic or methodology can be described as an upward movement of thought.[41] After the preliminary stage of a *historiola Mentis,* a purification of the intellect must be performed through a separation between intellect and imagination. This yields clear and distinct knowledge of the properties of the intellect, which in turn is supposed, through "extraction," to give us a sufficient insight into the nature of the intellect to serve as a foundation for the discovery and development of the idea of God. This idea of the ultimate cause is absolutely necessary for a methodical (rule-guided) discovery of new truths about reality without a waste of forces and especially for the discovery of the truth about ourselves, including the complete, adequate idea of the nature of the intellect. The idea of God is the starting point for a downward movement of thinking, that is, deductive knowledge through the cause.[42] The method discussed in the *Treatise* is the instrument (reflection on a given true idea) to lead, in a quick and nonhaphazard way, to self-awareness of the intellect and to adequate understanding of real things—first of all, of God.

Spinoza's concept of methodical thinking displays a number of inevitable circularities, of which he was well aware.[43] The method is supposed to give us insight into how to think properly, but this insight seems possible only if we already are capable of thinking properly—that is, if we already have some pure intellectual idea as an innate tool. Another, related circularity is present at the end of the *Treatise:* knowledge of the properties of the intellect cannot be full-fledged unless one possesses knowledge of the essence of the intellect. Yet, given this clear and distinct knowledge of the properties, we must somehow know the essence of the intellect, or at least be capable of constructing this knowledge. Furthermore, a circularity is present in the purpose of the logic, or methodology, itself. How can students be brought to recognize this method as a good method, unless they are capable of performing the reflection for themselves, in which case they would not need the exposition of the method?

These circularities are not vicious circles. They express the condition of the actually existing human mind, which, as part of God's intellect, is necessarily in possession of the elements of eternal truths but at the same time is living in the real world, which usually obstructs the actual possession of fully developed knowledge. One or another catalyst is required to trigger the autonomous development of intellectual thinking. This hardly ever happens simply through good luck. The discovery of geometry, together with reflection on the intellectual thinking involved in it, is a powerful means to reach, in an *artful* manner, the adequate knowledge needed to achieve our ultimate aim.

In his methodology, Spinoza has tried to show that it is possible to arrive at a real knowledge of things, which is itself the basis of a new ethical life. The ethical dissatisfaction with the ordinary way of living can, in the reflection on this dissatisfaction itself, achieve some consolation. These moments of consolation in thinking should be transformed into a sustained reflection on the nature of intellectual thinking, which itself is the condition for adequate knowledge of ourselves and for real salvation. Showing people this "trick," as Spinoza does in the *Treatise,* will not be fruitful unless they are capable of actually performing this reflection for themselves.

Although logic, as it is developed here, is a way toward the kind of knowledge in which salvation is supposed to exist, another way is possible. Suppose that the master logician has himself arrived at knowledge of God, of man, and of his well-being; suppose he can expose this knowledge in a demonstrative way, as displayed in the *Ethics.* Would it not be possible that people, when confronted with this exposition, come to understand for themselves the truth of what is demonstrated and so come to know reflexively what truth means, thereby performing the necessary purification of the intellect through following the demonstrations? In this case, the *Ethics* would itself provide a shortened version of the way to salvation. The pedagogy is slightly different; the aim is the same. Since this pedagogy is a real possibility, Spinoza may have thought it not absolutely urgent to complete his logic.

| NOTES

1. Curley clearly subscribes to this opinion in his division of paragraphs in *TEI* § 49, rightly rejected by Don Garrett (1986, 87n. 2).

2. This view is followed by Rousset (Spinoza 1992, 393), De Dijn (1987), Bartuschat (Spinoza 1993, 89), and Garrett (1986).

3. Spinoza 1993, 120.

4. See Bartuschat's introduction to Spinoza 1993, xxiv–xxviii.

5. De Dijn 1987, 425.

6. Spinoza 1986, 446.

7. I have slightly modified Curley's translation here.

8. The same was true for the relationship between the first and second part: in the first part we discovered that it is important to "begin as soon as possible from the first elements, i.e., from the source and origin of Nature" (§ 75), and that we should get to know "how to define problems precisely, before striving for knowledge of them" (§ 80).

9. See Curley's comment in Spinoza 1985, 41n. 67.

10. See (among many) Koyré's comments in Spinoza 1990, 112–13; and Rousset's in Spinoza 1992, 393, both giving further references.

11. Cf. Thomas Aquinas 1957 (chap. 7).

12. Gueroult 1968, 245–48; De Dijn 1974a, 1983.

13. For example, Bartuschat in Spinoza 1993, 120–21.
14. Letter 64; *TTP,* Spinoza 1989, 145.
15. See Curley's comment in Spinoza 1985, 42n. 68.
16. This argues against Bartuschat's judgments in Spinoza 1993, xix, 121.
17. *TTP,* Spinoza 1989, 141, 145.
18. Ibid., 142.
19. G 4:276.
20. Spinoza 1985, 173ff.
21. Zweerman 1974.
22. Curley points this out in a comment in Spinoza 1985, 196.
23. See Bennett 1984, 20–25; and Curley's "nomological" interpretation of Spinoza in Curley 1969.
24. For example, Curley (Spinoza 1985, 42n. 70). Rousset (Spinoza 1992, 406), Bartuschat (Spinoza 1993, xix, 121), De Dijn (1986a, 59n. 24), and Marion (1972) hold the opposite opinion.
25. Bartuschat 1992a, 406.
26. *PPC* I, *Prolegomenon* (G 1:142).
27. See Bartuschat's comment in Spinoza 1993, 121.
28. See also *TEI* § 40 for another paradox.
29. See Curley's and Rousset's surveys in Spinoza 1985, 5; and Spinoza 1992, 427, respectively. In line with my own hypothesis, see Boss 1986; and Rousset's comments in Spinoza 1992, 47–51.
30. G 2:339. Curley's emendation—following Gebhardt's—is not really necessary.
31. See also *Ethics* I, P. 15, Sch., which discusses the distinction between quantity qua substance and quantity as affected in some or other way.
32. This is Hobbes's definition.
33. See also letter 12 and Gueroult's penetrating commentary on this letter in Gueroult 1968, appendix 9.
34. See *Ethics* II, Def. 5; II, P. 45, Sch.; V, P. 23; V, P. 29, Sch.; and Donagan 1988, 112.
35. *Ethics* II, P. 44, Cor. 2. On the idea of "common notions," see chapter 10, section 2.
36. See Curley's comment on the "Notice to the Reader," Spinoza 1985, 6.
37. Spinoza 1992, 423.
38. Gueroult 1968, 38, 67.
39. I use "amended" in Hobbes's sense; see De Dijn 1973, 716.
40. This argues against Walker 1985, 18 (and others).
41. Zweerman 1993, 194n. 41. This upward movement is what I understand by analysis; see De Dijn 1986a, 62–63.
42. I use "downward" to characterize a synthetic movement; see De Dijn 1986a, 62–63.
43. Zweerman 1974, 178–79; Boss 1986; De Dijn 1986b, 20–21.

Wisdom

On God (*Ethics* I)

My purpose here is not and cannot be to give a full, detailed interpretation of Spinoza's *Ethics* but to discuss the major steps by
which Spinoza implements the project of the *Philosophia* as announced in his *Treatise* (or *Logica*). At the same time, I will develop those points or topics touched upon in the *Treatise* but
awaiting further clarification in the *Philosophia*. As we have
seen, the *Ethics* is the culmination and completion of the logical
project, both in the sense that it is itself a methodical development of ideas leading to the ultimate aim indicated at the beginning of the *Treatise,* and in the sense that it realizes this aim in
knowledge.

God's Nature and Properties (*Ethics* I, P. 1–15)

As mentioned in the last chapter, the definitions and axioms of
Ethics I serve as a basis to elucidate one "real" definition (*Ethics*
I, Def. 6) and to draw conclusions from it that will be important
for the rest of our investigation. The proof that the definition of
God is a *real* definition, or the definition of a real thing, is given in
Ethics I, P. 11. This proof—or, more precisely, the definition used
in it—is prepared in the previous propositions in two phases. The
first phase is *Ethics* I, P. 1–8, where the notion of substance is
clarified through an examination of the sort of thing substance is
and through a deduction of its properties. In *Ethics* I, P. 9–10, the
application of the notion of substance to God is prepared.

In these propositions, Spinoza operates with notions he does
not define, such as thing, essence-existence, nature ("rerum natura," *Ethics* I, P. 5), nature-properties. All these terms are taken

from the *philosophia novantiqua* and are ultimately of Aristotelian origin. The way Spinoza operates with these terms and combines them leads to extraordinary results. For example, although he uses the term in a broad sense as encompassing everything, nature will turn out to be identical to, or to consist of only one substantial thing, God (*Deus sive Natura*).

Spinoza's conception of reality or of real things contains a number of basic, more or less Aristotelian intuitions that, combined with typical Spinozistic insights, are transformed into a revolutionary worldview. These intuitions are: first, that nothing can be real unless it is a "so and so"—that is, unless it has a certain particular nature or essence; second, that the degree of reality depends on the "richness" of the nature of the thing;[1] third, that a real thing is prototypically a substance or something that is "in itself" and that is the basis of "affections" that are "in another" (Spinoza calls these "modes"); and, fourth, that a thing cannot be real ("werk-elijk" in Dutch) unless it is working, unless it is a power actively producing "effects." Combined with these are important Spinozistic insights: first, that there are only *two sorts* of things "in Nature"—things that are "in themselves" and things that are "in another" (*Ethics* I, Ax. 1), such as substance(s) and modes; second, that the essence of a substance is constituted by one or more attributes (a term borrowed from Descartes and indicating a strictly essential quality or perfection constituting the essence of a substance) (*Ethics* I, Def. 4); third, that the effects of real things follow with *necessity* from their causes (*Ethics* I, Ax. 3); fourth, that substances with different attributes have nothing in common with each other (*Ethics* I, P. 2) and can therefore have no causal influence on each other (*Ethics* I, P. 3, 6); and fifth, that substances cannot produce other substances but only modes, and that these modes are necessarily produced immanently "in" their substances (this can be gathered from a combination of propositions: see *Ethics* I, P. 6, 16).

Before Spinoza can demonstrate the reality of his definition or conception of God, he clarifies the fundamental concepts that he uses in this definition and proof in a number of preparatory propositions. Indeed, we must first be absolutely clear about the relationship between substance, attribute, and mode. One of the most problematic points in this respect is the relationship between substance and attribute. "Attribute" is defined as "what the intellect perceives of a substance, as constituting its essence" (*Ethics* I, Def. 4). Some have taken this definition to imply that an attribute is not a constitutive principle or aspect of reality but only an intellectual perspective on substance through which substance is apprehended in a certain way; the only things there are are substance(s) and modes. This view, which is called the "subjectivist" interpretation of attribute, denies its ontological status.[2] The subjectivist interpretation clearly is mistaken.[3] The definition says that the intellect perceives (apprehends) an attribute as that which *constitutes* the *essence* of a thing; so it is a real constitutive principle of a thing. To say that "in Nature" there are only substance(s) and modes is not to deny that there are real constituting principles or aspects of things. Furthermore, the intellect is, for Spinoza, that which perceives things as they *really* are (*Ethics* I, P. 30, Dem.); so if it perceives an attribute as constituting the real essence of a thing, then the attribute *does* constitute the essence, as the "objectivist" interpretation holds.[4] The special reference to intellect in the definition of attribute is understandable because "that which constitutes the essence" is precisely the ontological principle of the intelligibility of the thing, that which exhibits or manifests the thing.[5] Also in other definitions (*Ethics* I, Def. 1, 3, 5) one finds an implicit reference to the intellect: the ontological order and constitution of things is, according to Spinoza, always "mirrored" perfectly on the epistemological level (the level of pure intellectual understanding). For example, what is in itself could not be such unless it were comprehensible through itself (*Ethics* I, Def. 3). Of course, being comprehensible is for an intellect; but this does not exclude that the thing is really comprehensible as it is in itself. Spinoza conceives the world as thoroughly intelligible by the intellect.

Far from being only a way of apprehending substance, an attribute—as constituting the essence of substance—determines the *sort* of activity that substance is capable of: it determines the sort of effects or modifications that follow from substance. (This is implied in many propositions, both in *Ethics* I and II; for example, I, P. 16, 21, 22.) Spinoza repeatedly uses expressions such as "whatever follows from some attribute of substance [or God]." This is consistent with his identification of essence and power ("essentia" and "potentia," *Ethics* I, P. 34): if the attribute constitutes the essence of a thing, it inevitably determines the causal activity of the thing as being the sort of causality it is.

Since an attribute really constitutes the essence of a substance, the same attribute cannot really constitute the essences of different substances; numerical difference between substances means real difference in nature or essence (*Ethics* I, P. 5). On the other hand, Spinoza does not accept that "really distinct" attributes are the sign of really distinct substances (*Ethics* I, P. 10, Sch.).[6] Nothing excludes the possibility of a substance with more than one attribute; on the contrary "[t]he more reality or being a thing [a substance] has, the more attributes belong to it" (*Ethics* I, P. 9). Here again, Spinoza appeals to a kind of Aristotelian intuition about reality: nothing can be real, unless it is a "so-and-so" (unless it has a quality or perfection); and the more real a thing is, the more it must have *essential* qualities or perfections, which also are the basis of its diversified activity (*potentia*, or power). Essential qualities (or perfections) of a substance are its attributes, each of which expresses an eternal and infinite essence (see *Ethics* I, Def. 6). Each attribute is "infinite in its own kind" and therefore different from all other attributes infinite in their own kind (*Ethics* I, Def. 6, Expl.). Each attribute is said to "express" an eternal and infinite essence of substance ("to express" means here both "to constitute" and "to manifest" to an intellect).[7]

The "infinitude" of an attribute should not be confused with the notion of the infinitely many or of that which has no boundaries (which Descartes calls indefiniteness).[8] When an attribute is called "infinite," it means that it is a certain nature *in its perfection,* lacking nothing as to the kind of "whatness" it is. The production of effects by a substance is "through" the attribute(s) it has: it produces infinitely many finite modifications according to the kind of each attribute that it has (*Ethics* I, P. 16). Therefore, modes of a substance are always modes "of a certain kind," belonging to or expressing certain attributes of substance. Unlike attributes that are infinite in their own kind, modes (or their essences) are "finite in their own kind" (*Ethics* I, Def. 2). This "kind" under or within which modes are finite modifications or affections of substance is, of course, the attribute of substance to which they belong. As we learned from the *Treatise,* attributes are somehow *genera* of the essence of finite things—these *genera* are themselves really constitutive of the essence of a substance; they are a kind of *singularium* (§ 101).

Since attributes are "essential qualities," each infinite in its own kind, they express or constitute certain natures *completely.* Things cannot "have something in common" unless they share the same nature or quality.[9] Since attributes are infinite qualities, expressing or constituting infinite natures or essences, they are necessarily *diversa* (different infinities). Causal influence presupposes "commonality"; therefore, things with different attributes—or depending on different attributes—cannot causally influence each other. This is why substances with different attributes cannot causally influence each other (*Ethics* I, P. 6). This also explains why a thing (or mode) that is finite in its own kind "can be limited [only] by another of the same nature" (*Ethics* I, Def. 2).

Since different attributes do not necessarily constitute the essences of different substances—since, on the contrary, the more real a substance is, the more it has attributes—"it is far from absurd to attribute many attributes to the one substance," whereby each attribute expresses "necessity, or eternity, and infinity" (*Ethics* I, P. 10, Sch.). Consequently, the notion of an *absolutely* infinite being "must be defined (as we taught in D 6) as a being that consists in infinite attributes, each of which expresses *a certain* eternal and infinite essence" (*Ethics* I, P. 10, Sch.; emphasis added). If diversity of infinite qualities, natures, or perfections does not indicate real diversity of substances, how can we know whether there is a diversity of substances in nature? Spinoza answers, "read the following propositions, which show that in Nature there exists only one substance, and that it is absolutely infinite. So that sign [of a diversity of substances] would be sought in vain" (*Ethics* I, P. 10, Sch.). In other words, the combination of the idea of an *absolutely* infinite being and the idea of substance leads to the definition of God. As substance, God necessarily exists. Since he possesses all possible attributes constituting essence, there can be no other substance besides him. Consequently, the divine substance is all there is in nature (as far as substance is concerned); God is nature ("Deus sive Natura," *Ethics* I, P. 29, Sch.).

Spinoza gives several proofs of God's necessary existence (*Ethics* I, P. 11). The most remarkable one is the last (*Ethics* I, P. 11, Sch.),[10] whose fundamental premise is that "the more reality belongs to the nature of a thing, the more powers it has, of itself, to exist." If this is true, then a being with infinite attributes has "an absolutely infinite power of existing. For that reason, he exists absolutely." Reality is equated here with perfection, and perfection "does not take away the existence of a thing, but on the contrary asserts it." Perfection, or reality, is constituted by "infinite natures" or attributes, which are considered here in an almost Leibnizian way as "demanding existence." Ultimately, God's necessary existence depends on his being *causa sui,* on his constituting himself in and through the perfections he unites in himself. As the attributes are essential constituents of God's nature, they are the grounds for his existence; likewise, they are the basis of his power and causal efficiency.

At this stage of *Ethics* I, we have obtained the required insight into the nature of the divine substance, and we are now in a position to prove not only the reality of this definition through the proof of God's necessary existence (*Ethics* I, P. 11) but also many other properties of God: his indivisibility (*Ethics* I, P. 12–13), his uniqueness (*Ethics* I, P. 14), the immanence of everything in him (*Ethics* I, P. 15), and all sorts of properties belonging to his being cause of himself and of everything else ("causa sui" and "causa omnium rerum," *Ethics* I, P. 16–20).

The change from an investigation of reality or of real things in nature (ontology) to an investigation of God (theological metaphysics) depends on the presence of an idea in our minds of God as "a being absolutely infinite" (*Ethics* I, Def. 6). Using the right "innate tools"—such as the notions of substance, attribute, and mode—we can come to a perfect, *adequate* idea of God's intrinsic nature as constituted by an infinity of attributes belonging to the unique substance. This substance is identical with nature itself. Through its infinite attributes as "channels," the divine substance is the immanent cause of everything else—that is, of an infinite infinity of modes; according to each of the infinite attributes, God produces an infinity of modes of a certain kind (*Ethics* I, P. 15–16). The presence of the idea of God as an *absolutely* infinite being is a *conditio sine qua non* for this concept of a unified nature. Spinoza does not feel compelled to argue for the presence of this idea in us: does not *everybody* accept this notion of God? In *Ethics* II, P. 45–47, he will demonstrate how this notion is of necessity present in every human mind.

Many commentators find that the definition of God presents a serious problem: how can the one essence of the divine substance be constituted by *different* attributes, each expressing an infinite and eternal essence?[11] To put the problem more sharply, how can an attribute, which by definition expresses a *certain* infinite and eternal essence ("unumquodque [attributum] aeternam, et infinitam certam essentiam exprimit," *Ethics* I, Def. 4; I, P. 10, Sch.), at the same time express the reality or being of the one divine substance ("unumquodque [attributum] realitatem, sive esse substantiae exprimit," *Ethics* I, P. 10, Sch.)? This seems particularly problematic, since, even as attributes constituting the essence of the same substance, they "must be conceived through themselves" (*Ethics* I, P. 10)—they remain, so to speak, "incommensurable." However difficult it may be to accept Spinoza's peculiar sort of monism, it is clear that it is the consequence of these basic assumptions: that substantial reality (and therefore power) can be a matter of degree, depending on the amount of whatness, qualities, or perfections; that diversity of attributes is no sign of diversity of things or substances; and that there is an absolutely infinite being. The consideration of an attribute on its own does not tell us whether it is an attribute constituting a rich or a poor substance; but once we know it is the attribute of an absolutely infinite being that works itself out through it, we know that its modes are necessarily matched by modes produced through other attributes (*Ethics* II, P. 6 and Cor.). Alan Donagan formulates Spinoza's monistic conception of the relation of God and his attributes in this way: "God or nature . . . is therefore a substance . . . such that, for every attribute that constitutes its essence, it is a law of nature that the essence it constitutes is also constituted by every other attribute that constitutes the essence of any substance."[12] In this connection, Thomas C. Mark talks about a sort of ontological synonymy between the attributes. To elucidate the relation of expression of the same substance in different attributes, he uses the analogy of the same musical composition transposed into different keys. "It is meaningless to ask whether the transpositions do or do not 'correspond to' the music. A transposition does not represent the music to us, it just *gives* us the music."[13]

We may ask ourselves how the "reality or being" of the same thing or substance can be expressed through radically different attributes without this threatening the unity of nature. The answer must be that if the unity of nature is clearly established in the idea of an absolutely infinite being, this question is superfluous. This shows how important it is to proceed in one's thinking in the right order—that is, to think the parts (the constitutive elements or attributes) not in separation from the whole (the divine essence). If the question is about how this unity shows itself, the answer must be that it shows itself in the fact that the same power—the same causal order and connection of things—shows itself in the different worlds of modes produced through each attribute. This is the basis of the so-called parallelism between thought and extension present in *Ethics* II. The power of the one substance displaying itself as immanent causation is a kind of "trans-attribute" relation;[14] this relation can only be understood —as to the kind of causation involved—by reference to the attribute through which it operates.

| God's Power (*Ethics* I, P. 16–29)

In the propositions dealing with the nature and properties of God, it is implied that God produces things or modes (*Ethics* I, P. 14, Cor. 2; P. 15). The question for Spinoza is not so much whether God produces but *what* he produces. Spinoza often has been accused of assuming without ground that God produces—that is, that the derivation of a creation of concrete things is not properly established. However, this objection runs counter to one of Spinoza's most basic insights: the concept of a real thing or of reality as unproductive would not be a conception of reality; the idea of a substance not producing modes would be the conception of a nonentity. On the contrary, a substance possessing an infinity of attributes must necessarily produce "infinitely many things in infinitely many modes [infinita infinitis modis]; (i.e., everything that can fall under an infinite intellect)" (*Ethics* I, P. 16). Spinoza compares this necessity to the necessity with which properties follow from the definition of a thing: "the more properties, the more the definition of the thing expresses reality" (*Ethics* I, P. 16, Dem.). "Infinita infinitis modis" can be read as "infinitely many things in infinitely many modes" or as "infinitely many things [modes] in infinitely many ways"—that is, according to the infinitely many attributes, which comes to the same thing. The reference to the intellect is not accidental: it stresses again the full *intelligibility* of Spinoza's world, as well as the *necessity* of the production or creation of the infinitely many "worlds" of modes that "mirrors" the "logical" (conceptual) necessity of intellectual thinking (*Ethics* I, P. 16, Dem.).

As God's essence is characterized by properties, so also is his power or productivity. God is characterized as an efficient cause (*Ethics* I, P. 16, Cor. 1); a cause through himself ("per se") and not accidental ("per accidens," *Ethics* I, P. 16, Cor. 2); an absolutely first cause ("absolute causa prima," *Ethics* I, P. 16, Cor. 3); a free cause (*Ethics* I, P. 17, Cor. 2); an immanent and not a transient cause (*Ethics* I, P. 18); and an immutable cause (*Ethics* I, P. 20, Cor. 2).

We know from *Ethics* I, P. 16, that God as cause necessarily produces an infinity of modes according to each attribute. The absolutely infinite cause produces an infinity of infinite modes, or an infinity of worlds consisting of infinitely many modifications. The absolute richness of the essence of the cause, which is constituted by an infinity of attributes or powerful expressions, is matched by an infinity of worlds consisting of infinitely many modes. God as cause, as *Natura Naturans* (naturing nature), is matched by the totality of his effects, or *Natura Naturata* (natured nature) (*Ethics* I, P. 29, Sch.). We already know the constitution of the *Natura Naturans:* it is the infinity of attributes through which all production must operate. Spinoza also discusses in detail the constitution of the *Natura Naturata* (*Ethics* I, P. 21–29).

The things or modes produced immediately by God must themselves be infinite and not finite: cause and effect must match each other; an infinite cause cannot be determined to produce one finite effect rather than another (*Ethics* I, P. 21 and Dem.). Consequently, God immediately produces infinite modes (termed, in the Spinoza literature, infinite immediate modes), one according to every attribute. For example, the infinite immediate mode of the attribute *Cogitatio* is the *Idea Dei*, or infinite intellect of God (*Ethics* I, P. 21, Dem.; I, P. 32, Cor. 2; II, P. 3, P. 4 and Dem.; V, P. 40, Sch.). The infinite immediate mode of the attribute *Extensio* is motion and rest, in which are inscribed the laws that extended nature always observes (*Ethics* I, P. 33, Sch.; II, P. 13, lemma 2; letter 64 to Schuller; *TTP*, 7 [G 3:102]). These infinite immediate modes contain the laws governing the concrete, causal relations between all modes of a certain kind (*TEI* § 101). The infinite immediate modes are not only infinite, they "have always had to exist," they cannot have a finite, determinate duration or existence (*Ethics* I, P. 21 and Dem.); they are present everywhere and their influence is everywhere (*TEI* § 101). From these infinite immediate modes follow necessarily infinite mediate modes, which are mediate because they are produced in God insofar as he already is modified by the infinite immediate mode; they also exist necessarily as infinite wholes (*Ethics* I, P. 22). Spinoza gives only one example, the "facies totius Universi" (letter 64),[15] which is nature, considered as a whole, as "one Individual, whose parts [all bodies] vary in infinite ways, without any change of the whole Individual" (*Ethics* II, P. 13, lemma 7, Sch.).

There is debate as to whether the "facies totius Universi" is the totality of all these individuals in all attributes or only the individual totality of all bodies.[16] In any case, it is clear that there must be an infinite mediate mode according to each attribute (*Ethics* I, P. 22). Another point of disagreement is over why there are two infinite modes, and not one or even an infinity of them. The answer could be that the infinite immediate mode is the unity of all "formal essences" of things modifying a certain attribute—a whole at the same time "embodying" the laws governing the whole of existing things, as coming into, and disappearing out of, existence, this last whole being the infinite mediate mode (this interpretation can be gathered from several statements taken together; see *Ethics* II, P. 8, Cor.; II, P. 13, lemma 2; V, P. 40, Sch.; *TEI* § 101; letter 64). Talk about laws governing real things may sound strange. Yet insofar as the infinite immediate mode effectively determines the behavior of all finite modes of a certain kind, the "laws inscribed in them" can be said to really operate on these finite modes (*TEI* § 101; *TTP* 7 [G 3:102]).

Finite modes are, of course, not infinite; nor do they have the kind of existence of the infinite modes. Their existence is not implied in their essence (*Ethics* I, P. 24). They are the effects of God, not only as to their existence but also as to their essence (*Ethics* I, P. 25). They are necessarily produced by God, not immediately but through the mediation of his infinite modes. This means that God produces the finite modes in his production of the infinite modes as wholes, of which the finite modes are parts.

God is the first, efficient, immanent cause of everything (*Ethics* I, P. 16, Cor. 1; Cor. 3; P. 18). As an efficient cause, he is also the proximate cause of everything (in opposition to a remote cause, "which is not conjoined in any way with its effect"; *Ethics* I, P. 28, Sch.). God is the *absolutely* proximate cause, and not the proximate cause only in his own kind, of things *immediately* produced by him—that is, of the infinite modes. Finite things do not follow "from his absolute nature," so God is not their absolutely proximate cause; God is their proximate cause only in his own kind (as *first* cause), because finite things do not follow from his absolute nature—from his attributes, as such—but only from his nature as already determined by his infinite modes. So the production of finite things by God as first cause is mediated by other factors. As we have seen, the absolutely proximate cause of the *essence* of a finite thing is a certain modification of God's attributes that is also a certain part of the infinite immediate mode. The absolutely proximate cause of things as to their *existence* is other existing things belonging to the same attribute in the infinite mediate mode.

The essences of things are eternal parts of the infinite immediate mode (*Ethics* II, P. 8, Cor.; V, P. 40, Sch.). Finite essences of things cannot, as essences, be produced by other finite things, of the same or of a different kind. For example, the essence of a man is not produced by other men (*Ethics* I, P. 17, Sch.). The concrete existence and operation of a finite thing or mode are determined by the existence and operation of other finite modes in an endless chain of causation (*Ethics* I, P. 28). This does not mean, however, that a finite mode is not itself an *active* principle in this chain: once it actually exists, each finite mode is a *conatus*, a finite determination of God's essence or power under a certain attribute (*Ethics* III, P. 4–8, based on I, P. 25, Cor.; I, P. 36). The existence and operation of a thing in reality ultimately is completely determined by God (*Ethics* I, P. 26, 27); it is conditioned by an infinite chain of causes (*Ethics* I, P. 28), and, of course, by its own essence, which also completely depends on God (*Ethics* I, P. 25). Spinoza seems to advocate determinism, which holds "that every occurrence is causally determined by antecedent conditions together with the laws of nature":[17] "In nature there is nothing contingent, but all things have been determined from the necessity of the divine nature to exist and produce an effect in a certain way" (*Ethics* I, P. 29). Spinoza also seems to accept necessitarianism, which is the doctrine "that things could not have been in any respect different than they are, or that the actual world is the only possible one":[18] "Things could have been produced by God in no other way, and in no other order than they have been produced" (*Ethics* I, P. 33).

In view of this one can say that although the essence of finite things does not of itself involve existence, yet, as an expression of God's powerful nature, it somehow does involve existence. This existence will necessarily come about when the chain of finite causes is such that the essence gets instantiated. The thing then becomes a *conatus*, an *actual* essence, which out of itself strives to persevere *indefinitely* in its existence (*Ethics* III, P. 4–8). This striving in the midst of other striving things leads necessarily to all sorts of effects (*Ethics* I, P. 36), some of which can be explained on the basis of the thing's essence and power alone (actions) and some of which can be explained only by the combination of the powers of things working on each other (passions) (see *Ethics* III, P. 3; IV, P. 2–4). What is remarkable is that a thing cannot be said to be active except as operating in the actual chain of causes; yet real (adequate) activity requires the sort of operation that is determined by the thing's essence and power alone. (See *Ethics* III, Def. 2: "I say that we act when something happens, in us or outside us, of which we are the adequate cause, i.e. [by D. 1], when something in us or outside us follows from our nature, which can be clearly and distinctly understood through it alone. On the other hand, I say that we are acted on when something happens in us, or something follows from our nature, of which we are only a partial cause.")

Since everything that we are and do we are and do on the basis of God's power, to say that something happens through man alone is to say that God acts "insofar as he is explained through the nature of [man alone], *or* insofar as he constitutes the essence [of man]" (*Ethics* II, P. 11, Cor.). Real activity is the development of an activity, in the midst of other things, that is strictly self-sufficient: *Deus quatenus modificatus* does not need anything besides the thing to do what he does.

Anti-anthropomorphism (*Ethics* I, P. 30–end)

In the last section of *Ethics* I, Spinoza brings together the insights concerning God's essence and properties and those concerning his power: "God's power is his essence itself" (*Ethics* I, P. 34). At the same time, he demonstrates the revolutionary nature of this concept of God by opposing it to the ordinary philosophical and theological concept of a personal God, free creator of a macrocosm in which man, the microcosm, occupies an exceptional position as a being created in God's image—that is, as having a free will. This section is a thorough criticism of the concept of God in the *philosophia novantiqua* (both in its more Scholastic and in its more Cartesian versions). Here we also encounter the astounding consequences with respect to man's spontaneous anthropocentrism, which follow inexorably if we take seriously the definitions at the beginning of the *Ethics* and develop their implications (I, App.).

God is nature ("Deus sive Natura," *Ethics* IV, Pref.): everything in or of nature is God, or in God; all infinite natures or powers are of God, and all things in nature are his modes. God is not nature's creator, God is not outside nature; he is one with nature. God also is not to be identified with something in nature. God is not, as both Scholastics and Cartesians think, infinite intellect and will. The intellect—whether finite or infinite—is, for Spinoza, an intellect in act (*in actu*); it is not a faculty, a pure potentiality; it is, as we have seen in the *Treatise,* the very activity of forming objective essences. It is by nature the power to think reality— God's attributes and God's affections, and nothing else (*Ethics* I, P. 30; P. 31, Sch.). The intellect is not separate from the will (*Ethics* I, P. 31; and especially II, P. 49). Neither intellect nor will constitute God's essence; they belong to the *Natura Naturata*, not to the *Natura Naturans* (*Ethics* I, P. 17, Sch.;[19] I, P. 31). They are infinite or finite *modes* of a certain "attribute of God, which expresses the eternal and infinite essence of thought [*Cogitatio*]"; they cannot be, or be conceived, without this attribute (*Ethics* I, P. 31, Dem.).

As modes, intellect and will are completely determined, both as to their existence and as to their operation, by God's nature, in the same way as motion and rest and all bodily modes are determined by God's *Extensio* (*Ethics* I, P. 32, Cor. 2). Consequently, the will is not free; and God certainly does not operate by a free will (*Ethics* I, P. 32 and Cor. 1) but rather as freely necessitated by his own nature (*Ethics* I, Def. 7).

The infinite intellect and will do not belong to God's essence; they are "creatures" of God, completely determined by him (the *Short Treatise* calls the infinite intellect the "Son of God"[20]). The infinite will not only does not belong to God's essence; it is not even a free cause but a determined effect. This forms a denial of the commonly accepted concept of God (*Ethics* I, P. 33, Sch. 2; I, App.; II, P. 3, Sch.), but it is not a denial of the *power* of the infinite intellect and will. The infinite intellect is the concrete activity that God—possessing the nature-power of *Cogitatio*—produces "in order" to think as objective essences whatever is "in nature"— that is, God and all his affections (*Ethics* I, P. 30, Dem.). Since God is unique, his idea (formed by the infinite intellect) is unique; and everything that follows from God, in reality, follows "objectively" from this *Idea Dei* (*Ethics* II, P. 4; P. 7, Cor.).

Spinoza's God is not a personal God, if being personal presupposes at least being intellect and will. To God's essence (*Na-tura Naturans*) belongs only the attribute *Cogitatio,* the ontological ground for all concrete activity of forming objective essences (in the first place, the objective essence of God himself, or the *Idea Dei*). Some have claimed that God as *Cogitatio* is self-conscious and therefore personal after all.[21] They conclude this on the basis of *Ethics* V, P. 35: "God loves himself with an infinite intellectual love." They forget that this love of God depends on his having, as *Cogitatio,* first the idea of God (*Ethics* V, P. 35, Dem.), so this love of God for himself belongs—like God's idea of himself, which it presupposes (*Ethics* II, Ax. 3)—to the *Natura Naturata* (see also *Ethics* I, P. 31, where it is said that the other modes of thinking "such as desire, love, etc., must be referred to *Natura Naturata,* not to *Natura Naturans*"). Furthermore, man's intellectual love of God is part of God's infinite love for himself. This intellectual love is therefore a whole, identical with the infinite intellect, or infinite immediate mode (*Ethics* V, P. 36, Dem.).

Infinite modes (as well as finite modes) depend completely on God or his attributes, without which they "can neither be nor be conceived" (*Ethics* I, P. 31, Dem.; I, App.). Yet, although "nothing can either be or be conceived without God," and although "God is the only cause of all things, both of their essence and of their existence," "nevertheless, God does not pertain [or belong; *pertinere*] to their essence" (*Ethics* II, P. 10, Sch. 2). "I say that to the essence of anything belongs that which, being given, the thing is necessarily posited and which, being taken away, the thing is necessarily taken away; or that without which the thing can neither be nor be conceived, and which can neither be nor be conceived without the thing" (*Ethics* II, Def. 2). Spinoza repeatedly claims that a mode (whether infinite or finite) cannot be or be conceived without God. Many philosophers think that since this is so, either God belongs to the nature of created things, or created things can be or be conceived without God.[22] They have a wrong conception of "what pertains to the essence of a thing"; this implies also "what can neither be nor be conceived without the thing," which excludes God (*Ethics* II, P. 10, Sch. 2). Some might object that Spinoza seems to forget here a fundamental proposition of *Ethics* I, which says that infinitely many things follow *necessarily* from God in infinitely many ways (*Ethics* I, P. 16). If they follow necessarily, does this not mean that God cannot be or be conceived without his modes; and does this not imply that God "belongs" to the essence of his modes? How can Spinoza escape this devastating consequence? Unlike his opponents, he "observe[s] the [proper] order of Philosophizing. For they believed that the divine nature, which they should have contemplated before all else (because it is prior both in knowledge and in nature) is last in the order of knowledge, and that the things that are called objects of the senses are prior to all. That is why, when they contemplated natural things, they thought of nothing less than they did of the divine nature; and when afterwards they directed their minds to contemplating the divine nature, they could think of nothing less than of their first fictions, on which they had built the knowledge of natural things, because these could not assist knowledge of the divine nature. So it is no wonder that they have generally contradicted themselves" (*Ethics* II, P. 10, Sch. 2). In other words, to interpret the necessary dependence of modes on substance as implying that substance "cannot be or be conceived" without the modes is to subvert the order of true thinking and therefore of reality; it is to disregard the absolute difference between substance and mode, to put modes on the same level as substance.

From this one has to conclude that although God is the *immanent* cause of everything (*Ethics* I, P. 18) and produces everything in himself (*Ethics* I, P. 15), this does not mean that one can neglect the difference between cause and effect (*Ethics* I, P. 17, Sch.), between *Natura Naturans* and *Natura Naturata* (*Ethics* I, P. 29, Sch.). Spinoza is not a pantheist; he is a panentheist[23] whose panentheism implies that God and his modes differ "entirely" (*toto coelo*), insofar as the effect or "what is caused differs from its cause precisely in what it has from the cause" (*Ethics* I, P. 17, Sch.). Although God is not "outside" nature, although God is not a transient or remote cause, although he necessarily expresses himself in an infinite infinity of things, yet he is not to be identified with his effects, not even with the *whole* of his effects (the universe). As *Natura Naturans,* he is fundamentally different from the universe (*Natura Naturata*); he is its *substance,*[24] and through his infinite natures or attributes he is the absolute ground of *what* things are and of the particular kind of power or activity they display. It is wrong to say that God only exists and operates in his modes; rather, his modes are nothing except through and in God. Therefore, I cannot agree with Donagan when he writes, "The infinite modes of the absolutely infinite substance are . . . not modes in the sense of things immanently caused by another thing. Rather they and the absolutely infinite substance are one and the same thing, of which a series of different concepts can be formed, those later in the series being 'conceived through' those earlier in it."[25]

If the intellect perceives the infinite modes as modes, they really are "in another," even though they are, as immediate effects, *infinite* modes. God does not transcend the world by being an inscrutable intellect and will, who as a free, transient cause creates things outside and independent of him. He transcends the world and things by being their *substance,* the ultimate ground of their being and their immanent cause. In order to understand Spinoza, we must take on the full seriousness of the claim that God stands to things as a substance to its affections or modifications—a relation that is totally unlike that between two substances or between substance and attribute. Furthermore, this relation of substance to modes is totally unlike the relation between a free, willing intellect and its supposed creation out of nothing (*creatio ex nihilo*) (*Ethics* I, P. 17, Sch.).

From the divine substance as *Natura Naturans* follows necessarily an infinite amount of modes according to each attribute of substance (the totality of *Natura Naturata*). The problem with this derivation is not that Spinoza cannot derive the world from God—in view of his conception of reality as spontaneous activity, the opposite, a nonproductive God, is unthinkable. The real problem is that the idea of an infinity of things does not lead to the consideration of one thing rather than another (*Ethics* II, Pref.). Therefore, in order to begin to think about the human mind and intellect—as is required in view of our ultimate aim—specific premises are necessary, to be delivered only by a purified self-experience (*Ethics* II, Ax. 2, 4).

Spinozistic philosophy originates in an ethical perspective, but the solution of the ethical problematic seems to require the adoption of an objective standpoint vis-à-vis oneself and one's place in nature (a view *sub specie aeternitatis*[26]). It is clear that the model of such a view was, for Spinoza, the newly developing

natural science, which Descartes had tried to underpin with a
foundational metaphysics. The new natural science revealed a
world totally different from that of our ordinary anthropocentric
categories (sweet and sour, light and heavy, near and far—but
also beautiful and ugly, harmonious and chaotic, good and evil[27]),
just as a distanced reflection discloses an unexpected view of our
ordinary life as leading inexorably from illusion to disillusion and
despair. Was it not natural to expect that somehow through this
scientific view one would reach an answer to one's ethical problems? However, according to Spinoza, obtaining this answer requires the development of the scientific view into a *metaphysical*
picture, which provides insights into the relationship between
man and the universe, and in which the ethical problem can be
formulated completely anew, taking into account a naturalistic
view not only of man's body but also of the human mind and of
social phenomena (such as the state).

In physics, the fundamental categories are the "common notions" (such as extension, figure, motion, and rest) and the general
laws that they imply concerning the nature and the interrelations
of modal configurations. At most, one obtains here insight into the
space-time continuum of all the parts or configurations and into
the law of the conservation of energy.[28] In metaphysics, however,
the whole is identified as an infinite, sempiternal whole, which is
but an infinite mode of the divine substance. The whole, studied
in physics by examining its parts (configurations of particles in
motion or rest vis-à-vis each other), is interpreted in metaphysics
as having not only a "surface" dimension (the whole constituted
by the parts) but also a dimension of "depth," the infinite substance that underpins each part as well as the whole. As *Natura
Naturata,* the whole can thus be seen to depend radically on substance, or *Natura Naturans,* God being at the same time immanent cause and substance "transcending" all its modes, without
being outside them. In this respect, it is not surprising that
Spinoza feels obliged to rethink the relation between extension
and motion (and rest) in line with his concept of *Extensio* as a divine attribute (see letter 83, of 1676, to Tschirnhaus). Without
this transformation of the new science into a metaphysics, the
"objective point of view" could not become relevant for the ethical
problematic.

If we take all this into account, it is not surprising that the
metaphysical doctrine of *Ethics* I so "unscientifically" results in a
vigorous attack on traditional and Cartesian-based anthropocentric views. This attack comes immediately after *Ethics* I, in the

appendix, one of Spinoza's strongest texts (it was already prepared in *Ethics* I, P. 30, and following). The affirmation of *Deus sive Natura* means the denial of a free, personal creator. That God is constituted by an infinity of attributes (all equally perfect expressions of God's essence) forms a denial in principle of the superiority of mind over body and of the exceptional place of mind in the order of things. The affirmation of determinism, and of the necessity of the actual world, as well as of the unity of intellect and will, results in the negation of our cherished conception of human freedom. The equation of reality and perfection (*Ethics* II, Def. 6) nullifies all ordinary ethical and religious views concerning good and evil, perfection and imperfection. Affirmation of the exclusive substantiality of God-nature, and of the modality of all other things, invalidates the spontaneous view of the self as a free agent, as a creative self-consciousness capable, in principle, of being transparent to itself and in full command of itself—a view completely in accordance with the deep vanity of all anthropocentric conceptions.

According to Spinoza, Descartes's metaphysics was far from adequate, not only because it did not succeed in providing a valid foundation for the new science but especially because it did not free itself from the basic assumptions of the traditional view of man and world (on the contrary, it tried to save that view). Spinoza wanted to develop a scientific metaphysics ("ordine geometrico demonstrata"[29]) without any mysterious entities (such as an inscrutable God and a free will). This metaphysics provided the ultimate context for the insights of the new science and for ethical and political considerations. Yet, unlike Hobbes's, this metaphysics does not consist in a *materialistic* worldview.[30] In the first place, Spinoza accepts the irreducible character of thought, whose capacity to present things "objectively" (as objective essences) cannot be explained away in terms of physical properties. Second, his concept of an absolutely infinite substance leads him to a worldview positing infinitely many worlds of modes according to each attribute of the divine substance. Third, his view of the world of finite things as parts of a *modal* network, combined with the ontological categories that he finds inescapable (substance-mode, essence-existence), results in a *naturalistic,* monistic metaphysics in which all concrete happenings and operations are seen as modal configurations of a deeper, divine power. As we will see, it is this peculiar kind of naturalism that will play a central role in the ethical problematic.

I NOTES

1. Compare Alan Donagan's principle of plenitude; see Donagan 1988, 77ff.

2. For example, Wolfson 1969, 146; Eisenberg 1990, 11n. 2.

3. This is argued by many commentators—for example, Gueroult 1968, appendix 3; Donagan 1988, 70.

4. The "objectivist" interpretation is also to be found in Gueroult 1968; Mark 1977; Jarrett 1977a; Martens 1978.

5. Mark 1977, 73.

6. Gueroult (1968) interprets *E* I, P. 1–8, as dealing with the notion of a substance with only one attribute and as being essentially a study of the *elements* of the divine substance—namely, substances with only one attribute. This interpretation is textually and philosophically untenable. As A. Doz (1976, 1980) conclusively shows, *E* I, P. 1–8, is Spinoza's ontology, or the study of basic reality or substance (with an indeterminate number of attributes). Gueroult is wrong because he interprets Spinoza as holding that difference in attributes normally indicates real difference in substance unless it can be shown that they must belong to the same substance.

7. Gueroult 1968, appendix 9. Mark (1977, 59–62) rightly denies that "expression" is a relation of representation—as if substance were one thing and the attribute another, so that we could ask whether an attribute *really* manifests substance.

8. Gueroult 1968, appendix 9.

9. Opposition also presupposes community of nature; see *E* IV, P. 29 (and *E* I, Ax. 5; I, P. 3; II, P. 6).

10. Donagan 1988, 80–84.

11. There is abundant literature on this problem. For references, see Donagan 1973, 1991; Gueroult 1968; Mark 1977.

12. Donagan 1988, 87.

13. Mark 1977, 63n. 12.

14. Gueroult 1968, 260–62; Donagan 1988, 87 (the expression "trans-attribute relation" comes from Bennett 1984, 144–45).

15. Literally, "face or form of the whole universe," that is, the macrocosmos.

16. Donagan 1988, 105; Allison 1987, 71; Gueroult 1968, 316–24.

17. Garrett 1990, 32.

18. Garrett 1990, 32 (see also Mark 1977, 82; Donagan 1988, 113ff.; and Friedman 1978). This view runs counter to Naess 1974.

19. For a defense of this reading of *E* I, P. 17, Sch., see Gueroult 1968, appendix 12 (referring to Koyré); Harris (1973, 38) argues against this reading.

20. *ST* I, chap. 9.

21. See, for example, Hubbeling 1973, 10–11. For an extensive discussion of this problem, see Kammerer 1992.

22. Spinoza here criticizes Scholastic philosophers, as well as Descartes; see Curley's comments in Spinoza 1985, 455nn. 24, 25.

23. Donagan 1988, 89.

24. Jarrett 1977b, 101, 103.

25. Donagan 1988, 106.

26. This expression should not be translated (as Curley does) by "under a species of eternity" but by "under the aspect of eternity"; see Donagan 1988, 121 (following Gueroult 1974, appendix 17, 609–15).

27. *E* I, App.

28. This is a condensed reformulation of Spinoza's physics based on *E* II, P. 13, Sch.

29. This is the subtitle of the *Ethics*.

30. Donagan 1988, 119.

CHAPTER
T   E   N | **On Man (*Ethics* II)**

Spinoza is not interested in the furthering of the new science as such. His purpose is the development of knowledge in the service of a specific aim: salvation. This is true not only for the Spinoza of the *Treatise* but also for the Spinoza of the *Ethics*. In the preface to *Ethics* II, we read that of the infinitely many things that follow from God, Spinoza is going to study "only those that can lead us, by the hand, as it were, to the knowledge of the human Mind and its highest blessedness." *Ethics* II constitutes the first step in this endeavor: it is the study of "the Nature and Origin of the Mind." Since the human mind is explained as "the idea of the human body," we find here Spinoza's "Theory of Man."

Matheron has claimed that Spinoza has no full-fledged "philosophical anthropology."[1] In a sense he is right: Spinoza's insights into the nature of man are simply the application of general insights, relevant in principle to the understanding of many different kinds of complex ideas (of complex bodies). Again it is clear that his aim is not a theory of man developed for its own sake; his aim is to reach, as quickly as possible, the insights required to achieve salvation.

Ethics II consists of three sections: an analysis of the nature of the human mind in its relation to the body (II, P. 1–15); an analysis of the properties of the human mind—that is, of the nature and the extent of human knowing (II, P. 16–47); and an analysis of the human will in relation to human knowing, which also contains a critique of the ordinary concept of human freedom (II, P. 48–49). This last section prepares the ground for Spinoza's concept of man as a dynamic-affective being (*Ethics* III), which is pivotal to his ethics.

The Relation between Mind and Body (*Ethics* II, P. 1–15)

In *Ethics* I we were taught that God exhausts nature as its only, unique substance, which consists in an infinity of attributes and necessarily produces an infinity of worlds of infinitely many modes. We did not learn what these attributes are or which sorts of modes there actually are. If specific attributes or modes were mentioned (such as *Cogitatio* or *Idea Dei* or motion and rest), it was by way of example only. It is only on the basis of experience, expressed in axioms, that the leap can be made from this purely "formal" insight into God's nature and production to a concrete insight into specific attributes and modes, as well as to an understanding of concretely existing modes. The crucial axioms are axioms 2, 4, and 5, which contain the following affirmations, based on our self-awareness: "man thinks" (or "we know that we think"[2]); "[w]e feel that a certain body is affected in many ways"; and "[w]e neither feel nor perceive any singular things, except bodies and modes of thinking." Our self-awareness—whereby we experience thought itself, certain bodily affections, and no affections of any other kind—leads, given the ontological framework of the interpretation of *Ethics* I, to the following affirmations: that there must be attributes of God, such as thought (*Cogitatio*) and extension (*Extensio*), of which the indicated modifications are actually existing modes (II, P. 1, 2).

The attribute of thought must contain an infinite mode—the *Idea Dei,* or the infinite intellect of God[3]—which is the whole of all ideas that express in thought all things that follow from God in both their essence and their existence (II, P. 3). From this *Idea Dei,* which is a unity, follow "infinitely many things . . . in infinitely many ways" (II, P. 4). This derivation is, at the same time, a logical-deductive sequence and a causal succession: "whatever follows from God's infinite nature follows objectively in God from his idea in the same order and with the same connection" (II, P. 7, Cor.). It is a "logical" derivation because the order of formal essences is deducible as an order of objective essences from the idea of God. This logical derivation is also a *real* sequence of objective essences, which is necessarily complicated because it is, first of all, a sequence of ideas of eternal things (*res aeternae*)—that is, a sequence in which the act of thinking God is necessarily effectively related to the act of thinking God's infinite modes as containing all eternal essences (II, P. 8 and Cor.). Second, this sequence of "objective essences" also is the sequence of actually existing acts of thought that are causally related in the way that their formally existing objects are causally related (as far as their existence is concerned) (II, P. 9). Only in possessing this sequence of actually existing ideas does God know, in his infinite intellect, the concrete reality of things.

Spinoza next discusses the way ideas in the attribute of thought relate to bodies in the attribute of extension and, generally speaking, to other modes in other attributes. First, ideas as formal realities are not caused by their *ideata,* or objects or modes in other attributes (of which they are the objective essences) (II, P. 5). Generally speaking, "[t]he modes of each attribute have God for their cause only insofar as he is considered under the attribute of which they are modes, and not insofar as he is considered under any other attribute" (II, P. 6). This is a logical consequence of Spinoza's view of the "incommensurability" of the attributes, which we discussed in connection with *Ethics* I, P. 10. Therefore, "the formal being of things which are not modes of thinking does not follow from the divine nature because [God] has first known things; rather the objects of ideas follow and are inferred from their attributes in the same way and by the same necessity as that with which we have shown ideas to follow from the attribute of Thought" (II, P. 6, Cor.). Yet, although there is no interattribute causation, "[t]he order and connection of ideas is the same as the order and connection of things" (II, P. 7). That it is the same follows from the fact that in each of the attributes, or through each of the attributes, God produces everything that can be produced, according to the kind of perfection or nature constituted by each attribute. This is the basis of the so-called parallelism between an idea and its counterpart in another attribute—for example, of the parallelism between mind and body. Immanent causation is, as Donagan puts it, a transattribute relation—that is, a relation that operates equally in or through each attribute.[4] Yet, Donagan adds, "like its *relata,* immanent causation can only be understood through some attribute." Or, as Michael Della Rocca has it, causation as such is "referentially opaque": we need a description of the kind of context (*genus*) in which it operates in order to know whether it is true that God (as substance) is the immanent cause of a certain finite mode, or whether a certain mode (say, a body) causes another mode (say, another body).[5] The fact that causation is referentially opaque expresses that there is parallelism—but without *inter*-attribute causation (II, P. 7, Sch.).

The *Idea Dei* (and therefore the attribute of thought) contains not only the ideas of all modes of extension but also those of all other modes of all other attributes. Hence, God's power of thinking ("potentia cogitandi"), working itself out in the *Idea Dei*, is equal to God's power of acting ("potentia agendi") (II, P. 7, Cor.). The attribute of thought is the ground for an infinite infinity of ideas (corresponding to the infinite infinity of modes in all attributes), which are unified in the *Idea Dei* (II, P. 4). According to many commentators, this destroys the parallelism between the attribute of thought and other attributes. But one could argue that it is the parallelism that requires this exceptional situation in the attribute of thought. Precisely because immanent causation can be understood only through some attribute, ideas expressing causation in one attribute must be separate from ideas expressing it in other attributes, although they are all ideas of the same trans-attribute acts of causation. This is the reason that although human beings are a unity of mind and body, and although these modes are necessarily paralleled by modes in other attributes, we do not know these other modes concretely, and the human mind is not "united" with them as it is with the human body because they are expressed in thought in separate ideas (see also letter 64). These and other remarkable features of the world of thought should not be wondered at too much; they are the consequences of the peculiar *nature* of thought itself, which is different from all other infinite natures of God and which forms true presentations of these other "incommensurable" natures and their modifications.

Next, Spinoza discusses what it means that the idea of singular things are said to *actually exist*. Spinoza distinguishes the actual existence of things in the midst of other things from their being "comprehended" as formal (real) essences in a certain attribute (II, P. 8 and Cor. and Sch.). Whether ideas of things are actually existing or only comprehended (as the objective essences of things) in the infinite idea of God again depends on the parallelism between ideas and what they express: "when singular things are said to exist, not only insofar as they are comprehended in God's attributes, but insofar also as they are said to have duration, their ideas also involve the existence through which they are said to have duration" (II, P. 8, Cor.). Why is there this special reference to the *Idea Dei* rather than to the attribute of thought? The ideas are, "from all eternity," effectively formed by the infinite intellect in the infinite idea of God, whereas the essences of bodies are contained in the attribute of extension as pure possibilities. *Actual* existence, as opposed to merely "being comprehended," is the same as "to have duration" in the midst of other enduring things.

How, then, does the mind originate? How does it achieve duration? "The idea of a singular thing that actually exists has God for a cause not insofar as he is infinite, but insofar as he is considered to be affected by another idea of a singular thing which actually exists; of this [idea] God is also the cause, insofar as he is affected by another third, and so on, to infinity" (II, P. 9). In other words, in the same way as the existence of things depends on their insertion in a chain of causes, so also the actual existence or duration of ideas is dependent on a chain of already existing ideas. God knows the actual existence of bodies by possessing in his infinite intellect the actually existing ideas corresponding to these bodies. In and through his intellect, God knows not only the essences of things but also the whole truth of the realm of the existence of things.

Next, Spinoza explains, God also knows what is actually happening *in* the existing object of any idea; but he can know this only insofar as he first has the idea itself of this object (II, P. 9, Cor.). This means that any change in a human body, for example, is known only insofar as God has the actually existing idea of this body, or insofar as its mind is part of God's intellect (II, P. 11 and Cor.). In other words, God knows the details of what happens in the world of bodies only through his having, as parts of his infinite intellect, actually existing ideas, which stand to each other in the way that the objects of these ideas themselves (the bodies) are causally related to each other. God knows what is happening in (or to) these objects only insofar as he first has the ideas of these objects themselves; these ideas themselves can then be said to *have* ideas or perceptions of these changes in their *ideata* (II, P. 12, Dem.).

What is man? "[T]he essence of man is constituted by certain modifications of God's attributes" (II, P. 10, Cor.). On the basis of axioms 2 and 4, we know that these modifications are modes of thought and of extension, mind and body (II, P. 11, 13, resulting in P. 13, Cor.). But we want to talk about *real*—that is, actually existing—man: "[t]he *actual being* of a human Mind is nothing but the idea of a singular thing which *actually exists*" (II, P. 11, emphasis added); this singular thing is "the Body, or a certain mode of Extension which actually exists, and nothing else" (II, P. 13). The human mind is the complex idea of a complex, compound body (II, P. 13, Sch.). This insight explains the peculiar union of mind and body (II, P. 13, Sch.), which is not, as Descartes thought, a unity of two incommensurable substances miraculously fused together and nevertheless influencing each other causally (*Meditations* 6). The union of mind and body is the union of an idea, being the objective essence of the body and the actually existing essence of this body; this is a union of perfect "expression," the result of trans-attribute causality operating in different attributes. This union is felt strongly because there is no affection of or in the body that is not automatically expressed in the mind as an experience of the body. This experience can contain even an affective (emotional) element, depending on whether the body's power to operate is increased or diminished in the affection (see III, Def. 3; P. 11, Sch.). The mind *being* the idea of the actually existing body necessarily endeavors to affirm the existence of the body (III, P. 10, Dem.). In his *Short Treatise,* Spinoza called this endeavor the mind's love for its own body, implied in the union of mind and body.[6]

The mind *is the idea* of an actually existing body. This does not imply that the mind *consciously has* the idea of its body (whether adequately or inadequately). What are the conditions for the mind—being the idea of the body—to perceive something, or to *have* the idea of something (for example, of itself)? That the mind has ideas, or perceives, means "that God, not insofar as he is infinite, but insofar as he is explained through the nature of the mind, or insofar as he constitutes the essence of the human mind, has this or that idea" (II, P. 11, Cor.). In other words, for the mind to *have an idea* of x, or to *perceive x,* it is required that *God's* having the idea of x is (at least in part) linked to God's constituting the nature of the human mind or to God's being explained through this nature (that is, to God's being modified accordingly).

What, then, are the ideas that the mind *has?* They are those ideas that God can have only insofar as he constitutes the human mind: namely, ideas of what is happening in the object of the idea constituting the human mind—that is, the actually existing human body (II, P. 12). God does not have the idea of the human body as existing insofar as he simply constitutes the nature of the human mind because God's having the idea of the human body as existing does not follow (even in part) from God's constituting the nature of the human mind. God has this idea only insofar as he has an endless number of other ideas of other bodies. Consequently, the human mind does not have the idea of its body or know it simply by being the idea of the body (II, P. 19). As we will see, all the ideas the mind ever *has* somehow find their origin in, or are occasioned by, these ideas of what is happening in the body.

The distinction between the idea that the mind *is* and the idea that it *has* can be rephrased as the distinction between primary and derivative ideas.[7] This distinction explains how the idea of Peter's body that Paul has can be different from the idea of Peter's body that constitutes Peter's mind, although both are ideas in God's intellect. The idea of Peter in Paul's mind depends on the presence—among the ideas in Paul's mind expressing all the changes and affections in and of Paul's body—of the idea of an affection of Paul's body that is a bodily image of Peter's body (II, P. 17, Sch.). God's intellect has the idea of Peter differently, according to whether it simply has the idea of Peter—as a primary idea—or whether it has the idea of Peter insofar as it first has the idea of Paul. Insofar as it has the idea of Paul, it has the idea of Peter only derivatively and partially, as involved in the idea of a particular affection of Paul's body referring to Peter's body. God's having the idea of Peter simply, or in a primary sense, does not necessarily imply that God has the idea of Peter derivatively; as we will see in the next section, God, as having the idea of Peter in a primary sense, only has the idea of Peter in a derivative sense through his having ideas of modifications of Peter's body.

The human body, like all bodies, is a unity or an individual because its parts, although continually renewed, preserve, through all sorts of changes, the same *ratio* of motion and rest vis-à-vis each other (see the short theory of the body after *Ethics* II, 13, Sch.).[8] If we want to know the difference between the human mind and other things, we should know the nature of its object. But, says Spinoza, "[w]hat this nature is, I am unable to explain here, but that is not necessary for what I am going to show" (II, P. 13, Sch.). Certain general truths will do—for example: as "a body is more apt than others for performing many actions at the same time, or receiving many actions performed at the same time, so is its mind more apt than others for perceiving many things at the same time; and according as the actions of a body depend more solely on itself, and according as fewer other bodies concur with its action, so its mind is more apt for distinct understanding" (II, P. 13, Sch.). On the basis of experience and of the general theory of the body, we can prove that the human body is a complex body, and that "[t]he idea that constitutes the formal being [*esse*] of the human Mind is not simple, but composed of a great many ideas" (II, P. 15). Because the human body "can be disposed in a great many ways," the human mind is correspondingly "capable of perceiving a great many things" (II, P. 14).

What are these "many things?" They are, in the first place, but not only, "whatever happens in the object of the idea constituting the human Mind" (II, P. 12). They are, as we will see, also such things as the mind itself, its body, and other bodies (II, P. 17ff.). Many commentators have expressed doubts about the possibility of the human mind having ideas of whatever happens in the human body. This proposition would mean only that nothing occurs in the organism that does not have its mental correlate.[9] The problem is that Spinoza really speaks of having the idea of, or perceiving, everything that is happening in the body. A better solution is to understand Spinoza as saying that the perceptions that the mind has somehow reflect whatever happens in the body. One should bear in mind that Spinoza is not saying that we have an adequate idea of each occurrence or change in the body, or that we perceive these changes distinctly.[10]

We know now what a human being is, albeit in rather general terms. We also know what it is for the mind—being the idea of a complex body—to have ideas or to perceive or to know. The being of the mind is explained here as both an effect completely determined by God as immanent cause, and a part of God's infinite intellect, which is the total comprehension that God has of everything. The mind's own having of ideas, or its activity of thinking, is understood here as God's having of ideas of certain things insofar as he constitutes the mind's being. The mind's own activity is the activity of *Deus quatenus modificatus*. This does not mean that the mind does not have its own perspective; on the contrary, its own perspective on the world is through its being the objective essence expressing an actually existing body and consists in having all sorts of ideas related to its having ideas of affections of its body. Yet this peculiar perspective is "only" a modification of God's power to think everything. Man's activity of thought is the formation in God of a peculiar perspective that is needed concretely to think certain changes happening to and in a certain actually existing human body. Paradoxically, this perspective is somehow the perspective of the mind itself; and what is more, it will allow certain minds to think the absolute itself. Spinoza tries to show in the second section of *Ethics* II that the mind, as existing in time, can, through knowledge of what is eternal, come to a certain "internal" determination in time. This internal determination should be understood not as Cartesian self-determination but as God's own activity of thinking something, working itself out in us without the cooperation of anything else.[11]

| Sorts of Human Knowing
| (*Ethics* II, P. 16–47)

In this section, Spinoza explains how the mind can have the mental life it has—or, in terms of the *Treatise,* how it can be imagination and intellect.

All ideas that the mind originally has are ideas of affections of its body. But the ideas of these affections "involve the nature of the human Body and at the same time the nature of the external body" responsible for the affection (II, P. 16). "From this it follows, first, that the human Mind perceives the nature of a great many bodies together with the nature of its own body" (II, P. 16, Cor. 1). The mind will perceive the external body responsible for the affection of the body "as actually existing, or as present to it, until the Body is affected by an affect[ion]¹² that excludes the existence or presence of that body" (II, P. 17). In this way Spinoza explains the mind's capacity to perceive (in the ordinary sense) external things, as well as mental phenomena, such as hallucinations (II, P. 17, Cor.). Spinoza calls the affections of the human body by other bodies "images,"¹³ and the perceptions (or hallucinations) in the human mind of external bodies that correspond to these images "imaginations" (*imaginationes*) (II, P. 17, Sch.). On the same basis, he explains mental phenomena such as recollection, memory, and association (II, P. 18 and Sch.). All these mental phenomena are grouped together under the term *imaginatio.*

The mind as imagination knows its own body (II, P. 19), itself (II, P. 20–23), the affections of its body and the ideas of these affections (II, P. 22), the parts of its own body (II, P. 24), external bodies (II, P. 25–26), and the duration of its own body and of external bodies (II, P. 30–31).

The mind knows none of these things by simply being the idea of the body. The only things that the mind can know are things somehow given in the ideas that it has of the affections of its body (in its *imaginationes*). Indeed, what is it for the mind to perceive *x?* As we said before, for the mind to perceive *x,* God's having the idea of *x* must be linked (at least in part) to God's *constituting* the nature of the human mind (II, P. 11, Cor.). If God's having the idea of *x* cannot somehow be linked to God's constituting the nature of the human mind, the mind does not have the idea of *x.* For example, God does not have the idea of the human body *as existing* insofar as he simply constitutes the nature of the human mind. Rather, God has this idea of the human body as existing only insofar as he is considered to be affected by a great many other ideas (other than the human mind), which do explain the presence of this idea—the mind as idea of the actually existing body—in God (II, P. 19, Dem.). The idea of the body as existing can be in God—insofar as he constitutes the nature of the human mind—only if there are ideas of affections of the body in God, which are necessarily in God precisely insofar as he constitutes the nature of the human mind (II, P. 12). Something similar can be demonstrated concerning the mind's having other ideas: their presence in the mind is conditioned by the mind having ideas of affections of the body. Somehow, the presence of the idea of a bodily affection in the mind must be transformed from pure appearance (from a pure "being appeared to" in a certain way) into a thought characterized by intentionality, by affirming or denying the existence of a certain thing. Spinoza gives no explanation of this, however. Neither does he explain in detail how the same idea of a bodily affection leads to the having of such different ideas as the idea of the external body, the idea of an affection of the body, or the idea of the body as a whole.[14]

There is also necessarily an idea of the mind in God, and this idea is united to the mind in the same way as the mind is united to the body (II, P. 20–21). "In the same way," should be understood in terms of trans-attribute causality. Still, since the idea of the mind is an idea not of a body but of an idea—and therefore constitutes the *form* of the first idea insofar as this is a mode of thinking—the unity of mind and idea of mind is peculiar (II, P. 21, Sch.). Self-awareness of the mind as the expression of an actually existing body can only be had through the perception of the ideas of the bodily affections (II, P. 23).

Awareness of bodily affections is the only starting point from which the mind can perceive its world and itself. Unfortunately, this starting point produces a distorted perspective on what is perceived (II, P. 24ff.) because, of the things perceived on this basis, God has an idea "not only insofar as he constitutes the nature of the human Mind, but insofar as he also has the idea of another thing together with the human Mind"; and "then we say that the human Mind perceives the thing only partially, *or* inadequately" (II, P. 11, Cor.). For example, "[t]he idea of any affection of the human Body does not involve adequate knowledge of an external body" (II, P. 25) because the knowledge of the external body is given only partially in the awareness of our body's affection by it, whereas God's full knowledge of this external body is present in God insofar as he has many other ideas apart from the ones that the human mind has (II, P. 25, Dem.). Indeed, the mind's knowledge of external bodies "indicate[s] the condition of our own body more than the nature of the external bodies" (II, P.

16, Cor. 2).[15] For similar reasons, the mind's awareness of bodily affections does not yield adequate knowledge of the other things it can imagine. On the contrary, "so long as the Mind perceives things from the common order of nature, it does not have an adequate, but only a confused and mutilated knowledge of itself, of its own Body, and of external bodies" (II, P. 29, Cor.). To perceive things "from the common order of nature" is to be "determined externally, from fortuitous encounters with things" (II, P. 29, Sch.).

We now have an explanation of the *imaginatio* and of the inevitably inadequate character of its ideas. Strangely enough, as Gueroult observes, Spinoza never calls the ideas of a bodily affection themselves *in*adequate but rather *non*adequate.[16] They are simply the expressions of some bodily image (*imago*). But they inevitably lead to inadequate ideas because they give rise to partial ideas of one's own body, of external bodies, and so on, which are spontaneously *affirmed* as being thus-and-such (and not otherwise). Now Spinoza can explain error, or falsity, which is not due, as Descartes thought, to rashness of the will. The *imaginationes* "considered in themselves contain no error": they are the inevitable expressions in the mind of processes in the body; and "the Mind does not err from the fact that it imagines, but only insofar as it is considered to lack an idea"—for example, "to lack an idea that excludes the existence of those things that it imagines to be present to it" (II, P. 17, Sch.). "Falsity, then, consists in the privation of knowledge which inadequate, *or* mutilated and confused, ideas involve" (II, P. 35).

According to Spinoza's theory of truth and falsity (II, P. 32–36), no idea considered in itself can be negative: it cannot be the presentation of nothing. "There is nothing positive in ideas on account of which they are called false" (II, P. 33). Then how can there be falsity? Spinoza's answer seems disappointing: falsity consists in lack of knowledge. Falsity, however, is not the same as ignorance (II, P. 35, Dem.). Spinoza explains falsity by *partiality* of knowledge involved in having inadequate ideas. This partiality, together with affirmations (and linkages or exclusions) of ideas, constitutes falsehood.

Spinoza gives two revealing examples (II, P. 35, Sch.). People think they are free. This thinking expresses something positive in their actions; but at the same time, they lack awareness of the causes of their actions. They say, of course, that their actions depend on their will; "but these are only words for which they have no idea." It is this partiality in thinking in which falsity consists:

our thinking is cut off from most of the ideas that are linked with it in God's thinking of reality.[17] Another example is the idea that the sun is about two hundred feet away. The error consists in this: that while one is "imagining" this, one is ignorant of the true distance and the cause of the *imaginatio*. That there is something positive in this idea is proven by the fact that even when one comes to know the true distance and the mechanism of perception, one continues to see the sun at the same distance. But now the error is gone because we have enough knowledge to be in the truth (IV, P. 1 and Sch.). Falsity can exist only insofar as there are finite minds (II, 36, Dem.). But insofar as inadequate ideas are considered to be part of the realm of God's ideas, there is no falsity in them (II, P. 32). The production of inadequate ideas in the finite mind is as necessary as the production of adequate ideas (II, P. 36).

Man has an idea of x if God's having the idea of x can be linked to God's constituting the nature of the human mind. Man has an inadequate idea of x if God's having the idea of x can be linked to his constituting the nature of the mind only partially. Man has an adequate idea of x if God's having the idea of x can be linked to his constituting the nature of the human mind on its own (II, P. 11, Cor.). Since all ideas that God has are true, adequate ideas are true (II, P. 34). But if it is true that "so long as the human Mind perceives things from the common order of nature [that is, "so long as it is determined externally, from fortuitous encounters with things, to regard this or that" (II, P. 29, Sch.)], it does not have an adequate idea . . . of itself, of its own Body, and of external bodies" (II, P. 29, Cor.), do we ever actually have adequate ideas?

Spinoza clearly envisions the possibility that the mind "is determined internally, from the fact that it regards a number of things at once, to understand their agreements, differences, and oppositions. For so often as it is disposed internally, in this or another way, then it regards things clearly and distinctly, as I shall show below" (II, P. 29, Sch.). Spinoza accepts that the human body is capable of doing many things at once or of being acted on in many ways at once, and that it can depend on itself alone so that it does not need other bodies (II, P. 13, Sch.); and, accordingly, that the mind is capable of perceiving many things at once, and of understanding distinctly. As he shows from *Ethics* II, P. 37, onward, this leads to adequate understanding.

However, man is capable of "perceiving many things at once" in two radically different ways. Spinoza uses this difference to explain two radically different kinds of knowledge: imagination and reason. Imagination is the mental operation "of perceiv[ing] many things and [of] form[ing] universal notions" on the basis of sense perception, memory, and hearsay. Reason is the activity of perceiving many things and of forming universal notions "from the fact that we have common notions and adequate ideas of the properties of things" (II, P. 40, Sch. 2). The mind's perceiving "many things at once" does not *automatically* lead to distinct understanding. On the contrary, it usually leads to confused ideas—for example, universal and transcendental ideas, which are formed because the imagination cannot keep track of the slight differences between the multiple "imaginations" of singular things of a certain kind (for example, human beings, leading to the universal "man"; or bodies, leading to the transcendental term "thing" or "being"[18]). We even form "second notions" (concepts of the way we classify things or speak about things, such as "genus, species, word," which we sometimes even confuse with real things) (II, P. 40, Sch.1).[19]

Since all these ideas and notions are formed on the basis of the accidental encounters of one's body with other bodies, it is not surprising that there are so many differences and controversies concerning them (II, P. 40, Sch. 1). How, then, can we perceive "many things at once" *and* understand "distinctly"? When is our body depending "on itself alone," and the mind "disposed internally," so that it understands the "agreements, differences, and oppositions" between things and "regards them clearly and distinctly"? The answer is given in Spinoza's doctrine of the common notions (*notiones communes*), which are the cornerstones of adequate understanding in the form of *ratio,* a specific kind of intellectual thinking.

The mind becomes reason through the perception of certain "things" that are common to all bodies and that are both in the part and in the whole of each body. The idea of these "things" will be completely in God insofar as he constitutes the human mind or insofar as he has the ideas of bodily affections of the human body itself and of external bodies in the human mind. Every human mind will thus conceive them adequately, which means that the notions of what is common are common to all people (II, P. 37, 38 and Cor.). This is Spinoza's version of the Cartesian idea that in every perception are clear and distinct ideas of the fundamental common characteristics of all things and of all bodies are present. These common notions are undoubtedly notions like cause-effect, thing-property, whole-part, essence-existence, motion-rest, extension, and figure.[20] There is no reason not to add notions like idea and object, idea and affect.

Spinoza goes one step further: there are not only notions common to all things or all bodies but also *specific* common notions. Since there are characteristics "common to, *and peculiar to*, the human Body and *certain* external bodies by which the human Body is usually affected, and [which are] equally in the part and in the whole of each of them," ideas thereof will be adequate in the human mind; God has these ideas completely insofar as he constitutes the human mind on its own (II, P. 39, emphasis added). The mind will actually have these specific common notions when the affections of its body by external bodies are happening precisely through what these bodies have specifically in common with each other (II, P. 39, Dem.). From this it follows that the more the human body has in common specifically with other bodies, the more the mind is capable of perceiving many things adequately (II, P. 39, Cor.). What does Spinoza have in mind here? What, for example, is common to my human body and to certain other human bodies, both as to the whole and as to their parts, such that it can strike us as common in this way? Is it the peculiar life form of human beings, which allows us to notice also the "agreements, differences, and oppositions" with other life forms? Comprehending this fully will require the elaboration of a theory of the human body explaining how it can perform the extravagant acts it does (see III, P. 2, Sch.).

When the mind is having ideas of affections of the body, it necessarily has ideas of what is common to all things and to all bodies, and it *occasionally* can have ideas of what is "common and peculiar" to its body and certain other bodies. In this way, it can understand the "agreements, differences, and oppositions" between many things and regard them "clearly and distinctly." This is particularly so for the human mind, which "is the more capable of perceiving many things adequately as its Body has many things in common with other bodies" (II, P. 39, Cor.).

Reason (*ratio*) is the *sequence* of adequate ideas following from these general and specific common notions (II, P. 40). Whether a human mind possessing these common notions will effectively develop rational capacities depends on the success with which the mind can develop adequate thinking, being "disposed internally" to understand "the agreements, differences, and oppositions between things."

Spinoza reformulates what he has been saying about the mind as imagination and intellect in a résumé of the different kinds of knowing, two of which have to do not only with the perception of many things at once but also with the formation of "universal notions" (II, P. 40, Sch. 2). Knowledge of the first kind, called "opinion or imagination," consists of two elements: "Knowledge from random experience," which we obtain "from singular things which have been represented to us in a way that is mutilated, confused, and without order for the intellect (see P 29 C)"; and knowledge "from signs, e.g., from the fact that, having heard or read certain words, we recollect things and form certain ideas of them which are like them, and through which we imagine the things (P 18 S, dealing with memory and association)." Both of these elements yield inadequate knowledge of singular things (and their relations) as well as universal and transcendental notions.

Knowledge of the second kind, called "reason" (*ratio*), also leads us to "perceive many things and [to] form universal notions," "from the fact that we have common notions and adequate ideas of the properties of things (see P 38 C, P 39, P 39 C, and P 40)." Presumably, the adequate ideas of the properties of things form the understanding of what is "common to and peculiar to" certain sorts of things.

The third kind of knowledge, called "intuitive knowledge" (*scientia intuitiva*), is mentioned separately as something to be discussed in what follows. It "proceeds from an adequate idea of the formal essence of certain attributes of God to the adequate knowledge of the . . . essence of things." This kind of knowledge, then, has not been demonstrated as to its origin in the previous propositions. It is not understood as falling under the heading of "knowledge which consists in the perception of many things and in universal notions." As we will see, it is knowledge of the *singular* essence of things as comprehended in the formal essence of certain attributes of God (see, for example, V, P. 36, Sch.).

As in the *Treatise* (§ 23–24), Spinoza gives the example of the different kinds of knowledge concerning the proportionality of cardinal numbers. As I observed in my commentary on the *Treatise,* this example highlights only certain aspects of the third kind of knowledge, particularly its "immediacy."[21]

Spinoza demonstrates that the second and third kinds of knowledge are adequate and therefore true (II, P. 41); that they teach us "to distinguish the true from the false" (II, P. 42); and that they lead to certainty and to elimination of all doubt, reflection on them giving us the standard of truth and falsity (II, P. 43 and Sch.). So what we obtained in the *Treatise,* in a reflection on a given true idea, is demonstrated in the *Ethics* on the basis of an explanation belonging to the second kind of knowledge, or reason. At the same time, Spinoza repeats the basic ideas of the *Treatise* as to how the human mind can effectively develop its rational instruments. What is required is not only the possession of general and specific common notions but also the actual reflection on these notions so as to discover the standard of truth, which will guide us in the full development of rational knowledge, whereby the mind is "disposed internally" and not by the fortuitous encounters in ordinary life. The real difference with the *Treatise* is that the process of forming adequate ideas of the essences of things on the basis of the fixed and eternal things (*res fixae et aeternae*) is spelled out here more explicitly as the process of arriving through reason (in terms of general and specific common notions) to intuitive knowledge. Intellectual thinking is thus a two-stage process, as is elucidated in the last propositions of this section (II, P. 44–47).

First, Spinoza gives the fundamental characteristics of reason: "It is of the nature of Reason to regard things as necessary, not as contingent" (II, P. 44). The view of things as contingent, in respect to both the past and the future, depends only on the imagination (II, P. 44, Cor. 1; see also II, P. 31, Cor.). The view of things as contingent depends on "a defect of our knowledge. For if we do not know that the thing's essence involves a contradiction, or if we do know very well that its essence does not involve a contradiction, and nevertheless can affirm nothing certainly about its existence, because the order of causes is hidden from us, it can never seem to us either necessary or impossible" (I, P. 33, Sch. 1). Because the concrete order of causes is hidden from us, we cannot affirm their existence with certainty either in the past or in the future (II, P. 44, Cor. 1). On the contrary, "[i]t is of the nature of Reason to regard things as necessary" or "to perceive things under a certain [aspect] of eternity" (*sub quadam aeternitatis specie*) (II, P. 44, Cor. 2). This "perception" from the point of view of eternity[22] presents things as *necessary* consequences or effects: in this way, the thinking of these things can be "according to the order of the intellect, by which the Mind perceives things through their first causes, and [this order] is the same in all men" (II, P. 18, Sch.). What is meant here is an explanation of things not on the basis of their concrete causal links but on the basis of general common notions, which do not explain the essence of any singular thing (II, P. 44, Cor. 2, Dem.). It is an explanation of things on the basis of general notions (such as extension, motion, and rest) and the general laws related to them (such as Galileo's laws of falling bodies), an explanation prototypically present in the new science (and hinted at in *Treatise* § 102–3). Is such an explanation capable of explaining the singular essence of singular things? Before we answer this question, let us consider the origin of the third kind of knowledge.

The third kind of knowledge, intuitive knowledge, "proceeds from an adequate idea of the formal essence of certain attributes of God to the adequate knowledge of the essence of things" (I, P. 40, Sch. 2). Clearly, it is necessary first to have an adequate idea of the formal essence of a certain attribute of God. That this idea is necessarily present in the human mind as an adequate idea is proven in *Ethics* II, P. 45–47. First Spinoza shows that the idea of every actually existing thing involves the concept of the attribute of which the thing is a mode; in other words, it involves the concept of an eternal and infinite essence of God. This concept is involved in the idea of everything, whether it is considered to be the whole or only a part. So what gives knowledge of an eternal and infinite essence of God is common to all ideas, whether of the whole or of parts. Since this knowledge is not only common to all these ideas but is also knowledge of what is common to whole and parts, it is adequate and perfect.

The next question is whether the human mind itself actually has this kind of knowledge. The mind has ideas of all sorts of things as actually existing; so it must have, involved in these ideas, the adequate knowledge of an eternal and infinite essence of God. Spinoza concludes that "[f]rom this we see that God's infinite essence and his eternity *are known* to all. And since all things are in God and are conceived through God, it follows that we *can* deduce from this knowledge a great many things which we know adequately, and so can form that third kind of knowledge of which we spoke in P 40 S 2 and of whose excellence and utility we shall speak in part V" (II, P. 47, Sch.; emphasis added).

Spinoza's claim here is that every human mind necessarily has the idea of God according to a certain infinite and eternal essence (or attribute). In other words, since each human mind has the idea of something actually existing, it has in it the principle of intuitive knowledge. Anything actually existing is existing not simply in the abstract sense of having a certain measurable duration in the context of other things (this is the idea of existence we form through the imagination).[23] An actually existing thing ultimately exists because it is a modification of God's power, which makes it into a force to exist and operate (a *conatus;* see II, P. 45, Sch.; and III, P. 7). This force, of course, refers to God. Spinoza claims here (II, P. 45 and Sch.) that it is not possible to have the idea of anything actually existing without somehow knowing about this sort of existence, and therefore about God. (Again we are reminded of Descartes's claim that in our daily, confused perceptions innate, clear, and distinct ideas are present.)

Why is it, then, that so few people seem to possess the intuitive knowledge of God? In the first place, although they have the idea of God, they do not easily attend to it. This idea is totally alien to the imagination, which differentiates it from the common notions concerning bodies, which are related to *imaginationes*. The word "God" often is associated with something totally different, something imaginable. This does not mean that people really err concerning God; in what they say about God, they actually talk and think confusedly about something else (II, P. 47, Sch.). In the meantime, they do not develop intuitive knowledge, even though they effectively possess its principle.

How do we fully obtain intuitive knowledge as being "the adequate knowledge of the essence of things" on the basis of "an adequate idea of the formal essence of certain attributes of God"? And what do we know according to this kind of knowledge? The *desire* to know things by intuitive knowledge "cannot arise from the first kind of knowledge, but can indeed arise from the second" (V, P. 28). That is, reason, which is based on common notions, teaches us to understand things from the point of view of eternity. Still, reason does not teach us the *singular* essence of things; at best, it gives us an insight into what is common to certain sorts of things (into what is "common and peculiar" to certain things). How, then, can reason help us to reach intuitive knowledge?[24]

Let us first clarify what it is we can know intuitively. There is in God "necessarily an idea that expresses the essence of *this or that* human body, under [an aspect] of eternity" (V, P. 23; emphasis added). The mind forms this idea in demonstrations concerning human nature; and in these demonstrations the mind *experiences itself* as eternal (V, P. 23, Sch.). The demonstrations are the work of reason (V, P. 29, Dem.); but the "application" of this rational knowledge to one's experience of oneself yields an insight into one's *own singular* essence as eternally related to God (V, P. 30). In other words, rational knowledge of human nature can result in intuitive knowledge of oneself, provided it is joined to the mind's experience of itself and of its own bodily affections as "eternal" modifications of God. The experience and understanding of oneself must be linked to the idea of certain attributes of God (see also V, P. 14, prepared by V, P. 11–13).

All other intuitive knowledge will, presumably, be equally prepared by rational understanding and triggered by the awareness of singular things as necessary modifications of God. Involved in all intuitive knowledge is the intuitive knowledge of oneself (V, P. 31, Sch.). All intuitive knowledge is of particular things, not only of their essence but also of their existence, although this existence is perceived as the intrinsic force of existence, which belongs to things as expressions of God's power. This intuitive knowledge of the intimate relation between God, oneself, and other things will be the major ethical factor leading to real happiness (V, P. 32–42, announced in II, P. 47, Sch.).

In discussing the three kinds of knowledge in his *Ethics,* Spinoza has kept his promise of the *Treatise* to explain imagination and intellect theoretically. At the same time, he has deduced them as effects or properties from his understanding of the human mind as a peculiar idea of an actually existing body. The insight into these effects or properties is based on an understanding of the mind through its proximate cause—that is, as a certain modification of a certain attribute of God (*Deus quatenus modificatus*). It is true that this proximate cause is described only in a general sense (without a detailed physical understanding of the human body, for example). Yet this general, genetic description is sufficient to give an accurate account of how this finite modification of an attribute of God can actually succeed in having adequate and true knowledge of certain things that is not substantially different from the knowledge of the infinite intellect (although not as extensive). This theoretical insight into the nature of the human mind as imagination and intellect can be transformed into intuitive knowledge, having the "ethical" consequences described in *Ethics* V.

It is striking how, in the course of his explanation of the human mind and its different sorts of knowledge, Spinoza is always careful to talk about what is *real.* He takes great pains to show that although the mind is nothing but a modification of certain attributes of God, nevertheless God actually has ideas through the human mind—that is, the human mind really has certain, and adequate, ideas. At the same time, we noticed that the three kinds of knowledge cannot actually be had by a human mind, except insofar as this mind is the idea of an actually existing body having ideas of bodily affections: this is the ontological foundation for the mind's really being an intellect. Although intuitive knowledge (unlike reason) is not explained in terms of the perception of many things at once and of the formation of universal notions related to this perception, it could not come about if the mind did not actually have ideas of existing things and if it were not capable of taking the rational point of view (which is necessarily related to perception). The three kinds of knowledge form the one life of certain actually existing human minds. Thus there is no ground for saying that Spinoza underestimates, let alone advocates a rejection of, the first kind of knowledge, imagination.[25]

Human Willing
(*Ethics* II, P. 48–49)

The theory of the human mind as "a certain and determinate modification of thinking" (II, P. 48, Dem.) is completed with an account of human willing, which is accompanied by a critique of the ordinary and Cartesian concepts of free will (a critique to be found also in *Ethics* I, App., but produced here in a geometrical or demonstrative way). There is a certain parallelism between Spinoza's discussion of God and his discussion of man:[26] after Spinoza has explained the nature and properties of the human mind, he demonstrates that this essence, in itself and in its properties, is *power:* power to think, to present as real, to affirm what is expressed "objectively." This power is called the will. Like God's will, man's will is not characterized by freedom of choice and is seen as identical with the intellect.

By willing, Spinoza in the first place understands the affirmation or negation present in an idea as the presentation of a formal reality in thought (II, P. 49, Dem.). Later he speaks about another form of willing, desire (III, P. 9, Sch.; see also II, P. 48, Sch.), which is a form of willing related to the fact that the mind is not only idea but also emotion or affect. The mind as power to think, which displays itself in affirmation or negation, can be affected positively or negatively, leading to all sorts of emotions and desires.

Spinoza rejects the existence of *faculties* of understanding and willing: these are nothing but *entia imaginationis* (or "Metaphysical beings," II, P. 48, Dem.), universals, not existing in reality. Faculties are understood as separate capacities (potentialities) that are uniformly deployed in certain activities. For Spinoza, there only is the one activity of the mind, which is characterized both as idea and as willing. The mind is not a potentiality but consists of *acts* of conceiving and affirming or denying things (II, P. 48, Dem. and Sch.; II, P. 49, Cor. and Sch.). These acts are not the results of an independent faculty or potentiality expressing itself evenly in all affirmations or negations. Rather, the mind's power of affirmation is *coextensive* with its acts of affirmation, each act being different from the other. This means that the affirmation of one idea can be "more perfect" than another—for example, the affirmation of what is true requires "more power" than the affirmation of what is false (*Ethics* II, P. 49, Sch., [III.B.(iii)])—and that the "certainty" of a false idea is totally different from the certainty of an adequate idea (*Ethics* II, P. 49, Sch. [I]).

In this doctrine of the unity of idea and willing, of intellect and will, Spinoza not only criticizes implicitly philosophers such as Bacon and Hobbes, who conceive of thinking as the formation of mental representations ("as mute pictures on a panel," II, P. 49, Sch.); he also attacks those, like Descartes, who separate intellect and will and for whom the intellect is only the understanding or conceiving of things, the will being responsible for affirmation or negation (that is, for judgment). Error, for Descartes, is due to the human will's being distinct from, and more extensive than, the intellect, sometimes affirming or denying too rashly, without sufficient evidence.[27]

Spinoza strongly rejects this Cartesian conception of the will and of the origin of error. Error does not originate in the will but "only in the privation that mutilated and confused ideas [which inevitably contain an affirmation or negation] involve" (II, P. 49, Sch. [I.]). The concept of the will as extending more widely than the intellect, as being a free power to suspend judgment or to freely affirm and deny, is criticized on each count. The will is seen to extend more widely than the intellect only because it is conceived abstractly, as a universal, and because one does not see that its concrete extension operates as widely as the extension of our perceptions (which are broader than purely intellectual acts) (II, P. 49, Sch. [III.B.(i)]). Spinoza flatly rejects that we have a free power of suspending judgment or of affirming or denying. Suspension of judgment is due not to freedom of the will but to doubt, which comes through the presence of new ideas going against the original, spontaneous affirmation present in the first idea. Furthermore, it is not true "that we require an equal power of thinking, to affirm that what is true is true, as to affirm that what is false is true" (II, P. 49, Sch. [III.B.(ii), (iii)]). Against such a denial of freedom of will, it sometimes is objected that it is then conceivable that someone could fall into a state of equilibrium like Buridan's ass, which was confronted with two stacks of hay between which it could not decide, so that it died from hunger; this individual is less than human unless allowed the power or "faculty of going where he wills and doing what he wills." Spinoza answers that such a state of equilibrium is not impossible, and that an individual's being in such a state is only as incompatible with the nature of man as the behavior of such people as those who hang themselves and madmen (II, P. 49, Sch. [III.B.(iv)]).

Spinoza ends his explanation of "the nature and properties of the human Mind" (II, P. 49, Sch.) with an indication of the usefulness of this doctrine in life, of the "ethical" advantages of this doctrine, which are developed in what follows:

> "[I]t teaches that we act only from God's command, that we share in the divine nature, and that we do this the more, the more perfect our actions are, and the more we understand of God." This implies the equation between knowledge of God, action, virtue, freedom, and happiness.
>
> "[I]t teaches us how we must bear ourselves concerning matters of fortune, or things which are not in our power, i.e., concerning things which do not follow from our nature — that we must expect and bear calmly both good fortune and bad. For all things follow from God's eternal decree with the same necessity as from the essence of a triangle it follows that its three angles are equal to two right angles."
>
> "[It] contributes to social life, insofar as it teaches us to hate no one, to disesteem no one, to mock no one, to be angry at no one, to envy no one; and also insofar as it teaches that each of us should be content with his own things, and should be helpful to his neighbor, not from unmanly compassion, partiality, or superstition, but from the guidance of reason, as the time and occasion demand. I shall show this in the Fourth Part."
>
> "Finally, this doctrine also contributes, to no small extent, to the common society insofar as it teaches how citizens are to be governed and led, not so that they may be slaves, but that they may do freely the things that are best."

It is striking that Spinoza, in mentioning the ethical consequences of his theory of man, uses vocabulary that is not strictly philosophical but is taken from religious commonsense language, such as "God's command or decree" and "fortune." He clearly trusts that the reader is capable of understanding these terms in their true — that is, Spinozistic — meaning. The use of these terms establishes a bridge between metaphysical and ethical considerations. Such a bridge was unproblematic in traditional metaphysical thinking because of its peculiar conception of God as a law-giver and of man as possessing free will. But it is less straightforward in a naturalistic conception. The intellectual understanding of things "from the point of view of eternity" is not simply supposed to be a neutral view, interesting in itself, but also is to have a real bearing upon our affective and desiring life. Why should such a view of things lead us, for example, to "bear calmly both good fortune and bad," to treat others in a new way, and to try to establish a certain political order? How can a theory about what is teach us how to behave in a new way and reject "the old way of life?"[28] Before this link is explained, Spinoza thinks it necessary to develop a theory of human desire and affectivity. Book 3 of the *Ethics* serves as this bridge between the "scientific" (naturalistic) theory of man and the ethics, properly speaking. In the meantime, it is clear that the theory of man is worked out only insofar as was necessary to enable us to develop the ethical insights.

If *Ethics* I, with its doctrine *de Deo,* is a shock to the reader who is used to the *philosophia novantiqua, Ethics* II contains a no less revolutionary doctrine: *de homine.*[29] Man is only a modification of an impersonal substance. The human mind is understood as the idea of the body (and the human body is considered to possess extraordinary qualities that are not attended to in the ordinary dualistic way of thinking; III, P. 2, Sch.).[30] It is an idea that is had by God as part of his infinite intellect. The will is not free but is identical with the acts of understanding. This doctrine of man is expressed in neutral, objective language, as if we were describing a curious, complex organism. It is not surprising that present-day philosophers, attempting a "decentration of man," [31] have seen a precursor in Spinoza. Yet in Spinoza's eyes, this doctrine was not meant to belittle man or to teach us a lesson of metaphysical humility. Rather, this naturalistic vision of man, stressing also his *real* power (which is concentrated in adequate understanding), was supposed to be a *medicina mentis,* to become a "doctrine suprême,"[32] leading to real salvation.

I NOTES

1. Matheron 1978; but Bartuschat (1992a) claims that Spinoza's philosophy is basically a theory of man.
2. This is Curley's alternative version in Spinoza 1985, 448n. 3.
3. The identity between *Idea Dei* and *intellectus (infinitus) Dei* is obvious from the way these concepts are handled in Spinoza's demonstrations, for example, in *E* II, P. 4, Dem.
4. Donagan 1988, 87 (see also Gueroult 1968, 1974).
5. Della Rocca 1993, 186ff. (referring also to Charles Jarrett).
6. *ST* II, chap. 19, § 14 (Spinoza 1985, 133): "And because the first thing the soul comes to know is the body, the result is that the soul loves the body and is united to it."
7. Donagan 1988, 134–35.

8. Gueroult compares this to the relation between part and whole in a pendulum; Gueroult 1974, appendix 5 (and appendix 8); see also Donagan 1988, 124.

9. Parkinson 1954, 110–11.

10. Allison 1987, 95.

11. This view argues against Bartuschat 1992a, 63.

12. See Curley's comment in Spinoza 1985, 464n. 41.

13. This is in accord with the physiology of the time; see Gueroult 1974, 205–13 (and appendix 9).

14. But see Gueroult 1974, chap. 7.

15. See Curley's reference to Gueroult 1974, 196–97, in Spinoza 1985, 463n. 42.

16. Gueroult 1974, 225–29.

17. Donagan 1988, 144.

18. Transcendental ideas confound an operation involved in all ideas with qualities shared by everything real; see Donagan 1988, 50–51.

19. About "second notions," see Curley's comment in Spinoza 1985, 476n. 62 (with further references).

20. Donagan 1988, 136–37.

21. Donagan 1988, 138–39; Matheron 1986.

22. For a contemporary treatment of "the viewpoint from eternity," see Nagel 1986.

23. About Spinoza's conception of the relation between duration, time and measure, see letter 12 (Spinoza 1985, 200–205) and Gueroult's commentary on this letter in Gueroult 1968, appendix 9.

24. Again, there is much debate about this problem. For an extensive discussion, see Gueroult 1974, chap. 16; see also Matheron 1988; Hubbeling 1986.

25. De Deugd (1966) is right to stress this point.

26. Allison 1987, 120.

27. See Descartes's *Meditations* IV.

28. This problem is discussed in an interesting way in Strawson 1974. For a confrontation between Spinoza and Strawson on this point, see De Dijn 1985; see also chapter 11.

29. Allison 1987, 122.

30. This is stressed in Deleuze 1968, chap. 14.

31. As in French structuralist and Marxist thinking. See, for example, the interest in Spinoza of Althusser (and his students, such as Balibar and Macherey), Negri, Matheron, and Deleuze, some of them discussed in Zweerman 1979.

32. This is the title of a Spinozistic book by Benoit (1967).

Once we know the truth about nature (*Ethics* I) and about ourselves as knowers (*Ethics* II), we can take the last step in our investigation, which is to determine what adequate knowledge — especially of God and of our relation to him — can achieve with respect to our happiness. This happiness, or "blessedness" consists "in the knowledge of God alone, by which we are led to do only those things which love and morality advise" (II, P. 49, Sch. [IV-A]). Happiness, virtue, and freedom are the same: they ultimately consist in, or closely depend upon, intuitive knowledge. To clarify these connections, announced at the end of *Ethics* II, we must investigate the link between knowledge and the dynamic-affective element in man — the power of adequate knowledge in restraining the emotions. Indeed, the wretchedness of our condition consists in the hold upon us of certain negative emotions related to all sorts of illusions. In order to determine the power of adequate knowledge in restraining the emotions, it is necessary first to understand the nature and origin of the emotions (*Ethics* III); second, to come to an insight into the inevitable bondage of man, which reason cannot overcome easily (*Ethics* IV); and third, to show that a life of freedom, through intuitive knowledge, is not altogether impossible (*Ethics* V).[1]

The answer to the question of what adequate knowledge can achieve requires an investigation into a kind of power struggle in humans between "external" influences, which are expressed in the passions (passive emotions), and the "internal force," which takes the form of adequate thinking and "active" emotions. We return full circle here to the "ethical" problematic of the beginning of the *Treatise*. But this time we are in a position to develop this problematic together with the master or the philosopher, because we are ourselves in possession of the truth about nature and man: we have experienced the pleasures of adequate thinking, and we desire the true and the highest good. Spinoza's *ethics* (in the strict sense) requires, in a preliminary step, an understanding of man's actual essence as a *power* expressing itself in emotions and desires (*Ethics* III). The ethics falls into two parts. In *Ethics* IV Spinoza investigates the power struggle as it is lived by rational man—how rational man's ethical life is determined by the formation of the notions of what is really good and bad, of rational rules for the good life, and of the ideal of free man. At the same time it is shown that the desire of rational man, as determined by this ideal and these notions and rules, is nevertheless neither effective nor free. In *Ethics* V the conditions of *real* freedom are laid out (the *remedies* against the passions): they consist in intuitive knowledge and the active affects related to it. Here Spinoza shows how knowledge can constitute real happiness or blessedness, which is, at the same time, real virtue or power. This part contains Spinoza's alternative for the traditional religious doctrine of salvation. It provides the final answer to the questions about happiness posed at the beginning of the *Treatise*.

Power, Emotion, and Desire (*Ethics* III)

In the preface to *Ethics* III, Spinoza circumscribes the topic of his ethics, properly speaking: "I shall treat the nature and the powers of the Affects,[2] and the power of the Mind over them." At the same time, we encounter here the famous dictum, "I shall consider human actions and appetites as if it were a question of lines, planes, and bodies," thereby expressing his naturalistic approach to human emotionality and to ethics.

The initial propositions of *Ethics* III (P. 1–3) are an explicit critique of the Cartesian concept of the emotions as having to do with the interaction of mind and body, the passions of the soul finding their origin in actions of the body, which can and should be countered by the will's influence on the body. As we know, Spinoza rejects all causal influence between mind and body; he also redefines actions and passions as belonging to the mind, which at one moment has adequate, at another inadequate, ideas —the actions and passions of the mind expressing in thought the actions and passions of the body.[3]

But how can the mind be understood as active or passive? In order to explain this, Spinoza introduces his well-known notion of *conatus*. There are many problems related to this notion of *conatus* and the propositions in which it is elucidated, which cannot be discussed in detail here.[4] It is clear that Spinoza conceives *conatus* as a positive force, a force by which a thing, once it is functioning, continues to function, unless something opposes it (we are reminded here of the principle of *inertia* in Galileo's physics).[5] According to Spinoza, this notion implies that nothing in the thing, considered as a whole or as to a part constituting this whole, could terminate its own functioning (III, P. 4).[6] In other words, destruction always comes from outside; there can be no death wish (III, P. 5). Each thing strives "as far as it can by its own power . . . to persevere in its being" (III, P. 6) for an indefinite time (III, P. 8). Since the *conatus* of finite things can always be overpowered by a combination of other things, no finite thing actually lasts indefinitely (IV, Ax.). Being a self-maintaining force—which excludes self-destruction—the *conatus* is not a mere capacity but a real force that necessarily works itself out unless it is hindered by other things. If it is hindered, it will oppose the things contrary to it. Each *conatus* is also considered as a force tending toward self-expansion (III, P. 12, 13), as if an organism could not successfully conserve its existence unless it actively strives to increase its power.[7] This increase is determined by conditions having to do with the sort of organism in question (for example, a horse can never change into a man; see III, P. 57, Sch.).

Each thing, being *Deus quatenus,* expresses God's power in a peculiar way and to a certain degree (I, P. 34; III, P. 6). Just as God's necessarily existing essence is a power to produce an infinite infinity of things, so also each *conatus* is a real striving, in principle having indefinite duration, to produce certain effects in the real world (III, P. 7, 8). It cannot be such a striving unless it is an *actual* essence, operating in the real world of existing things. The *conatus,* being a "striving by which each thing strives to persevere in its being," "is nothing but the actual essence of the thing" (III, P. 7). This sort of perseverance in existence—the concrete *conatus*—is determined by the sort of actual essence in question and by the way the actual essence is actually modified. A horse does not strive to persevere as a man but as a horse. The *conatus* of a human being takes the form of concrete reactions and operations according to the actual modifications of the actual essence. These operations and/or reactions are performed "either alone, or with others" (III, P. 7, Dem.). All this explains why the *conatus* of human beings is not a striving to persist in "pure biological existence," and why the *conatus* of different human beings can take such different forms. Let us consider the case of the human body. In its encounters with other bodies, the human body may be annihilated, or its "power to operate" may be increased or diminished (III, Post. 1). This means that the form of the body (the fixed ratio of motion and rest between its parts) may be conserved, and yet its capacity to act and react may increase or diminish through the encounter with, or the affection by, other bodies. This increasing or decreasing of the body's power to operate (or to produce effects in the line of self-conservation and self-expansion) Spinoza calls emotion or affect (*affectus*) of the body (III, Def. 3). *Affections* of the body by other bodies—in which this power to operate is increased or diminished—produce *affects*.[8] These affects in turn give rise to reactions that are called bodily *appetites* (III, P. 9, Sch.; III, Def. Aff. 1, Expl.).

How does this apply to the mind? The *conatus* of a human being is at work in the mind insofar as the mind is the idea of an actually existing body. The modifications of the *conatus* as body will necessarily be expressed in modifications of the *conatus* as mind. And in the same way as the *conatus* of the body reacts to certain modifications of the body (affections), the *conatus* of the mind reacts to modifications of the mind (the mind's having certain ideas). Thus the mind strives to preserve itself, both insofar as it has adequate, and insofar as it has inadequate, ideas; furthermore, since the mind is conscious of itself, it also is conscious of its striving (III, P. 9).

At this point, Spinoza again introduces the notion of the will (*voluntas*), together with the notions of appetite (*appetitus*) and desire (*cupiditas*). The will is not only the affirmation or negation present in every idea as a real objective essence. It is the *conatus* itself, insofar as it "is related only to the Mind." (As we will see immediately, the will is, more concretely, the negation of what restrains or diminishes the body's power and the affirmation of what increases or aids the body's power to operate.) According to Spinoza, there is no fundamental distinction among will, appetite, and desire: will is the fundamental striving of the mind; appetite is this same striving "as related to Mind and Body together"; and desire is "appetite together with consciousness thereof" (III, P. 9, Sch.).

The appetite of man or the will or desire of the mind is not to be conceived as an abstract principle, any less than the will as affirmation or negation could be conceived as a faculty. The mind's desire "is man's very essence, insofar as it is conceived to be determined, *from any given affection of it,* to do something" (III, Def. Aff. 1; emphasis added). This determination to do something may arise from an affection or constitution that is innate or external; the affection, and therefore the determination, belong to the mind or the body, or both. If the affection belongs to the body and the mind, the determination is a human appetite; if it is combined with consciousness, it is a desire (III, Def. Aff. 1, Expl.). A desire arises from a certain affection of the mind (and the body) of which one is conscious. Desire (or appetite) is "man's very essence . . . insofar as it is conceived to be determined . . . to do something"; it necessarily takes the form of a concrete desire (or appetite) originating in a particular "affection" or "constitution of which the mind can be conscious." "Here, therefore, by the word *Desire* I understand any of man's strivings, impulses, appetites and volitions, which vary as the man's constitution varies, and which are not infrequently so opposed to one another that the man is pulled in different directions and knows not where to turn" (III, Def. Aff. 1, Expl.).

One should not make the mistake, as many philosophers do, of thinking that the mind operates because there is an external, finalistic principle moving it (the principle of "the good"). Although "everyone necessarily wants, or is repelled by, what he judges to be good or evil" (IV, P. 19), the force that makes us want or desire something is the *conatus* itself; it is because our *conatus* takes on a particular form on the basis of a certain affection that we can judge something to be good or evil, and that we desire what is good and are repelled by what is evil (III, P. 9, Sch.).

The "affections" or "constitution" from which concrete desires arise are said to be either innate or external; in the first case man can be said to be active; in the second case, to be passive (III, Def. 1, 2). In both cases, being a *conatus,* man will persevere in being, as determined in a certain way. A human being is a body that can be affected in many ways by other bodies without being destroyed. By these "affections," the body's "power of acting" can be increased or diminished (III, Post. 1). These affections of the body are also called affects (III, Def. 3). These affects/affections of the body will be expressed in the mind as ideas of these affections; these, too, are called affects (III, Def. 3). Affects of which we are not the adequate or full cause are called *passions*. If the affects of the body and the corresponding ideas of the increase of the power of the body find their origin in us or if we are their adequate (or full) cause, then we call these affects *actions* (III, Def. 3; see also III, P. 58–59).

In *Ethics* III, Spinoza concentrates on the passions of the mind (thus rewriting Descartes's *Les passions de l'âme*). A passion, or passive affect, of the mind is the expression in the mind of a bodily affection. Spinoza accepts three fundamental passions:

laetitia (pleasure or joy), *tristitia* (pain or sadness), and *cupiditas* (desire) (III, P. 11, Sch.). Pleasure or joy is defined as "a man's passage from a lesser to a greater perfection" (III, Def. Aff. 2). Pain or sadness is "a man's passage from a greater to a lesser perfection" (III, Def. Aff. 3). Spinoza explains that pleasure and pain are not a state but the transition itself of the body toward greater or lesser perfection, which is felt in the mind (III, Def. Aff. 3, Expl.), and this feeling constitutes pleasure or pain. The feeling of pleasure or pain should not be understood as the act of comparison between two states of the body's *conatus;* "the idea which constitutes the form of the affect affirms of the body something which really involves more or less of reality than before" (III, Gen. Def. Aff.). This affirmation of a change of the body toward more or less reality is something "which increases or diminishes, aids or restrains, our Mind's power of thinking" (III, P. 11). So this affirmation constitutes pleasure or pain as the emotion or feeling of the mind itself whereby the mind itself passes to greater or lesser perfection.

It is curious that Spinoza lists desire as the third fundamental emotion, although he first seems to explain it as equivalent to the thing's *conatus* itself—that is, as the basis of all emotions. But this is not as strange as it may seem at first. Spinoza defines desire not only as *conatus*—appetite with consciousness thereof. Indeed, this conscious striving of the actual essence of man is always necessarily determined by one affection or another (III, Def. Aff. 1)—that is, it is a reaction to pleasure or pain. Since desire is not the same as pleasure or pain but is a reaction to it, and as such is the basic motivating force in human behavior, it can be considered as a third fundamental emotion.[9]

Affects, such as love and desire, are modes of thinking that presuppose the fundamental mode of thinking—that is, an idea as acquaintance with one or another object. There can be an idea even though there is no other mode of thinking, but not vice versa (II, Ax. 3). An emotion is the affirmation of a greater or lesser force of the body; this affirmation constitutes by itself a positive or negative feeling or a positive or negative desire. Emotion or desire presupposes an affection of the body referring to other bodies (whether they are actually present or not). Therefore, it always presupposes an *idea* of one external thing or another that is supposedly involved in the affection of the body. But an emotion is itself an idea through which a fluctuation of the power of the body—which is the bodily *affectus*—is affirmed (albeit confusedly) (III, Gen. Def. Aff.). Because of all this, an emotion is really cognitive *and* affective. The desires related to it are dynamic as well as cognitive: "The Mind, as far as it can, strives to imagine those things that increase or aid the Body's power of acting" (III, P. 12); "when the Mind imagines those things that diminish or restrain the Body's power of acting, it strives, as far as it can to recollect things that exclude their existence" (III, P. 13).

From the three basic, or primitive, emotions all other emotions can be derived. For this derivation, one must take into account certain factors and laws concerning man's existence in "the common order of nature." For example, the affections of the body—and the corresponding emotions of pleasure, pain, and desire—refer to objects that cause these affections and the corresponding emotions. This explains emotions like love or hate ("Love is a Joy, accompanied by the idea of an external cause," III, Def. Aff. 6). Factors such as memory and the modal conceptions of things as necessary, impossible, possible, contingent, past, or future give rise to all sorts of emotion ("Despair is a Sadness born of the idea of a future or past thing concerning which the cause of doubting has been removed," III, Def. Aff. 15). Emotions also can be contrary to each other or reinforce each other ("Vacillation of the mind" is the "constitution of the Mind which arises from two contrary affects," III, P. 17, Sch.).

Association based on similarity, contrast, or contiguity is the source of a whole train of emotions. Association explains "how it can happen that we love or hate some things without any cause known to us, but only (as they say) from Sympathy or Antipathy. And to this must be related also those objects that affect us with Joy or Sadness only because they have some likeness to objects that usually affect us with these affects" (III, P. 15, Sch.).

A factor that plays a significant role in our emotional life is related to our social nature: it is "the imitation of the affects" (III, P. 27, Sch.). This gives rise to emotions such as pity, emulation, and benevolence ("Emulation is a Desire for a thing which is generated in us because we imagine that others have the same Desire," *Ethics* III, Def. Aff. 33). This imitation of the emotions does not necessarily lead to positive attitudes toward others, such as pity and benevolence; paradoxically, it also can lead to emotions such as ambition, envy, and jealousy (see III, P. 31ff.).[10]

Because Spinoza tries to explain the emotions on the basis of their proximate cause, it is not surprising that his definitions do not necessarily follow the usual understanding of the common terminology of the emotions, even though he tries to conserve as much as possible of this terminology and meaning (see, for example, his definition of indignation in III, Def. Aff. 20, Expl.). Spinoza does not claim to have explained all possible emotions and "conflicts of mind" but only the main ones. "Indeed, from what has already been said I believe it is clear to anyone that the various affects can be compounded with one another in so many ways, and that so many variations can arise from this composition that they cannot be defined by any number" (III, P. 59, Sch.). Furthermore, "[e]ach affect of each individual differs from the affect of another as much as the essence of the one from the essence of the other" (III, P. 57). This means that each emotion in its concreteness is as particular as each individual *conatus* of which it is a modification ("there is no small difference between the gladness by which a drunk is led and the gladness a Philosopher possesses," III, P. 57, Sch.). That this does not exclude the possibility of a general explanation of the sorts of emotions belonging to human nature is also indicated by Spinoza's claim that "the affects of the animals which are called irrational . . . differ from men's affects as much as their nature differs from human nature" (III, P. 57, Sch.).

In *Ethics* III Spinoza claims to "have explained and shown through their first [proximate] causes the main affects and vacillations of the mind which arise from the composition of the three primitive affects, *viz*. Desire, Joy, and Sadness." And, he adds, "From what has been said it is clear that we are driven about in many ways by external causes, and that, like waves on the sea, driven by contrary winds, we toss about, not knowing our outcome and fate" (III, P. 59, Sch.). Yet the mind can also be characterized by *active* emotions. The primitive active emotions take the form either of joy (pleasure) or of desire, never of sadness (pain) (III, P. 59). The active emotions and desires are related to the mind insofar as it is active and not passive—that is, insofar as it understands and at the same time considers itself as active. The active mind is necessarily characterized by active joy and active desires flowing from it. "All actions that follow from affects related to the Mind insofar as it understands I relate to Strength of character [*fortitudo*]" (III, P. 59, Sch.). The desires related to *fortitudo* can be directed either toward oneself or toward others. Spinoza calls the active desires of the first kind forms of tenacity or courage (*animositas*), which is "the Desire by which each one strives, solely from the dictate of reason, to preserve his being"; those of the second kind he calls nobility (*generositas*), which is "the Desire by which each one strives, solely from the dictate of reason, to aid other men and join them to him in friendship." *Generositas* displays itself in friendship (IV, P. 71, Dem.), gratitude (IV, P. 71, Sch.), honesty (IV, P. 72 and Sch.), and morality (*pietas*) (IV, P. 73, Sch., referring to IV, P. 37, Sch. 1). *Animositas* (tenacity) shows itself in religion (*religio*), which is the desire to act on the basis of having the idea of God (IV, P. 37, Sch. 1); in wisdom, which "is a meditation on life, not on death" (IV, P. 67); and in true heroism (IV, P. 69). The active emotions and desires are discussed primarily in *Ethics* IV. In *Ethics* III, Spinoza concentrates on the passions, which one must explore extensively in order to determine precisely the power of the mind with respect to them. In desire, or willing, but also in the emotions of pain and pleasure and in their multiple derivations, we clearly form our own proper perspective on things, however inadequate this perspective may be.[11]

On Human Bondage (*Ethics* IV)

Ethics, or morals, is concerned with the question of the good life, a question that is intrinsically linked to problems such as freedom and responsibility in human activity. Today, the question of the good life often is narrowed down to what we should or should not do vis-à-vis other human beings or beings also capable of experiencing pain and pleasure. For Spinoza, as for his time, ethics has primarily to do with the pursuit of virtue or self-perfection, which is normally considered to imply also being good to others. The aim of this broad ethics is to show the way to self-perfection, real well-being, or virtue—all of these terms have the same meaning. The big question is how this self-realization is possible in view of the fact that "[i]t is impossible for man not to be part of nature and not to follow the common order of nature" (IV, App. 7)—that is, not to be free from passions. Accordingly, ethics is centered on the theme of freedom versus slavery vis-à-vis one's passions and on the means to escape slavery and reach real freedom through following the dictates of reason or finding the remedies against the passions. Since Spinoza rejects the notion of a free will, his ethics is not one of responsibility or duty but one of freedom in the sense of self-realization. For him, the notions of good and evil do not refer to what is good or evil in itself but to what is known to be the means to reach real freedom (IV, Def. 1, 2).

Nothing is good or evil in itself; things just are necessarily what they are. Notions of good or bad arise in the mind because it experiences pleasure and pain and desires what gives pleasure and flees what gives pain (IV, P. 8; IV, Pref.). But why would philosophers continue to talk about good and evil if these notions "indicate nothing positive in things, considered in themselves," if they are nothing "other than modes of thinking or notions we form because we compare things to one another" (IV, Pref.)? Indeed, "[i]f men were born free [rational], they would form no concept of good and evil so long as they remained free" (*Ethics* IV, P. 68).

But this hypothesis clearly is false: human beings inevitably encounter setbacks and form the notion of what is evil and of what is good (IV, P. 68, Sch.); they construct the model of a more perfect human nature than the one already enjoyed (IV, Pref.). What is more, even though we have become rational and know that the notions of good and bad and of an ideal human nature are not objective concepts that express things as they are in themselves, yet "we must retain these words. For because we desire to form an idea of man, as a model of human nature which we may look to, it will be useful to retain these same words ["good" and "evil," "perfect" and "imperfect"] with the meaning I have indicated" (IV, Pref.). The "we" who "must retain these words" are clearly the rational readers of the *Ethics* who have followed and understood Spinoza this far and who are not different from other rational people engaged in ethical endeavor. Rational people too form the idea of a perfect model of human self-realization (or full freedom or virtue); they, too, in function of this ideal, form notions of what is the *true* good (a certain means to reach perfection) and of what is the *highest* good (virtue itself, consisting in knowledge of God; IV, P. 28). These notions of good and evil, and of ideal man, are not fictions of the imagination:[12] they are the inevitable product of the developing rationality of human beings.

Obviously, Spinoza takes up here the ethical problematic expressed at the beginning of the *Treatise* and fully endorses it. First he had to engage in logic, metaphysics, and the theory of man (the study of the cognitive and dynamic-affective nature of man) before he could develop this problematic. But if we are capable of rational as well as intuitive knowledge and of the active emotions related to them, why did Spinoza not simply go straight to the discussion of the relation between intuitive knowledge and blessedness (*Ethics* V), thus collapsing the central aim of logic, metaphysics, and ethics, which is to reach the intuitive knowledge of God?[13] Why first engage in a description of the causes of human infirmity and inconstancy (IV, P. 1–18)? Why try to establish the precepts of reason (*dictamina rationes*) (IV, P. 19–37) and, in the light of these, to investigate which passions agree with reason and which not (IV, P. 38–58)? Why attempt to construct a picture of a life lived "under the dictate of reason alone" (IV, P. 59–66) or of the free person (IV, P. 67–end)?[14]

The reason is clearly that we are not born free, that even rational people are living in the real world, which is not there for the purpose of man. It is inevitable that even rational people are assailed daily by passions and suffer all sorts of setbacks (IV, Ax. 1). Rational man, who has already experienced the special pleasures involved in rational activity, inevitably desires more of this, forms the picture of the ideal human nature, and judges everything as good or evil on the basis of this desire and this ideal. Rational people form the notions of the true and the highest good because, on the basis of their knowledge of human nature, they can know which passions are compatible with their desire and which not, and what activity can really fulfill this desire. The move from knowledge of human nature and passions to knowledge of what is good and evil is possible (and inevitable) because of rational man's self-experience and desire.

Within the context of the desire of rational man, the scientific truths about the origin of the emotions and their consequences are transformed into hypothetical imperatives (the precepts of reason).[15] Ideas of what is good and evil are nothing but the consciousness of what gives pleasure or pain (IV, P. 8). It is no different in rational people: their knowledge of what is good and evil is an expression of their awareness of the pleasures of the activity of reason (IV, P. 63, Cor.). But with rational people, these pleasures and the desire to conserve them are informed by rational insight into the relations between *means and ends*. So they possess *true* knowledge of what is good or evil (IV, P. 15, Dem.).[16]

Rational man's striving toward the ideal of free man is inevitable in view of what rational man knows and desires. It is a striving informed by the precepts of reason. Spinoza realizes that knowledge, even knowledge of good and evil, cannot restrain any emotion simply because this knowledge is true, but only when it takes the form of an emotion (IV, P. 14). This means that it is not sufficient to know the hypothetical imperatives related to true knowledge of good and evil, in order to make, and keep, one's life rational. The rational insight that certain things are damaging to a certain sort of *conatus* can be part of "the view from nowhere." As such, it is incapable of any real influence. But this rational insight can be inserted into the proper point of view of a concrete striving individual with his or her own experiences of pain and pleasure (see the reference to IV, P. 8, in IV, P. 14, Dem.).[17] Then this knowledge becomes *relevant* for the individual who is striving.

An ethics consisting of precepts and ideals (of the rational life, of free man) arises because of the *interim position* of man, because of the clash between interiority and exteriority. People can become rational, but even when rational, they inevitably are overwhelmed by passions from time to time. The rational individual has tasted the pleasures of reason yet is caught in a struggle in which he inevitably encounters defeat and the resultant longing to reach peace again. It is this predicament that gives rise to the strange science of what is really good and evil, and of the ideal of freedom—a practical science that consists of precepts and models, a science of which the central notions are beings of reason (*entia rationis*) (like those of geometry and of architecture[18]) that do not express reality.

This science, which is to be applied in the reality of the struggle of daily life, is inevitably abstract and a mixture of imagination and reason. The scientific knowledge of good and evil is "only abstract, or universal" (IV, P. 62, Sch.). Because rational people are confronted with an unknown future, with possibilities and contingencies (IV, P. 16, 17), their knowledge of good and evil must be combined with judgments concerning the future and the likely outcome of things—judgments that are more imaginary than real (IV, P. 62, Sch.).

Thus one can easily see that even though the rational individual possesses true knowledge of good and evil, and even though this knowledge has affective force, he inevitably succumbs to passions—for example, to the desire for things that are pleasing in the present (IV, P. 16, 17), and that they do form the notion of what is evil (IV, P. 64, Cor.). The paradoxical truth is that "the *true* knowledge of good and evil arouses disturbances of the mind, and often yields to lust of every kind" (IV, P. 17, Sch.). In one's concrete daily struggle, to know what is really good and evil means to see the real difficulties of obtaining the good and to encounter discouraging setbacks. Spinoza quotes here the words of Ovid: "video meliora, proboque, deteriora sequor" ("I see and approve the better, but follow the worse," *Metamorphoses* 7.20–21), and borrows from Ecclesiastes: "He who increases knowledge increases sorrow" (Eccles. 1:18)—which, of course, is not to say that "it is better to be ignorant than to know, or that there is no difference between the fool and the man who understands when it comes to moderating the affects" (IV, P. 17, Sch.). Nevertheless, one could say (with Victor Goldschmidt) that the science of good and evil is part of the weakness and servitude of rational man.[19] Jon Wetlesen rightly says that "[t]he model of a free person . . . should not be confused with the free person himself."[20]

Some commentators have expressed surprise at the title of book 4 of the *Ethics* and claim that it does not seem to correspond to the content of the book. How can a book that contains the

doctrine of the free individual bear the title "On Human Bondage"? Many parts of this book seem to belong to the topic of *Ethics*
V, "On the Power of the Intellect or on Human Freedom." After
what we have said about human weakness in the ethical struggle,
even of rational man, we can see the whole of *Ethics* IV as dealing
with human bondage. The perspective of *Ethics* IV clearly is set by
the only axiom we find at the beginning of book 4: man is a part of
nature, which can always be overpowered by something stronger.
It is the weakness of people—more precisely, of rational people—
which gives rise to the peculiar ethical problematic both at the
beginning of the *Treatise* and of *Ethics* IV.

The question that looms at the end of book 4 is whether "we,"
living the concrete life of the rational human being described in
Ethics IV, P. 1–18, can ever realize the picture of a really rational
life (IV P. 59–66) or of the free individual (IV, 67–end)—in other
words, whether rational people can ever go beyond this stage of
constant struggle and longing. The question is whether we can
ever lead a life that is, at least for a while, a *consistent* flow of
active thinking, feeling, and desiring (IV, P. 63; P. 65, Cor.; and
P. 66, Cor.), a life in which one is not easily affected by bad emotions (V, P. 10, Sch.) even though one remains a part of nature
(IV, App. 32); a life in which the passions constitute the smallest
part of the mind (V, P. 20, Sch.). This question about the possibility of an at least partial escape from longing, of a stage of ethical
life "beyond good and evil," is answered in *Ethics* V, P. 1–20.

Spinoza's precepts of reason often are presented as being in
strong opposition to traditional Christian values. For example,
many highlight his rejection of pity (IV, P. 50), humility (IV, P.
53), and repentance (IV, P. 54) and stress his anti-asceticism (IV,
45, Sch. 2) and his condemnation of a superstition-based aversion
to pleasure, which is usually combined with praise of impotence
(IV, P. 35, Sch.; and App. 31). What they forget is that Spinoza
also says that the human being who is moved neither by reason
nor by pity is rightly called inhuman (IV, P. 50, Sch.) and that, insofar as people rarely live according to the precepts of reason, humility, and repentance (but also hope and fear), they do more
good than evil. So it is not surprising for Spinoza to find that the
prophets greatly commend these virtues (together with reverence); furthermore, the person liable to these emotions is more
easily led to live under the guidance of reason (IV, P. 54, Sch.).
We should not forget that when Spinoza rejects these emotions in
the *Ethics,* it is because he addresses himself to the *friends* who
are trying to become men of reason. Common morality, for the
majority, should be based, as the *Tractatus Theologico-Politicus*

shows, on a purified Judeo-Christian religion, on the religious precepts of obedience, justice, and charity, and on nonsuperstitious forms of other commonly advocated virtues.

Spinoza's ethics is, in a sense, hedonistic: "Pleasure clearly is not evil but good; but pain, on the contrary, is clearly evil" (IV, P. 41). Of course, there are different sorts of pleasure (IV, P. 42, 43), and one should look for nonexcessive forms of pleasure and especially for the pleasures of reason. Spinoza stresses in his ethics the importance of society, of other people. Although man is often a wolf to man (IV, P. 34), yet "man is [also] a God to man" (IV, P. 35, Sch.; IV, App. 7, 9). Outside the community of men or outside the state, real human life is practically impossible (this is why, in IV, P. 37, Sch. 2, after a group of propositions in which Spinoza lays the foundation governing interhuman rational life,[21] he mentions the central tenets of his political philosophy[22]).

Spinoza's utterances have an undeniable utilitarian ring: he constantly talks about the usefulness of other people—also of other rational people—for the rational human being; furthermore, he equates the good with what is useful (IV, Def. 1). Yet it would be wrong to interpret Spinoza as a straightforward utilitarian or even as an intellectualist egoist. Although he says that what can be most useful to an individual is other people, this does not mean that the rational human being has a purely utilitarian attitude to other people. The true good that rational people desire for themselves they genuinely desire for other people as well (IV, P. 37, Alt. Dem.), and the bond between free people is characterized by friendship and gratitude (IV, P. 71 and Sch.). Thus the relations between rational people are based not on strictly utilitarian considerations but on their common interest in reason and on the pleasure of seeing others join in their interest (IV, P. 37 and Dem. 1, 2).[23] Although at a deep level there is the inescapable egoism (not to be confused with egocentrism) of the fundamental *conatus,* this ontological egoism is not incompatible with the bond of friendship between rational people who genuinely want others to progress in rationality and virtue.

Among the precepts of reason are many recommendations that, however interesting they may be, it is impossible to go into here: remarks concerning sexual lust (IV, App. 19), marriage (IV, App. 20), the care for the poor (IV, App. 17), attitudes toward animals (IV, P. 37n. 2 and App. 26), money (IV, App. 28), care for the body (IV, App. 27), the rejection of pride (IV, P. 55–57)—but not of honor or love of esteem (IV, P. 58)—and many others. The passage concerning the wise man is well known: "It is part of a wise man, I say, to refresh and restore himself in moderation with pleasant food and drink, with scents, with the beauty of green plants, with decoration, music, sports and theater, and other things of this kind, which anyone can use without injury to another" (IV, P. 45, Sch.); it clearly establishes Spinoza's anti-asceticism.

The last words of *Ethics* IV (App. 32) are a reminder of the very beginning of that book (IV, Ax. 1): "But human power is very limited and infinitely surpassed by the power of external causes. So we do not have an absolute power to adapt things outside us to our use." The recommendation is then to "bear calmly those things which happen to us contrary to what the principle of our advantage demands, if we are conscious that we have done our duty, that the power we have could not have extended itself to the point where we could have avoided those things, and that we are part of the whole of nature, whose order we follow." With respect to the past, rational people should not feel guilty: if they have been overpowered, this was inevitable; with respect to the future, they should strive toward the good with all their might and insight. In short, we should strive "to act well and rejoice" ("bene agere et laetari") (IV, P. 73, Sch.). Even our "moral defeats" can be occasions for rejoicing in what can be seen, from the point of view of nowhere, as an expression of the power of nature as present partly also in our own, limited power. And in our striving to act well, we should bear in mind that this striving, too— whether or not successful—is an expression of the necessity of nature. In this way, "insofar as we understand, we can want nothing except what is true. Hence, insofar as we understand these things rightly, the striving of the better part of us agrees with the order of the whole of nature."

Toward the end of *Ethics* IV, Spinoza announces *Ethics* V as the place where he will demonstrate "how far human virtue can go in the attainment of those things," and what it is capable of with respect to "acting well and rejoicing" (IV, P. 73, Sch.). These questions are appropriate, because it still is not clear how and under what conditions people can effectively reach these attitudes. It is not sufficient to know the recommendations to implement them in one's life. It is not sufficient to desire to have these attitudes to be really capable of them. Therefore it is always possible that these desires might be thwarted and instead lead to the peculiar sorrows of the rational man who sees and approves the better but follows the worse. The realization of these desires requires that we forget to desire and transcend the level of good and evil and of trying to follow the precepts of reason.

I On Human Freedom (*Ethics* V)

The question remaining at the end of book 4 was, Can we go beyond the stage of ethical struggle, the stage of knowledge of good and evil, of trying to live up to the model of the free human being, with all the fluctuations and contradictions that go with it? A positive answer to these questions is given in book 5, "the remaining Part of the Ethics" (V, Pref.). The ethics of the model of free man is only provisional.[24] The solution to the ethical struggle of the rational person is to reach knowledge of the third kind—intuitive knowledge—and the active emotions (such as the intellectual love of God) going with it.

Some interpreters of Spinoza's ethics claim that what is offered here, particularly in *Ethics* V, is a kind of therapy against the passions or a strategy of self-liberation and self-realization.[25] This idea seems basically right, yet it is surprising to see that these interpretations turn out to be very different, almost incompatible. Curley, for example, understands Spinoza's ethics as a kind of *cognitive therapy* against the passions.[26] Since the passions contain an element of insight and belief, we can, through our attempt to reach better beliefs, bring about changes in our emotional life (Spinoza is compared here with Nietzsche). For example, by taking an objective standpoint with respect to other people's behavior, we will be much less prone to hate them. However, we should not have unrealistic hopes about the effectiveness of this cognitive therapy.[27] Wetlesen's presentation of Spinoza's ethics is more elaborate and diversified, and much more grandiose. He distinguishes two radically different levels in the ethical development: gradual strategies of liberation (*Ethics* IV) and instantaneous strategies of liberation (*Ethics* V).[28] Wetlesen compares Spinoza's ethics in detail with great religious traditions of self-liberation and self-realization, such as Mahayana Buddhism.[29] A close look at Spinoza's texts reveals that although his ethics can be seen as a kind of cognitive therapy, it advocates a more sophisticated and unusual way to well-being and salvation than one would expect in a rationalist and naturalist framework. It is a therapy that can, indeed, be compared to what is advocated in some religious traditions. Especially in *Ethics* V, Spinoza offers his alternative to the religious doctrine of blessedness through grace[30] and of the "last things."[31]

How does one go beyond the stage of striving in terms of good and evil? Spinoza's solution, as demonstrated in *Ethics* V, P. 1–20, is that real freedom is possible through "the understanding alone." This statement should not be seen as an identification of this second stage of the ethics with logic: Spinoza explicitly distinguishes the two in the preface to book 5. The ethics is not the emendation of the intellect, as such; it concerns the relation between the intellect and the passions. Whereas logic has to do with purifying the intellect so that it can develop its knowledge as if it were a spiritual automaton, ethics has to do with how this knowledge can mean "salvation from despair."[32] What is required in ethics is not more knowledge for knowledge's sake but rather a peculiar kind of knowledge of a peculiar kind of object: knowledge of *our own* emotions. This knowledge is supposed to give rise to a train of active emotions that effectively produce a way of life predominantly free from the passions.

Vocabulary and notions related to the previous stage (guidance, precepts, ideals) are replaced by vocabulary and notions indicating real forces and real changes (the new tone is set by the two axioms of book 5 dealing with power relations). Before engaging in his analysis, Spinoza indicates what the solution to the ethical predicament and the weakness of reason does not consist in (V, Pref.). The solution cannot be the work of Stoic asceticism, nor can it be the work of an absolutely free will that is supposed to be enlightened by reason (this is the harshly rejected Cartesian solution). The solution, Spinoza continues, is actually experienced (to a certain degree) by everyone but is not accurately noticed or distinctly seen as a solution, probably because people are blinded by the ideology of free will and/or because of their immersion in the daily struggle.

The change from book 4 to book 5 is the change from a level in which one tries to implement *precepts* of reason and strives toward an *ideal* to a level in which one finds *remedies* "in understanding alone," in just acting. The theory of what should be striven for is replaced by a theory of what it is to *be* free.[33] We have to move *from* an attempt to apply—externally, as it were[34]—certain abstract truths about good and evil to our life *toward* a different level of ethical activity, indicated by the remedies, that is beyond striving for an ideal. This new therapy is the one in which we "forget" about precepts concerning good and evil and simply act in such a way that even our passions are transformed into occasions of self-realization. The solution is to "lose ourselves" in a meditative activity and in the specific active emotions going with it. Through these "actions of the mind," the passions are not exterminated but function as occasions for further intuitive knowing and active emotions. The striving of the person of reason in book 4 is fundamentally paradoxical: it is a desire for a state (of freedom or self-realization) that is such that if one has attained it, one can no longer have this desire (for example, in a state of freedom one no longer cares about the future; see IV, P. 62).[35] In order to really reach the goal set in book 4, one has to transcend striving toward this goal; one has to engage in an activity in which all longing is forgotten.

Virtue and freedom are not the result of the striving to dominate the passions; *being* virtuous and free is the best remedy against the passions (similarly, the real remedy against sickness is good health, the real remedy against insanity is sanity). This is not to say that the human being of reason is not yet rational and free to a certain degree; but the full realization of freedom requires a sort of leap to another level, thanks to the actual development of a life dominated more and more by intuitive knowledge and the active emotions that accompany it.

What are these remedies against the passions? The five remedies listed in *Ethics* V, P. 20, Sch., are none other than the life of intellectual understanding of an intuitive kind, whereby one is free and active, and blessed. The first remedy is *knowledge of the emotions*. As is clear from *Ethics* V, P. 4, Sch. (taken in context), Spinoza means knowledge of our *own* emotions: "We must . . . take special care to know each affect clearly and distinctly (as far as this is possible)." This knowledge produces power over the emotions because if we form a clear and distinct idea of an emotion, this idea will be distinguished only conceptually from the emotion and, as it were, fuse with it (*Ethics* V, P. 3, Dem.). This neutral, scientific conception of our *own* emotions can thus really affect our emotional states in such a way that, although they do not disappear, their passive character is changed. The adequate understanding in question must undoubtedly be a kind of meditative activity in which one's *concretely felt* emotion is *confronted* with the view from nowhere on the emotions (as made possible by the scientific psychology of *Ethics* III). In this confrontation, cognition produces a kind of not strictly cognitive effect.

The second remedy consists "in the fact that it separates the affects from the thought of the external cause, which we imagine confusedly" (V, P. 2, Sch. with reference to V, P. 2; P. 4, Sch.). As is clear from *Ethics* V, P. 4, Sch., this remedy is closely connected to the first: if the first remedy is implemented, we can no longer link our emotions with their supposed external causes. This brings to a halt the usual train of passions and desires related to the first emotion. Having separated the emotion "from the thought of an external cause and joined [it] to true thoughts" (V, P. 4, Sch.), a whole new train of internally determined emotions, desires, and activities will arise.

The first and second remedies thus consist in a peculiar combination of seeing passions really occurring in us in light of our adequate understanding of them. This requires that we succeed in forming a kind of meditative awareness of our passions (informed by adequate knowledge about them) whereby they are encapsulated and defused by being taken up into a different context. In this way, whatever happens to us becomes the occasion for adequate thinking and active emotions, for the further free flow of activity.

The next remedy consists in the presence or systematic production of active emotions. These emotions, which are species of *fortitudo* (strength of character) (III, P. 59, Sch.), are all characterized by a profound joy and quietude.[36] In discussing these remedies, Spinoza shows how having adequate knowledge of our own emotions produces these active emotions (as experiences of our power), and how they can spontaneously override many passions due to the very laws governing both kinds of emotions (such as laws having to do with the sorts of cause they have and with their relation to time and modalities). The very way that things are seen in this combination of detached understanding and meditative awareness means that the active emotions accompanying such cognitive activity will be stronger than many passions. The train of adequate thinking and active emotions constitutes a kind of life that is a formidable remedy against the passions. The systematic production of these actions is stressed particularly in the fifth remedy, which consists "in the order by which the mind can order its affects and connect them to one another" (see P. 10, 12, 13, 14). Although the five remedies cannot remove the passions entirely, they can bring about that the flow of active thought and feeling grows into an almost unassailable stronghold, or, in any case, that the passions constitute proportionally the smallest part of the mind (V, P. 20, Sch.).

In the propositions referred to in relation to the fifth remedy (*Ethics* V, P. 10, 12, 13, 14), Spinoza stresses the role of the *bodily* counterparts of our active ideas and emotions—that is, bodily images and bodily fluctuations of power.[37] The ease with which many images of things can be linked with images corresponding to adequate ideas and vice versa—as well as the ease with which bodily affects corresponding to active emotions can be evoked by images of things—creates a real flow of activity. Each thing we encounter can become a further occasion for adequate thinking and active emotions.

Spinoza's concept of the ethical importance of a meditative yet detached self-knowledge relates him to older, ethical-religious traditions. However, what is typical for Spinoza is that the meditative self-knowledge is closely linked to a scientific psychology modeled after the newly established study of nature. Another feature that brings to mind older traditions of wisdom is the connection made between this meditative self-knowledge and the intuitive knowledge and intellectual love of God. This indicates that the ethical remedies have a significance that goes far beyond conventional wisdom with respect to the passions ("tricks" discussed in *Ethics* V, P. 10, Sch.—for example, certain mnemonic-technical devices—belong to the provisional morality, which is superseded when one reaches the level of the remedies in action). If the meditative self-knowledge succeeds in being linked to the idea of God (V, P. 14), then the human mind will be characterized by the intellectual love of God ("amor intellectualis Dei," V, P. 15, 36–37). It is called *intellectual* love because it is dependent on the intellect, on adequate knowledge, and does not have the drawbacks of ordinary love. "This Love towards God must engage the Mind most" (V, P. 16). It is "the most constant of all affects, and insofar as it is related to the Body, cannot be destroyed, unless it is destroyed with the Body itself." It "cannot be tainted by any of the vices which are in ordinary love, but can always be greater and greater (by P 15), and occupy the greatest part of the Mind (by P 16), and affect it extensively" (V, P. 20, Sch.).

This love is not reciprocal: "He who loves God cannot strive that God should love him in return" (V, P. 19), because "[s]trictly speaking, God loves no one, and hates no one" (V, P. 17, Cor.). Although, later on, Spinoza demonstrates that our own love of God "is part of the infinite love by which God loves himself" (V, P. 36, Dem.), this does not contradict the statement that God is not characterized by affects at all. The infinite love by which God loves himself, and of which our love of Him is a part, does not belong to God as *Natura Naturans;* it is the love had by God *insofar* as he constitutes his *Idea Dei* (V, P. 36, Dem.). It is God's intellect that "contains" God's love for himself; therefore, our love can really be part of this love. This state of love produces the highest quietude (*acquiescentia*) (*Ethics* V, P. 38, Sch.) and constitutes "our salvation, *or* blessedness, or Freedom"; therefore, it is rightly "called Glory [*gloria*] in the Sacred Scriptures" (V, P. 36, Sch.).

The intellectual love of God is not simply delight in the intelligibility of things.[38] It is love of God and love of oneself; it is "an action by which the Mind contemplates itself, with the accompanying idea of God as its cause" (V, P. 36, Dem.). It is the perfect acceptance of oneself, of anything that happens to oneself; it is *acquiescentia* (*in se ipso*), a kind of "being at peace with oneself"

(V, P. 27). Intuitive knowledge, and the concomitant intellectual love of God, is always accompanied by the idea of oneself and of one's body as eternal essences belonging to God (V, P. 30, 36).

Salvation (or blessedness) does not consist simply in knowledge; rather, it consists in knowledge of a very special kind, not simply knowledge formed in demonstrations but knowledge that is awareness and love of one's concrete self as an eternal expression of God's power that modified itself in a mode that actively loves its cause: "we feel and know by experience that we are eternal. For the Mind feels those things that it conceives in understanding no less than those it has in the memory. For the eyes of the mind, by which it sees and observes things, are the demonstrations themselves" (V, P. 23, Sch.).

The intellectual love of God that accompanies intuitive knowledge is not mentioned as a separate remedy against the passions. It is the major active affect that blossoms whenever we succeed in knowing ourselves and our passions intuitively, which implies knowledge of God. It is the culmination of the system of remedies. It is that affective-dynamic state in which we are perfectly satisfied—blessedness. It is an experience that has to do with the presence of eternity in time. So it is not surprising that Spinoza discusses it in the second part of *Ethics* V, dealing with "those things which pertain to the Mind's duration without relation to the body" (V, P. 20, Sch.).

Blessedness (or salvation) is not the independent reward of virtue or of the striving toward the ideal and for the good. To be virtuous is to be beyond good and evil, beyond the striving for the ideal; it is to be active in knowing and feeling; this virtue *is* blessedness (V, P. 42).

If the first part of *Ethics* V (P. 1–20) is the object of controversy, this is even more the case with the second part (V, P. 21–end). Here Spinoza discusses the eternity of the human mind as characterized by intuitive knowledge and the intellectual love of God. Such a mind is eternal (V, P. 31–33) and can be considered "without relation to the Body's existence" as "an eternal mode of thinking" (V, P. 40, Sch.). It is unclear whether "eternity" should be understood here as opposed to duration or is the same as immortality after death.[39] It is obvious that for Spinoza, immortality cannot mean that we would recollect that we existed before the body actually existed (V, P. 23, Sch.) or that we would remember part or the whole of what happened to us in "the common order of nature" (V, P. 21: "The Mind can neither imagine anything, nor recollect past things, except while the Body endures"). Spinoza even seems to deny immortality when he says that "we do not attribute to the human Mind any duration that can be defined by time, except insofar as it expresses the actual existence of the Body" (V, P. 23, Dem.). However, Spinoza also says that there is "part of the Mind that remains": the intellect (V, P. 40, Cor.), which is, of course, self-conscious and which is "an eternal mode of thinking" belonging to God's eternal infinite intellect (V, P. 40, Sch.). This intellect "remains" insofar as it necessarily belongs to the eternal essence of the mind, which—unlike the essence of the body—is a real individual part of God's infinite intellect or idea (see the reference to *Ethics* II, P. 8, Cor., in V, P. 23, Dem.).[40] Spinoza notes that we "conceive things as actual in two ways: either insofar as we conceive them to exist in relation to a certain time and place or insofar as we conceive them to be contained in God and to follow from the necessity of the divine nature. But the things we conceive in this second way as true, or real, we conceive under a species [aspect] of eternity" (V, P. 29, Sch.). This "eternal existence" should not be conceived in terms of an endless time; it should be understood as a reality—that is, an irreducibly essential expression of God's power, even if it has an actual existence of only a few moments in a life span. Eternity, then, is not what is opposed to duration, but what is *in* duration, pure activity; it is the joyful self-awareness of an expression of God's power, fully accepting itself as God's modification in a moment of and in time. The intellectual love of God is a conscious experiencing of "our eternal essence" *in* time. Einstein, who calls himself a Spinozist, rephrases these experiences of extraordinary joy and glory as "cosmic religious feeling."[41]

It is time now to take up our original question: How can knowledge, especially the sort of metaphysical knowledge of God and man modeled after the new science, bring about happiness? The answer that one could most easily accept is that the activity of scientific-metaphysical understanding itself constitutes its own special delight. In the activity of viewing things *sub specie aeternitatis,* one forgets all one's troubles; and the more one is capable of engaging in this activity, the more one escapes the emotional troubles of ordinary life. It is interesting to note that Bertrand Russell at one point identified Spinoza's intellectual love of God with the emotional state accompanying intellectual discovery.[42] But later he came to see that this could not be the whole story, that in order to understand the relationship between intuitive knowledge and intellectual love of God, we must understand the relationship between the joy of thinking and a metaphysical view *of nature* (and of oneself).[43] For knowledge (especially scientific or objectifying knowledge) to produce experiences of joy and love—which can be understood as states of blessedness—it must not simply be known as a piece of information, it must become *relevant* for us personally. We all know that we must die, but this does not make us panic, as it does Lev Tolstoi's Ivan Illich. We can know that things are part of nature, but "this does not affect our Mind as much as when this is inferred from the very essence of any singular thing which we say depends on God" (V, P. 36, Sch.). And only a truth "which affects the mind" can influence us deeply.

Spinoza clearly believes that knowledge of the emotions can have an effect upon them. But this can only happen, as we have seen concerning the five remedies, when we succeed in "meditatively applying" this knowledge to *our own* emotions. The meditative application of an objective view about ourselves to ourselves can indeed be successful in defusing our ordinary emotional states and changing them into something active. In this application of the truth about ourselves to ourselves, a sort of delusion that is present in our ordinary way of life, in our ordinary conception of ourselves, seems to give way in an estrangement from our ordinary self. This change toward "a real, lived confrontation" with the truth about oneself is produced by the felt contrast between the objective view and the ordinary, involved attitude vis-à-vis oneself. But the full truth about ourselves is that, whether we are passive or active, we always are modes of the divine substance, which produces everything without any end in view. Even when we succeed in transcending our ordinary lives of passive emotions, we realize that we still are nothing but expressions of God's power. When this truth hits us, and when we accept it—accepting ourselves as being like "the clay in the hand of the potter"[44]—we can come to a kind of religious experience in which we are reconciled with the truth about ourselves, in which we love the impersonal deity or nature without expecting any love in return.

This paradoxical experience in which we glorify in our being *Deus quatenus* is real salvation or blessedness (V, P. 36, Sch.). Salvation does not lie in taking from time to time an objective point of view upon ourselves, succeeding in momentarily transcending our ordinary selves in an identification with "the view from nowhere." Salvation is related to the experience that even when we are most "ourselves," we are "in/of another"; this results in the strange love toward something that does not return love because it is impersonal being. The specific character of Spinoza's conception of salvation is undoubtedly related to the Spinozistic metaphysical insights that inform the religious experience: they are anti-anthropocentric insights about a nature to which we, of course, belong, of which we are an expression, but which is not there for us, which infinitely transcends all our concerns. What is happening here is exactly the opposite of what is described in *Ethics* I, App., where certain passions—mainly hope and fear—are mixed with illusions about being free and being preferred to others by a personal God. Here, the truth about nature and about ourselves transforms itself into love for the impersonal substance.

T. L. S. Sprigge has described Spinozistic religiousness as characterized by a reverence for "the terrifying side of nature."[45] The surprising fact is that just as the objective view of ourselves sometimes can lead to a kind of self-acceptance, so the "terrifying" truth of Spinozistic metaphysics can lead to an experience of highest blessedness. It is Spinoza's genius to have seen that a form of salvation is possible in connection with a scientific-metaphysical view of nature and of ourselves that is thoroughly disenchanting. Enchantment is possible through disenchantment.[46]

| N O T E S

1. Excellent detailed studies of these parts of the *Ethics* are found in Matheron 1969 and Bartuschat 1992a.
2. Curley translates *affectus* as "affects"; I also use the term "emotions."
3. Curley (1988, 87–107), extensively discusses the differences between Descartes, Hobbes, and Spinoza.
4. For a discussion of these problems, see Donagan 1988, chap. 8; and Allison 1987, 124–40.
5. Walther 1971, 102–3; Allison 1987, 130–31; Curley 1988, 107–8.
6. Donagan 1988, 150; Curley 1988, 109–12.
7. Allison 1987, 136, which refers to Hobbes to underpin this interpretation.
8. Spinoza is not always consistent in the terminological difference between *affectio* and *affectus;* see for example, Curley's remark in Spinoza 1985, 464n. 43.
9. Allison 1987, 137.
10. Donagan 1988, 161.
11. Bartuschat 1992a, 154ff.
12. Bartuschat 1992a, 195ff.
13. See *Ethics* IV, App. 4: "In life, therefore, it is especially useful to perfect, as far as we can our intellect, *or* reason. In this one thing consists man's highest happiness, *or* blessedness. Indeed, blessedness is nothing but that satisfaction of the mind that stems from the intuitive knowledge of God. But *perfecting the intellect is nothing but understanding God,* his attributes, and his actions" (emphasis added).
14. This division of *Ethics* IV can also be found in Matheron 1969 (for indications confirming this division, see *Ethics* IV, P. 18, Sch.; IV, P. 37, Sch. 1; IV, P. 58, Sch.; IV, P. 66, Sch.).

15. Concerning the "precepts," see also Donagan 1988, 167. Concerning the problem of the link between Spinoza's theory of nature and humanity, and his ethics properly speaking, see Frankena 1975, 1977; McShea 1976; Mattern 1978; Curley 1973.

16. *True* knowledge of good or bad should not be understood as knowledge that just happens to correspond to what is really useful. It is knowledge based on reason, as is clear from IV, P. 15, Dem. Therefore, it is too easy to say (like Wetlesen 1979, 303 and passim) that it belongs to knowledge of the first kind, or imagination.

17. Allison 1987", 146.

18. See *E* IV, Pref.

19. Goldschmidt 1978, 114: "For Spinoza it is in this very science of good and bad that slavery consists, and this is the reason why the code of 'the precepts of reason' necessarily had to be delivered in the book [of the *Ethics*] which bears this term [slavery] in its title. Freedom does not consist in knowing the precepts of reason or in following them. . . . It consists in not needing these precepts, more precisely in ignoring them."

20. Wetlesen 1979, 277.

21. Matheron 1969, 258ff.

22. This is discussed in Matheron 1969, part 3.

23. Bartuschat 1992a, 192–93.

24. Wetlesen 1979, 130.

25. See especially Hampshire 1967; but also Curley 1988; Wetlesen 1979.

26. Curley 1988, 128ff.

27. Curley 1988, 134–35.

28. Wetlesen 1979, 217, 319.

29. Wetlesen 1979, 308.

30. Allison 1987, 172–73.

31. Donagan 1988, 201.

32. I take this term from Harris 1973.

33. Bartuschat 1992b, 339.

34. Compare the marginal note in *KV* II, cap. 4, §3: "The second effect is that it [true belief] makes us rationally appreciate the thing which it indicates and displays as being outside us; that is, it is clear and distinct knowledge, not of the thing itself, but of what the thing has to be [i.e., its model]" (Spinoza 1982, 305).

35. For an analysis of such contradictory states, attitudes, and desires, see Elster 1985, 43ff.

36. For an enumeration of the active emotions, see Wetlesen 1979, 209.

37. So Wetlesen's talk of a kind of meditative body awareness as a major element in Spinoza's instantaneous strategies of liberation does not seem to be completely unjustifiable after all; see Wetlesen 1979, 313.

38. This argues against the view in Allison 1987, 173.

39. For further discussion and references, see Allison 1987, 167–68; Donagan 1988, 198.

40. Concerning this immortality of the mind, see Allison 1987, 167; and Matheron 1969, 575–76.

41. About Einstein and Spinoza, see De Dijn 1990, 1992b.

42. Blackwell 1985, 118.

43. Blackwell 1985, 149.

44. This expression can be found repeatedly in Spinoza, for example in letter 75; *TP* II §22; *TTP* chap. 16n. 34.

45. Sprigge 1984, 158.

46. See also De Dijn 1990, 1992b.

| Some Notes on the
| Spinoza Literature

The literature on Spinoza is vast and continues to grow. In the 1960s and 1970s the study of Spinoza's philosophy was revived by a number of French studies, especially those by Gueroult and Matheron; these had an enormous influence on studies elsewhere. Since the 1980s, some very good new works have appeared in English, both books (for example, the studies by Curley, Bennett, and especially Donagan) and articles. This appendix offers suggestions of reliable and stimulating works; it makes no pretense to completeness. Full details on all the works mentioned here are found in the bibliography.

I Biography

The groundbreaking work was done by Freudenthal. On Spinoza's youth and Jewish background, see the studies by Vaz Dias and Van der Tak, Revah, and the *Cahiers Spinoza* 3(1980). Meinsma's study of the circle around Spinoza should be complemented by De Vries's biography for a general picture of Spinoza's life and work in the context of the seventeenth-century Netherlands. Hubbeling and Van Suchtelen, of the international association Het Spinoza-huis (both one-time editors of the Mededelingen vanwege het Spinozahuis) stimulated a lot of research on Spinoza's reception in the Netherlands; for information about this, see Siebrand 1988.

Recently a controversy has arisen concerning Spinoza's debt to Van den Enden, some of whose anonymous works have been rediscovered (see Klever 1991, Van den Enden 1992, and De Dijn 1994).

Allison 1987, Donagan 1988, and Brad Gregory (in Spinoza 1989) offer good, short biographies.

I General Books

The major studies of this century are Gueroult's *Spinoza* (1968, 1974), and Matheron's *Individu et communauté chez Spinoza* (1969). Whereas Gueroult completed only his studies on *Ethics* I and II, the other parts of the *Ethics* and Spinoza's theological-political thought were analyzed by Matheron. Gueroult's work should be read together with the critical commentary of Doz (1976, 1980). Gueroult himself refers to two older but excellent studies: Lewis Robinson's *Kommentar zu Spinoza's Ethik* (1928) and Victor Delbos's *Le spinozisme* (1968).

A work generally referred to in recent English studies is Jonathan Bennett's *A Study of Spinoza's* Ethics (1984). Bennett is often too quick and impatient in his criticism of Spinoza.

The most important study of recent years—more resourceful than Bennett's and building carefully on insights of Gueroult and Matheron—is Alan Donagan's *Spinoza* (1988). Curley (1988) and Allison (1987) offer good general introductions. Older studies relied upon in recent English publications are Wolfson (1969) and Hampshire (1967).

There are also good general German studies on Spinoza. Of the more recent ones, see Walther, *Metaphysik als Anti-Theologie* (1971), and especially Bartuschat's *Spinoza's Theorie des Menschen* (1992), in which Spinoza's philosophy is interpreted as a new general human science.

I Proceedings and Collected Essays

Since the beginning of the 1970s Spinoza scholars have met regularly at international conferences. Many of the papers in the proceedings of these conferences are recommended. Here is an incomplete list of the successive proceedings: Van der Bend 1974; Wetlesen 1978; De Deugd 1984; Giancotti 1985; Bouveresse 1988; Curley and Moreau 1990; and Dominguez 1992. Some of the conferences were organized by, or with the active support of, the international association Het Spinozahuis, Rijnsburg, The Netherlands.

Since 1987, the Jerusalem Spinoza Institute has organized a series of conferences in which each book of the *Ethics* (as well as Spinoza's political thought and his life and sources) are investigated; the series runs until 1999. Two proceedings have appeared so far: Yovel 1991 and 1994.

There are a number of other valuable collections: Grene 1973; Freeman and Mandelbaum 1975; Hessing 1977; Kennington 1980; Grene and Nails 1986; Shanan and Biro 1978.

| Journals on Spinoza

The most important journal is undoubtedly *Studia Spinozana*, which has been in publication since 1985. Each yearly issue contains articles on a central theme and several specialized sections.

The international association Het Spinozahuis issues one or more Mededelingen vanwege het Spinozahuis each year, mostly in Dutch but sometimes also in English and German.

| Other Journals; Newsletters

Chronicon Spinozanum. Hagae Comitis, curis Societatis Spinozanae, 5 vols. (1921–27).
Cahiers Spinoza. Paris: Replique (since 1977).
Bulletin de l'Association des Amis de Spinoza. Paris (since 1979).
Guest Lectures and Seminar Papers on Spinozism. Rotterdam: Erasmus Universiteit (since 1986).
Travaux et documents du Groupe de Recherches Spinozistes. Paris: Presses de l'Université Paris-Sorbonne (since 1989).
North American Spinoza Society Newsletter (since 1992).

| Studies on the
| *Tractatus de Intellectus Emendatione*

Some interesting older studies are Joachim's well-known commentary *Spinoza's Tractatus de Intellectus Emendatione* (1940), itself critically assessed in Parkinson's *Spinoza's Theory of Knowledge* (1954). Valuable information also is found in the introduction and notes to Koyré's translation of the *TEI* (Spinoza 1990).

A recent, in-depth commentary of the *TEI*, with an extensive introduction, can be found in Rousset's edition (and French translation) of the *TEI* (Spinoza 1992). This is a must for any serious student of this work.

The biographical introduction to the *TEI* is masterfully analyzed, with great attention to the rhetorical element, in Theo Zweerman's *L'introduction à la philosophie selon Spinoza* (1993). Wolfgang Bartuschat has recently edited the Latin text of the *TEI* with a new German translation and an interesting introduction and commentary in the series Philosophische Bibliothek (Spinoza 1993).

Some articles that give good analyses and commentary on central elements of the *TEI* include Boss, "Méthode et doctrine dans le *Traité de la réforme de l'entendement"* (1986); Garrett, "Truth and Ideas of Imagination in the *Tractatus de intellectus emendatione"* (1986), and "Truth, Method, and Correspondence in Spinoza and Leibniz" (1990); Mark, "Truth and Adequacy in Spinozistic Ideas" (1978); Matheron, "Les modes de connaissance du 'Traité de la réforme de l'entendement'" et les genres de connaissance de 'l'Ethique'" (1988), "Pourquoi le *Tractatus de Intellectus Emendatione* est-il resté inachevé?" (1987), "Idée, idée d'idée et certitude dans le 'Tractatus de Intellectus Emendatione' et dans l'"Ethique'" (1989); Zweerman, "The Method in Spinoza's *Tractatus de Intellectus Emendatione"* (1974).

Filippo Mignini is preparing a new critical edition of the *TEI* (as he did of the *Korte Verhandeling, or Short Treatise*). He makes the still-debated claim that the *Korte Verhandeling* is posterior to the *TEI* (see Mignini 1979; Spinoza 1986b).

I Studies on the *Ethics*

Here I refer to the studies listed under "General Books"; the general study of Spinoza concentrates on his major, comprehensive work, the *Ethics*. A good introductory article on the *Ethics* is Friedman's "An Overview of Spinoza's *Ethics"* (1978).

Books and articles on *Ethics* I include Donagan, "Essence and the Distinction of Attributes in Spinoza's Metaphysics" (1973), "Substance, Essence and Attribute in Spinoza, *Ethics* I" (1991); Doz, "Remarques sur les onze premières propositions de l'*Ethique* de Spinoza" (1976); Jarrett, "Some Remarks on the 'Objective' and 'Subjective' Interpretations of the Attributes" (1977a), "The Concepts of Substance and Mode in Spinoza" (1977b); Mark, "The Spinozistic Attributes" (1977); Mason, "Spinoza on Modality" (1986). See also the papers in the first volume of the Jerusalem Spinoza Conferences (Yovel 1991).

Books and articles on *Ethics* II include Della Rocca, "Spinoza's Argument for the Identity Theory" (1993); Donagan, "Spinoza's Dualism" (1980); Mark, "Truth and Adequacy in Spinozistic Ideas" (1978), "Spinoza's Concept of Mind" (1979); Matheron, "Les modes de connaissance du 'Traité de la réforme de l'entendement' et les genres de connaissance de 'l'Ethique'" (1988), "L'anthropologie spinoziste?" (1978); Matson, "Spinoza's Theory of Mind" (1975); Van Peursen, "Le critère de la vérité chez Spinoza" (1978); Wilson, "Objects, Ideas and 'Minds': Comments on Spinoza's Theory of Mind" (1980). See also the papers in *Studia Spinozana* 2 on Spinoza's epistemology (1986); the papers in the second volume of the Jerusalem Spinoza Conferences (Yovel

1994); Parkinson's *Spinoza's Theory of Knowledge* (1954); and Bertrand, *Spinoza et l'imaginaire* (1983). Books and articles on *Ethics* III–V include Bartuschat, *Spinozas Theorie des Menschen* (1992a); Curley, "Spinoza's Moral Philosophy" (1973); Frankena, "Spinoza's 'New Morality': Notes on Book IV" (1975), "Spinoza on the Knowledge of Good and Evil" (1977); Naess, "Is Freedom Consistent with Spinoza's Determinism?" (1974). See also Wetlesen, *The Sage and the Way: Spinoza's Ethics of Freedom* (1979); Rousset, *La perspective finale de "L'Ethique" et le problème de la cohérence du spinozisme* (1968); Kammerer, *Die Frage nach dem (Selbst)-Bewusstsein Gottes im System Spinozas* (1992).

| Studies on Spinoza's Ideas on Method

First of all, one should consult the appropriate sections in Gueroult's studies of 1968 and 1974. See also De Dijn, "Conceptions of Philosophical Method in Spinoza" (1986a); Kennington, "Analytic and Synthetic Methods in Spinoza's *Ethics*" (1980); Mark, "*Ordine geometrica demonstrata:* Spinoza's Use of the Axiomatic Method" (1975); Schuhmann, "Methodenfragen bei Spinoza und Hobbes: Zum Problem des Einflusses" (1987); and Zweerman, "The Method in Spinoza's *Tractatus de Intellectus Emendatione*" (1974).

| Studies on Spinoza's Ideas on | Physics and Mathematics

See especially the papers in Grene and Nails, *Spinoza and the Sciences* (1986); Lachterman, "The Physics of Spinoza's *Ethics*" (1978); Van der Hoeven, "Over Spinoza's interpretatie van de cartesiaanse fysica en de betekenis daarvan voor het systeem der *Ethica*" (1973); d'Espagnat, "Spinoza et la physique contemporaine" (1988); and Lécrivain, "Spinoza et la physique cartésienne" (1977–78). Also important are several appendices in Gueroult 1968 (app. 1, 9, 10, 14, 15) and Gueroult 1974 (app. 4, 5, 7, 8, 9).

| Studies on the Political | Thought of Spinoza

The best English study is Den Uyl, *Power, State and Freedom: An Interpretation of Spinoza's Political Philosophy* (1983). Wernham's commentary to Spinoza, *The Political Works* (1958), also is valuable. There are some remarkable French studies on this subject: Matheron, *Individu et communauté chez Spinoza*

(1986); Tosel, *Spinoza ou le crépuscule de la servitude* (1984); Mugnier-Pollet, *La philosophie politique de Spinoza* (1976); and the excellent introduction by Balibar, *Spinoza et la politique* (1985).

Studies on Philosophy of Religion and Biblical Hermeneutics

Strauss's study of the *TTP*, "How to Study Spinoza's *Theologico-political Treatise?*" in his *Persecution and the Art of Writing* (1973), is well known. Influenced by Strauss is Tosel 1984. The best studies are in French: Zac, *Spinoza et l'interprétation de l'écriture* (1965); Malet, *Le Traité théologico-politique de Spinoza et la pensée biblique* (1966); Matheron, *Le Christ et le salut des ignorants chez Spinoza* (1971). A good recent study is Laux, *Imagination et religion chez Spinoza* (1993). Some papers on these subjects in Bouveresse 1988 and De Deugd 1984 also are worth reading.

Studies on Spinoza's Vocabulary, Style, and Early Translation

Here one should consult Akkerman's "Studies in the Posthumous Works of Spinoza: On Style, Earliest Translation and Reception, Earliest and Modern Edition of Some Texts" (1980), "Le caractère rhétorique du *Traité théologico-politique*" (1985). This work is continued in Akkerman and Steenbakkers, *Les textes de Spinoza: Etudes sur les mots, les phrases, les livres* (1996); and Steenbakkers, *Spinoza's* Ethica *from Manuscript to Print: Studies on Text, Form and Related Topics* (1994).

I Studies on Lexicography

Guéret, M., A. Robinet, and P. Tombeur. *Spinoza, Ethica; Concordances, index, listes de fréquences, tables comparatives.* Louvain-la-Neuve: Cétédoc, 1977.

Giancotti Boscherini, Emilia. *Lexicon Spinozanum.* 2 vols. The Hague: Martinus Nijhoff, 1970.

Wetlesen, J. *Internal Guide to the* Ethics *of Spinoza: Index to Spinoza's Cross References in the* Ethics, *Rearranged So As to Refer from Earlier to Later Statements.* Oslo: Filosofisk Institutt, 1974.

Naess, Arne. *Equivalent terms and notions in Spinoza's* Ethics. Oslo: Filosofisk Institutt, 1974.

I Bibliographies

Van der Linde, Antonius. *Benedictus Spinoza, Bibliografie.* 1871. Reprint, Nieuwkoop: B. de Graaf, 1965.

Oko, Adolph S. *The Spinoza Bibliography.* Boston, Mass.: G. K. Hall & Co., 1964.

Wetlesen, J. *A Spinoza Bibliography, Particularly on the Period 1940–1970*. Oslo: Universitetsforlaget (supplementary to Oko 1964), 1971.

Préposiet, J. *Bibliographie spinoziste: Répertoire alphabétique – Registre systématique – etc*. Paris: Les Belles Lettres, 1973.

Van der Werf, Theo, H. Siebrand, and C. Westerveen. *A Spinoza Bibliography 1971–1983*. Mededelingen vanwege het Spinozahuis, vol. 46. Leiden: E. J. Brill, 1984 (supplementary to Oko 1964, Wetlesen 1971, and Préposiet 1973).

Bulletin de bibliographie spinoziste (since 1979). In *Archives de philosophie* (last issue of each year).

Boucher, Wayne I. *Spinoza in English: A Bibliography from the Seventeenth Century to the Present*. Leiden: E. J. Brill, 1991.

Exhaustive ongoing bibliographical information on Spinoza is also to be found in the *International Philosophical Bibliography* (Leuven/Louvain – Institute of Philosophy), which also appears attached to the *Tijdschrift voor filosofie*.

This list includes all, and only, those works to which reference is made in the text and appendix. See the note on texts and abbreviations for details of references to Spinoza's own writings.

Abel, G. 1978. *Stoicismus und frühe Neuzeit*. Berlin: De Gruyter.

Akkerman, F. 1980. "Studies in the Posthumous Works of Spinoza: On Style, Earliest Translation and Reception, Earliest and Modern Edition of Some Texts." Ph.D. diss., University of Groningen.

———. 1985. "Le caractère rhétorique du *Traité théologico-politique*." In *Spinoza entre lumière et romantisme*, 381–90. Les Cahiers de Fontenay, nos. 36–38, E.N.S.: Fontenay-aux-Roses.

Akkerman, Fokke, and Piet Steenbakkers, eds. 1996. *Les textes de Spinoza: Etudes sur les mots, les phrases, les livres*. Assen: Van Gorcum; Naples: Bibliopolis.

Allison, Henry E. 1987. *Benedict de Spinoza: An Introduction*. Rev. ed. New Haven, Conn.: Yale University Press.

Altkirch, E. 1913. *Spinoza im Porträt*. Jena: Diederichs.

Aurelius, Marcus. 1964. *Meditations*. Harmondsworth: Penguin.

Balibar, Etienne. 1985. *Spinoza et la politique*. Paris: Presses Universitaires de France.

Bartuschat, Wolfgang. 1992a. *Spinozas Theorie des Menschen*. Hamburg: Felix Meiner.

———. 1992b. "Die Theorie des Guten im 4. Teil der *Ethik*." In *La Etica de Spinoza: Fundamentos y significado*, edited by Atilano Dominguez, 331–39. Ediciones de la Universidad de Castilla–La Mancha.

Beavers, Anthony F., and Lee C. Rice. 1988. "Doubt and Belief in the *Tractatus De Intellectus Emendatione*." *Studia Spinozana* 4:93–119.

Bennett, Jonathan. 1984. *A Study of Spinoza's Ethics*. Indianapolis, Ind.: Hackett.

Benoit, Hubert. 1967. *La doctrine suprême selon la pensée zen*. 4th ed. Paris: Le Courrier du Livre.

Bertrand, M. 1983. *Spinoza et l'imaginaire*. Paris: Presses Universitaires de France.

Biasutti, Franco. 1979. *La dottrina della scienza in Spinoza*. Bologna: Patron.

———. 1986. "Truth and Certainty in Spinoza's Epistemology." *Studia Spinozana* 2:109–27.

Blackwell, Kenneth. 1988. *The Spinozistic Ethics of Bertrand Russell*. London: Allen & Unwin.

Bloch, Olivier, ed. 1993. *Spinoza au XXe siècle*. Paris: Presses Universitaires de France.

Boss, Gilbert. 1986. "Méthode et doctrine dans le *Traité de la réforme de l'entendement*." *Studia Spinozana* 2:93–108.

Bouveresse, Renée, ed. 1988. *Spinoza: Science et Religion*. Actes du Colloque de Cerisy-la-Salle, 1982. Paris: Vrin.

Busche, Hubertus. 1991. "Die innere Logik der Liebe in Leibnizens *Elementa Juris Naturalis*." *Studia Leibnitiana* 23, no. 2: 170–84.

Curley, Edwin M. 1969. *Spinoza's Metaphysics: An Essay in Interpretation*. Cambridge, Mass.: Harvard University Press.

———. 1973. "Spinoza's Moral Philosophy." In *Spinoza: A Collection of Critical Essays*, edited by Marjorie Grene, 354–76. New York: Doubleday.

———. 1988. *Behind the Geometrical Method: A Reading of Spinoza's Ethics*. Princeton, N.J.: Princeton University Press.

Curley, Edwin M., and Pierre-François Moreau, eds. 1990. *Spinoza: Issues and Directions. The Proceedings of the Chicago Spinoza Conference*. Leiden: E. J. Brill.

De Deugd, C. 1966. *The Significance of Spinoza's First Kind of Knowledge*. Assen: Van Gorcum.

De Deugd, C., ed. 1984. *Spinoza's Political and Theological Thought: International Symposium, Amsterdam, 1982*. Amsterdam: North-Holland Publishing Company.

De Dijn, Herman. 1973. "Spinoza's geometrische methode van denken." *Tijdschrift voor filosofie* 35:707–65.

———. 1974a. "Historical Remarks on Spinoza's Theory of Definition." In *Spinoza on Knowing, Being and Freedom*, edited by J. G. Van der Bend, 41–50. Assen: Van Gorcum.

———. 1974b. "The Significance of Spinoza's *Treatise on the Improvement of the Understanding*." *Algemeen Nederlands tijdschrift voor wijsbegeerte* 66:1–16.

———. 1983. "Adriaan Heereboord en het Nederlandse Cartesianisme." *Algemeen Nederlands tijdschrift voor wijsbegeerte* 75:56–69.

———. 1985. "The Compatibility of Determinism and Moral Attitudes." In *Proceedings of the First Italian International Congress on Spinoza*, edited by Emilia Giancotti, 205–19. Naples: Bibliopolis.

———. 1986a. "Conceptions of Philosophical Method in Spinoza: *Logica* and *mos geometricus*." *Review of Metaphysics* 40:55–78.

———. 1986b. "Spinoza's Logic or Art of Perfect Thinking." *Studia Spinozana* 2:15-25.

———. 1987. "How to Understand Spinoza's Logic or Methodology." *Studia Spinozana* 3:419–29.

———. 1990. "Wisdom and Theoretical Knowledge in Spinoza." In *Spinoza: Issues and Directions*, edited by Edwin M. Curley and Pierre-François Moreau, 147–56. Leiden: E. J. Brill.

———. 1991. "Metaphysics as Ethics." In *God and Nature: Spinoza's Metaphysics,* edited by Y. Yovel, 119–31. Leiden: E. J. Brill.

——— 1992a. "Spinoza's *Ethics:* From the Sorrows of Reason to Freedom and Beyond." In *La* Etica *de Spinoza: Fundamentos y significado,* edited by Atilano Dominguez, 493–503. Ediciones de la Universidad de Castilla–La Mancha.

———. 1992b. "Einstein and Spinoza." In *Tradition and Renewal: Philosophical Essays Commemorating the Centennial of Louvain's Institute of Philosophy,* edited by D. A. Boileau and J. A. Dick, 1–13. Louvain: Leuven University Press.

———. 1994. "Was Van den Enden het meesterbrein achter Spinoza?" *Algemeen Nederlands tijdschrift voor wijsbegeerte* 86:71–76.

Delbos, Victor. 1968. *Le Spinozisme.* 1918. Reprint, Paris: Vrin.

Deleuze, Gilles. 1968. *Spinoza et le problème de l'expression.* Paris: Minuit.

Della Rocca, Michael. 1993. "Spinoza's Argument for the Identity Theory." *Philosophical Review* 102:183–213.

Den Uyl, D. J. 1983. *Power, State and Freedom: An Interpretation of Spinoza's Political Philosophy.* Assen: Van Gorcum.

Descartes, René. 1953. "Secondes réponses." In *Œuvres et lettres,* by R. Descartes, 366–98. Bibliothèque de la Pléiade. Paris: Gallimard.

d'Espagnat, B. 1988. "Spinoza et la physique contemporaine." In *Spinoza: Science et Religion,* edited by Renée Bouveresse, 209–14. Paris: Vrin.

De Vet, J. J. V. M. 1983. "Was Spinoza de auteur van *Stelkonstige reeckening van den reegenboog* en van *Reeckening van kanssen?*" *Tijdschrift voor filosofie* 45:602–39.

———. 1986. "Spinoza's Authorship of *Stelkonstige reeckening van den reegenboog* and of *Reeckening van kanssen* Once More Doubtful." *Studia Spinozana* 2:267–307.

De Vleeschauwer, H. J. 1964. "Il tema del *superuomo* in Arnold Geulincx." *Filosofia* 15:201–12.

De Vries, Theun. n.d. *Spinoza: Beeldenstormer en Wereldbouwer.* Amsterdam: Becht.

Dominguez, Atilano, ed. 1992. *La* Etica *de Spinoza: Fundamentos y significado.* Actas del Congreso Internacional, Almagro 1990. Ediciones de la Universidad de Castilla–La Mancha.

Donagan, A. 1973. "Essence and the Distinction of Attributes in Spinoza's Metaphysics." In *Spinoza: A Collection of Critical Essays,* edited by Marjorie Grene, 164–81. New York: Doubleday.

———. 1980. "Spinoza's Dualism." In *The Philosophy of Baruch Spinoza,* edited by R. Kennington, 89–102. Washington, D.C.: The Catholic University of America Press.

———. 1988. *Spinoza.* Philosophers in Context. New York: Harvester-Wheatsheaf.

———. 1991. "Substance, Essence and Attribute in Spinoza, *Ethics* I." In *God and Nature: Spinoza's Metaphysics,* edited by Y. Yovel, 1–21. Leiden: E. J. Brill.

Doz, A. 1976. "Remarques sur les onze premières propositions de l'*Ethique* de Spinoza: A propos du *Spinoza* de M. Martial Gueroult." *Revue de métaphysique et de morale* 81:221–61.

Doz, A. 1980. "Réponse à Mlle Dreyfus à propos du *Spinoza* de Martial Gueroult." *Cahiers Spinoza* 3:209–37.

Eisenberg, Paul D. 1971. "How to Understand *De Intellectus Emendatione.*" *Journal of the History of Philosophy* 9:171–91.

———. 1990. "On the Attributes and Their Alleged Independence of One Another: A Commentary on Spinoza's *Ethics* I P 10." In *Spinoza: Issues and Directions,* edited by Edwin M. Curley and Pierre-François Moreau, 1–15. Leiden: E. J. Brill.

Elster, J. 1985. *Sour Grapes: Studies in the Subversion of Rationality.* Cambridge: Cambridge University Press.

Frankena, William K. 1975. "Spinoza's 'New Morality': Notes on Book IV." In *Spinoza: Essays in Interpretation,* edited by E. Freeman and M. Mandelbaum, 85–100. La Salle, Ill.: Open Court.

——— 1977. "Spinoza on the Knowledge of Good and Evil." *Philosophia* 7:15–44.

Frankfurt, Harry G. 1986. "Two Motivations for Rationalism: Descartes and Spinoza." In *Human Nature and Natural Knowledge,* edited by A. Donagan, A. N. Petrovich, Jr., and M. V. Wedin, 47–61. Amsterdam: Reidel.

Freeman, E., and M. Mandelbaum, eds. 1975. *Spinoza: Essays in Interpretation.* La Salle, Ill.: Open Court.

Freudenthal, Jacob. 1899. *Lebensgeschichte Spinoza's in Quellenschriften, Urkunden und Nichtamtlichen Nachrichten.* Leipzig: Veit.

———. 1972. *Spinoza: Leben und Lehre.* 1927. Reprint, Heidelberg: C. Winter.

Friedman, Joel I. 1978. "An Overview of Spinoza's *Ethics.*" *Synthese* 37:67–106.

Garrett, Don. 1986. "Truth and Ideas of Imagination in the *Tractatus de Intellectus Emendatione.*" *Studia Spinozana* 2:61–92.

———. 1990. "Truth, Method, and Correspondence in Spinoza and Leibniz." *Studia Spinozana* 6:13–43.

Gebhardt, Carl. 1905. *Spinoza's Abhandlung über die Verbesserung des Verstandes: Eine entwicklungsgeschichtliche Untersuchung.* Heidelberg: C. Winter.

Giancotti, Emilia, ed. 1985. *Proceedings of the First Italian International Congress on Spinoza—Spinoza nel 350o Anniversario della Nascita.* Naples: Bibliopolis.

Goldschmidt, Victor. 1978. "La place de la théorie politique dans la philosophie de Spinoza." *Manuscrito: Revista de filosofia* 2:103–22.

Graeser, Andreas. 1991. "Stoische Philosophie bei Spinoza." *Revue internationale de philosophie* 45:336–46.

Grene, Marjorie, ed. 1973. *Spinoza: A Collection of Critical Essays.* New York: Doubleday.

Grene, Marjorie, and Debra Nails, eds. 1986. *Spinoza and the Sciences.* Dordrecht: Reidel.

Gueroult, Martial. 1968. *Spinoza.* Vol. 1, *Dieu (*Ethique, *I).* Paris: Aubier-Montaigne.

———. 1974. *Spinoza.* Vol. 2, *L'âme (*Ethique, *II).* Paris: Aubier-Montaigne.

Hampshire, Stuart. 1967. *Spinoza.* 1951. Reprint, Harmondsworth: Penguin Books.

Harris, Errol E. 1973. *Salvation from Despair: A Reappraisal of Spinoza's Philosophy.* The Hague: M. Nijhoff.

Henrard, Roger. 1977. *Wijsheidsgestalten in dichterwoord: Onderzoek naar de invloed van Spinoza op de Nederlandse literatuur.* Assen: Van Gorcum.

Hessing, Siegfried, ed. 1978. *Speculum Spinozanum, 1677–1977.* London: Routledge & Kegan Paul.

Hobbes, Thomas. 1961. *Opera Philosophica Quae Latine Scripsit Omnia* . . . Edited by G. Molesworth. 4 vols. Aalen: Scientia.

Hubbeling, H. G. 1964. *Spinoza's Methodology.* Assen: Van Gorcum.

———. 1973. *Logica en ervaring in Spinoza's en Ruusbroecs Mystiek.* Mededelingen vanwege het Spinozahuis, vol. 31. Leiden: Brill.

———. 1986. "The Third Way of Knowledge (Intuition) in Spinoza." *Studia Spinozana* 2:219–31.

Jarrett, Charles E. 1977a. "Some Remarks on the 'Objective' and 'Subjective' Interpretations of the Attributes." *Inquiry* 20:447–56.

———. 1977b. "The Concepts of Substance and Mode in Spinoza." *Philosophia* 7:83–105.

Joachim, H. H. 1940. *Spinoza's 'Tractatus de Intellectus Emendatione.'* Oxford: Clarendon Press.

Kammerer, Armin. 1992. *Die Frage nach dem (Selbst)-Bewusstsein Gottes im System Spinozas.* Innsbruck: Verlag des Instituts für Sprachwissenschaft der Universität Innsbruck.

Kasher, Asa, and Shlomo Biderman. 1990. "Why Was Baruch de Spinoza Excommunicated?" In *Sceptics, Millenarians and Jews,* edited by David S. Katz and Jonathan I. Israel, 98-104. Leiden: E. J. Brill.

Kennington, R. 1980a. "Analytic and Synthetic Methods in Spinoza's *Ethics.*" In *The Philosophy of Baruch Spinoza,* edited by R. Kennington, 293–318. Washington, D.C.: The Catholic University of America Press.

Kennington, R., ed. 1980b. *The Philosophy of Baruch Spinoza.* Washington, D.C.: The Catholic University of America Press.

Klever, Wim. 1986. "Axioms in Spinoza's Science and Philosophy of Science." *Studia Spinozana* 2:171–95.

———. 1991. "A New Source of Spinozism: Franciscus Van den Enden." *Journal of the History of Philosophy* 29:613–31.

Kristeller, Paul Oskar. 1985. "Stoic and Neoplatonic Sources of Spinoza's *Ethics.*" *History of European Ideas* 5:1–15.

Lachterman, David R. 1978. "The Physics of Spinoza's *Ethics.*" In *Spinoza: New Perspectives,* edited by R. W. Shanan and J. I. Biro, 71–111. Norman: University of Oklahoma Press.

Laux, Henri. 1993. *Imagination et religion chez Spinoza: La potentia dans l'histoire.* Paris: Vrin.

Lécrivain, A. 1977–78. "Spinoza et la physique cartésienne." *Cahiers Spinoza* 1:235–65; 2:93–206.

Malet, André. 1966. *Le Traité théologico-politique de Spinoza et la pensée biblique.* Paris: Les Belles Lettres.

Marion, J.-L. 1972. "Le fondement de la *Cogitatio* selon le *De Intellectus Emendatione:* Essai d'une lecture des §§ 104–105." *Etudes philosophiques* 3:357–68.

Mark, Thomas Carson. 1975. "*Ordine geometrica demonstrata:* Spinoza's Use of the Axiomatic Method." *Review of Metaphysics* 19:263–86.
———. 1977. "The Spinozistic Attributes." *Philosophia* 7:55–82.
———. 1978. "Truth and Adequacy in Spinozistic Ideas." In *Spinoza: New Perspectives,* edited by R. W. Shanan and J. I. Biro, 11–34. Norman: University of Oklahoma Press.
———. 1979. "Spinoza's Concept of Mind." *Journal of the History of Philosophy* 17:401–16.
Martens, Stanley C. 1978. "Spinoza on Attributes." *Synthese* 37:107–11.
Mason, Richard. 1986. "Spinoza on Modality." *The Philosophical Quarterly* 36:313–42.
Matheron, Alexandre. 1969. *Individu et communauté chez Spinoza.* Paris: Minuit.
———. 1971. *Le Christ et le salut des ignorants chez Spinoza.* Paris: Aubier-Montaigne.
———. 1978. "L'anthropologie spinoziste?" *Revue de synthèse* 3, nos. 89–91: 175–85.
———. 1986. "Spinoza and the Euclidean Arithmetic: The Example of the Fourth Proportional." In *Spinoza and the Sciences,* edited by Marjorie Grene and Debra Neils, 125–50. Dordrecht: Reidel.
———. 1987. "Pourquoi le *Tractatus de intellectus emendatione* est-il resté inachevé?" *Revue des sciences philosophiques et théologiques* 71:45–53.
———. 1988. "Les modes de connaissance du 'Traité de la réforme de l'entendement' et les genres de connaissance de 'l'Ethique.'" In *Spinoza: Science et Religion,* edited by Renée Bouveresse, 97–108. Paris: Vrin.
———. 1989. "Idée, idée d'idée et certitude dans le 'Tractatus de intellectus emendatione' et dans l'"Ethique.'" In *Méthode et métaphysique,* 93–104. Travaux et documents du Groupe de Recherches Spinozistes, vol. 2. Paris: Presses de l'Université Paris-Sorbonne.
Matson, Wallace I. 1975. "Spinoza's Theory of Mind." In *Spinoza: Essays in Interpretation,* edited by E. Freeman and M. Mandelbaum, 49–60. La Salle, Ill.: Open Court.
Mattern, Ruth. 1978. "Spinoza and Ethical Subjectivism." *Canadian Journal of Philosophy,* suppl. vol. 4, 59–82.
McShea, Robert J. 1976. "Spinoza in the History of Ethical Theory." *The Philosophical Forum* 8:59–67.
Medina, José. 1985. "Les mathématiques chez Spinoza et Hobbes." *Revue philosophique de la France et de l'étranger* 110:177–88.
Meinsma, K. O. 1980. *Spinoza en zijn Kring: Historisch-kritische Studiën over Hollandsche Vrijgeesten.* 1896. Reprint, Utrecht: HES-Publisher.
———. 1983. *Spinoza et son cercle: Etude critique historique sur les hétérodoxes hollandais.* Paris: Vrin.
Mignini, Filippo. 1979. "Per la datazione et l'interpretazione del 'Tractatus de intellectus emendatione' di Spinoza." *La cultura* 17:87–160.
———. 1988. "Per una nuova edizione del 'Tractatus de intellectus emendatione.'" *Studia Spinozana* 4:15–35.

Moreau, Joseph. 1971. *Spinoza et le spinozisme*. Paris: Presses Universitaires de France.

Moreau, Pierre-François. 1994. *Spinoza: L'expérience et l'éternité*. Paris: Presses Universitaires de France.

Mugnier-Pollet, L. 1976. *La philosophie politique de Spinoza*. Paris: Vrin.

Naess, Arne. 1974. "Is Freedom Consistent with Spinoza's Determinism?" In *Spinoza on Knowing, Being and Freedom*, edited by J. G. Van der Bend, 6–23. Assen: Van Gorcum.

Nagel, Thomas. 1986. *The View from Nowhere*. New York: Oxford University Press.

Oakeshott, Michael. 1984. "The Voice of Poetry in the Conversation of Mankind." In *Rationalism in Politics and Other Essays*, by M. Oakeshott, 197–247. 1962. Reprint, London: Methuen.

Pariset, G. 1906. "Sieyès et Spinoza." *Revue de synthèse historique* 12:309–20.

Parkinson, G. H. R. 1954. *Spinoza's Theory of Knowledge*. Oxford: Clarendon Press.

Paty, M. "Einstein et Spinoza." In *Spinoza and the Sciences*, edited by Marjorie Grene and Debra Nails, 125–50. Dordrecht: Reidel.

Proietti, Omero. 1985. "Aduluscens luxu perditus: Classici latini nell'opera di Spinoza." *Rivista di filosofia neo-scolastica* 77:210–57.

———. 1989. "Lettres à Lucilius: Une source du De Intellectus Emendatione de Spinoza." In *Lire et traduire Spinoza*, 39–60. Travaux et documents du Groupe de Recherches Spinozistes, vol. 1. Paris: Presses de l'Université Paris-Sorbonne.

Revah, I. S. 1959. *Spinoza et le Dr. Juan de Prado*. Paris: Mouton.

———. 1964. "Aux origines de la rupture spinozienne." *Revue des études juives* 3:359–431.

Rice, Lee C. 1969. "The Continuity of 'Mens' in Spinoza." *New Scholasticism* 43:75–103.

———. 1990. "Reflexive Ideas in Spinoza." *Journal of the History of Philosophy* 28:201–11.

Robinson, Lewis. 1928. *Kommentar zu Spinozas Ethik*. Leipzig: Felix Meiner.

Rousset, Bernard. 1968. *La perspective finale de "L'Ethique" et le problème de la cohérence du spinozisme: L'autonomie comme salut*. Paris: Vrin.

Saunders, J. L. 1955. *Justus Lipsius: The Philosophy of Renaissance Stoicism*. New York: Liberal Arts Pres.

Schneider, Ulrich J. 1981. "Definitionslehre und Methodenideal in der Philosophie Spinoza's." *Studia Leibnitiana* 13, no. 2: 212–41.

Schuhmann, Karl. 1987. "Methodenfragen bei Spinoza und Hobbes: Zum Problem des Einflusses." *Studia Spinozana* 3:47–86.

Shanan, R. W., and J. I. Biro, eds. 1978. *Spinoza: New Perspectives*. Norman: University of Oklahoma Press.

Siebrand, H. J. 1988. *Spinoza and the Netherlanders: An Inquiry into the Early Reception of His Philosophy of Religion*. Assen: Van Gorcum.

Spinoza, Baruch. 1958. *The Political Works: The* Tractatus Theologico-Politicus *in Part and the* Tractatus Politicus *in Full*. Edited and translated by A. G. Wernham. Oxford: Clarendon Press.

Spinoza, Baruch. 1966. *The Correspondence of Spinoza*. Translated by A. Wolf. London: Frank Cass.

———. 1972. *Spinoza Opera*. Edited by Carl Gebhardt. 4 vols. 1925. Reprint, Heidelberg: Carl Winter.

———. 1977. *Briefwisseling*. Edited, translated, and with introduction and commentary by F. Akkerman, H. G. Hubbeling, A. G. Westerbrink. Amsterdam: Wereldbibliotheek.

———. 1982. *Korte Geschriften*. Edited by F. Akkerman et al. Amsterdam: Wereldbibliotheek.

———. 1985. *The Collected Works of Spinoza*. Vol. 1. Edited and translated by Edwin Curley. Princeton, N.J.: Princeton University Press.

———. 1986a. *Verhandeling over de verbetering van het verstand*. Edited, translated, and with introduction and commentary by W. N. A. Klever. Baarn: Ambo.

———. 1986b. *Korte Verhandeling van God, de Mensch en deszelvs Welstand / Breve Trattato su Dio, l'Uomo e il suo Bene*. Edited and translated by Filippo Mignini. L'Aquila: L. U. Japadre Editore.

———. 1989. *Tractatus Theologico-politicus*. Translated by Samuel Shirley; introduction by Brad S. Gregory. Leiden: E. J. Brill.

———. 1990. *Traité de la réforme de l'entendement*. Edited and translated by A. Koyré. 1938. Reprint, Paris: Vrin.

———. 1992. *Traité de la réforme de l'entendement*. Edited, translated, and with introduction and commentary by Bernard Rousset. Paris: Vrin.

———. 1993. *Abhandlung über die Verbesserung des Verstandes — Tractatus de intellectus emendatione*. Edited, translated, and with introduction and commentary by Wolfgang Bartuschat. Hamburg: Felix Meiner.

Steenbakkers, Piet. 1994. *Spinoza's Ethica from Manuscript to Print: Studies on Text, Form and Related Topics*. Assen: Van Gorcum.

Sprigge, T. L. S. 1984. *Theories of Existence*. Harmondsworth: Penguin.

Strauss, Leo. 1973. *Persecution and the Art of Writing*. 1952. Reprint, Westport, Conn.: Greenwood Press.

Strawson, P. F. 1974. "Freedom and Resentment." In *Freedom and Resentment and Other Essays*, by P. F. Strawson, 1–25. London: Methuen.

Thomas Aquinas. 1957. *Opusculum de ente et essentia*. 3d ed. Turin: Marietti.

Tosel, André. 1984. *Spinoza ou le crépuscule de la servitude: Essai sur le "Traité théologico-politique."* Paris: Aubier.

Van den Enden, Franciscus. 1992. *Vrije Politijke Stellingen*, met een inleiding van Wim Klever. Amsterdam: Wereldbibliotheek.

Van der Bend, J. G., ed. 1974. *Spinoza on Knowing, Being and Freedom*. Assen: Van Gorcum.

Van der Hoeven, P. 1973. "Over Spinoza's interpretatie van de cartesiaanse fysica, en de betekenis daarvan voor het systeem der *Ethica*." *Tijdschrift voor filosofie* 35:27–86.

Van Peursen, C. 1978. "Le critère de la vérité chez Spinoza." *Revue de métaphysique et de morale* 83:518–25.

Van Suchtelen, Guido. 1985. "Mercator sapiens amstelodamensis." In *Proceedings of the First Italian International Congress on Spinoza*, edited by Emilia Giancotti, 527–37. Naples: Bibliopolis.

Vaz Dias, A. M., and W. G. Van der Tak. 1932. *Spinoza, mercator et autodidactus: Oorkonden en andere authentieke documenten betreffende des wijsgeers jeugd en diens betrekkingen.* The Hague: Martinus Nijhoff.

———. 1982a. "Spinoza Merchant and Autodidact: Charters and Other Authentic Documents Relating to the Philosopher's Youth and His Relations." *Studia Rosenthaliana* 16:113–71.

———. 1982b. "The Firm of Bento y Gabriel de Spinoza." *Studia Rosenthaliana* 16:178–89.

Vernière, P. 1982. *Spinoza et la pensée française avant la révolution.* 1954. Reprint, Paris: Presses Universitaires de France.

Violette, R. 1977. "Méthode inventive et méthode inventée dans l'introduction au 'De intellectus emendatione' de Spinoza." *Revue philosophique de la France et de l'étranger* 102:303–22.

Vulliaud, Paul. 1934. *Spinoza d'après les livres de sa bibliothèque.* Paris: Chacornac.

Walker, Ralph C. S. 1985. "Spinoza and the Coherence Theory of Truth." *Mind* 94:1–18.

Walther, Manfred. 1971. *Metaphysik als Anti-Theologie: Die Philosophie Spinozas im Zusammenhang der religionsphilosophischen Problematik.* Hamburg: Felix Meiner.

Wesselius, J. W. 1990a. "Spinoza's Excommunication and Related Matters." *Studia Rosenthaliana* 24:41–63.

———. 1990b. "De ban van Spinoza: Oude en nieuwe inzichten." *Geschiedenis van de wijsbegeerte in Nederland* 1:193–203.

Wetlesen, Jon. 1978a. "Spinoza's Philosophy of Man." In *Proceedings of the Scandinavian Spinoza Symposium 1977,* edited by Jan Wetlesen, 204–10. Oslo: Universitetsforlaget.

———. 1979. *The Sage and the Way: Spinoza's Ethics of Freedom.* Assen: Van Gorcum.

Wetlesen, Jon, ed. 1978b. *Proceedings of the Scandinavian Spinoza Symposium 1977.* Oslo: Universitetsforlaget.

Wilson, Margaret D. 1980. "Objects, Ideas and 'Minds': Comments on Spinoza's Theory of Mind." In *The Philosophy of Baruch Spinoza,* edited by R. Kennington, 103–20. Washington, D.C.: The Catholic University of America Press.

Wittgenstein, Ludwig. 1977. *On Certainty — Über Gewissheit.* Edited by G. E. M. Anscombe and G. H. von Wright, translated by Dennis Paul and G. E. M. Anscombe. Oxford: Basil Blackwell.

———. 1980. *Vermischte Bemerkungen — Culture and Value.* Edited by G. H. von Wright in collaboration with Heikki Nyman, translated by Peter Winch. Oxford: Basil Blackwell.

Wolfson, H. A. 1969. *The Philosophy of Spinoza.* Vol. 1. New York: Schocken Books.

Yakira, E. 1988. "Boyle et Spinoza." *Archives de philosophie* 51:107–24.

Yovel, Y., ed. 1991. *God and Nature: Spinoza's Metaphysics: Papers Presented at the First Jerusalem Conference (Ethica I).* Leiden: E. J. Brill.

———. 1994. *Spinoza on Knowledge and the Human Mind: Papers Presented at the Second Jerusalem Conference (Ethica II).* Leiden: E. J. Brill.

Zac, Sylvain. 1965. *Spinoza et l'interprétation de l'écriture.* Paris: Presses Universitaires de France.

Zanta, L. 1914. *La renaissance du Stoicisme au XVIe siècle.* Paris: Champion.

Zweerman, Theo. 1974. "The Method in Spinoza's *Tractatus de Intellectus Emendatione.*" In *Spinoza on Knowing, Being and Freedom,* edited by J. G. Van der Bend, 172–83. Assen: Van Gorcum.

———. 1979. *Spinoza en de hedendaagse kritiek op het humanisme als ideologie.* Mededelingen vanwege het Spinozahuis, vol. 34. Leiden: E. J. Brill.

———. 1993. *L'introduction à la philosophie selon Spinoza: Une analyse structurelle de l'introduction du* Traité de la réforme de l'entendement *suivi d'un commentaire de ce texte.* Leuven: Presses Universitaires de Louvain; Assen: Van Gorcum.

I N D E X

I Index of Names

I Index of Subjects